# TURNING POINTS
## IN
# *Film History*

# TURNING POINTS
## IN
# *Film History*

Andrew J. Rausch

**CITADEL PRESS**
Kensington Publishing Corp.
www.kensingtonbooks.com

CITADEL PRESS BOOKS are published by

Kensington Publishing Corp.
850 Third Avenue
New York, NY 10022

All Kensington titles, imprints, and distributed lines are available at special quantity discounts for bulk purchases for sales promotions, premiums, fund-raising, educational, or institutional use. Special book excerpts or customized printings can also be created to fit specific needs. For details, write or phone the office of the Kensington special sales manager: Kensington Publishing Corp., 850 Third Avenue, New York, NY 10022, attn: Special Sales Department; phone 1-800-221-2647.

CITADEL PRESS and the Citadel logo are Reg. U.S. Pat. & TM Off.

First printing: October 2004

10   9   8   7   6   5   4   3   2   1

Printed in the United States of America

Library of Congress Control Number: 2004106012

ISBN 0-8065-2592-4

This book is dedicated to my parents for conceiving me, and also Patricia Combs, who first lit the spark in me to write. She told me I'd be a writer, and she was right. . . .

Film as dream, film as music. No art passes our conscience the way film does, and goes directly to our feelings, deep down into the dark rooms of our souls.

—Ingmar Bergman

Film is more than the twentieth-century art. It's another part of the twentieth-century mind. It's the world seen from inside. We've come to a certain point in the history of film. If a thing can be filmed, the film is implied in the thing itself. This is where we are. The twentieth century is on film. . . . You have to ask yourself if there's anything about us more important than the fact that we're constantly on film, constantly watching ourselves.

—Don DeLillo

It's the movies that have really been running things in America ever since they were invented. They show you what to do, how to do it, how to feel about it, and how to look at how you feel about it. Everybody has their own America, and then they have the pieces of a fantasy America that they think is out there but they can't see.

—Andy Warhol

# Contents

# Foreword

HAVE YOU EVER WONDERED why film titles of the past are always followed by a date? We write *Easy Rider* (1969) and *The Sheik* (1921) and
*Kill Bill*—Vol. I (2003), and that date is considered forever and always
a point of reference for talking about the flick. And yet that may not be
the date the movie was actually written, or filmed, or edited. Most
films take two years or more from conception to screen, and many are
held from release for any number of reasons. A film could be conceived
in 1972, written in 1979, filmed in 1982, and not released until 1986.
But the only date that will matter is that last one, the release date—
because that's when the movie was unleashed and moved from the
private realm to the public. That's the moment it became part of us.

We need the release date because movies can't be watched out of
context. When we talk about novels, we don't write *War and Peace*
(1865) or *For Whom the Bell Tolls* (1940). When we talk about music,
we don't write Beethoven's Fifth Symphony (1808). And the reason is
that *War and Peace* doesn't change, and Beethoven's Fifth doesn't
change. Tolstoy's words remain the same today as they were for readers in 1865. Beethoven's Fifth can be variously interpreted, but overall it uses the same instrumentation and the same quiet spots and the
same fortissimos. It's only film, of all the art forms, that changes constantly. A film made in 1990 uses different technology than a film
made in 1980. A silent film made in 1926 is so fundamentally different from a talking picture made in 1929 that the earlier film becomes
all but obsolete. Once our eyes and ears have been educated to new
technology, we can't go back easily to the old one. So we can't think
of film history as a slow-moving stream, into which various "great
works" appear here and there. We have to think of it instead as a
series of fundamentally *different* art forms—many streams, located con-
tinents apart—that are born, flourish, mature, become obsolescent,
and die. The reason most people can't comfortably watch films made

before their own childhoods is that, without any preparation, it's alien terrain. It's almost a foreign language. It doesn't speak to their senses. It's part of a vanished culture.

And yet there are enough of us who do plunge into those musty old archives, even into the dark ages of silent films, especially in this era of the information-packed "special edition" DVD. The DVD is itself one of the latest technologies to alter the experience of film. Even though its technical quality is inferior to a silver-based Technicolor film of the 1930s, we've discarded that old technology just as surely as we discarded black-and-white cinematography. (Television executives have discovered, to their dismay, that at least half the viewers under the age of thirty-five won't watch a black-and-white movie at all. It's as off-putting to them as the pantomimic acting of a silent film.) Because film is the only art form that was created by scientists, it has always been shaped more by inventors than by producers, directors or stars. No matter how brilliant the filmmaker, he's ultimately a slave to the available technology.

This special quality of film is what is captured so expertly in Andrew Rausch's concise history of the key turning points in film history. As he aptly points out, especially in his chapters on Italian Neorealism and the French New Wave, nothing lasts in the film world. It's no more possible today to make an Italian Neorealist film than it would be possible to build a new Egyptian pyramid. That world is gone, and film is a "right now" thing. In some cases film history is shaped by outside forces—the Hays Office that effectively censored films for decades after 1934, the social revolution that fueled blaxploitation films, to name but two—but more often it's shaped by men in laboratories, whether they be in Edison's laboratory in New Jersey, or, a hundred years later, in the Pixar special-effects laboratory in Southern California. A sex scandal, like the Fatty Arbuckle affair, can have an impact on what we see on the screen for a time, but a new film emulsion process or innovative new camera can change the image on the screen itself. We tend to think of Hollywood as a place where rich and powerful people create movies. It would be more accurate to think of it as a place where people become rich and powerful by understanding what science and fashion demand that they make.

For many readers, these stories from movie history will be familiar, but Rausch recounts them with such precision and concision that they bring our film heritage into sharp relief, and occasionally his research into the oddities and chance occurrences of that heritage will startle even the jaded film buff. This is a mostly American story, and even though he gives credit to the French, Brits, Germans, Russians, Danes, and Italians where appropriate, that's as it should be. Film was invented in the United States, and with very few exceptions—the Lumiere brothers, Eisenstein, the Expressionists, André Bazin—it has found its highest expression in America. In fact, most of these ground-breaking films—*The Birth of a Nation* (1915), the work of Mae West, *Citizen Kane* (1941), *Sweet Sweetback's Baadasssss Song* (1971), *Jaws* (1975), *Star Wars* (1977), *Toy Story* (1995)—could not have been made anywhere else. Even when foreign filmmakers rebel against the traditions of Hollywood, as did the Dogme 95 group in 1995, the mainstream American film is the standard by which their rebellion is measured.

What I like about this book is that it takes what appears to be widely divergent eras, genres, and critical approaches, and somehow makes them part of one seamless continuum. What Rausch has done is to take all the elements of film that we take for granted as part of our subliminal experience, from the close-up to the soundtrack to the latest in computer-generated imagery, and shown that the only reason it *is* part of our experience is that hundreds of scientists and artists made it possible. And yet the strangest aspect of Rausch's story is that, in showing how men attempted to use technology to record "reality," he reveals that they couldn't do that after all. Even *Nanook of the North* (1922), the original reality film, seems hopelessly remote today. Film can create a version of experience, but not experience itself. Film is best at telling stories about "what might have been." Rausch, in the meantime, shows us how those stories came to be made.

—Joe Bob Briggs
New York, New York

JOE BOB BRIGGS has penned several books, including *Profoundly Disturbing: Shocking Movies that Changed History*, *Joe Bob Goes to the Drive-In* and its sequel, *Joe Bob Goes Back to the Drive-In*, as well as the novel *Evidence of Love* (as John Bloom). He hosted two long-running television series, *Joe Bob's Drive-In Theater* and *Monstervision*. He also appeared in a number of films, including *Stephen King's The Stand*, *Casino*, and *Face/Off*.

# *Introduction*

THEY SAY THAT EVERYONE remembers with absolute clarity the exact moment they fell in love with the love of their life. Like everyone, I'd experienced a few crushes which I'd naively mistaken for love. I'd even been married by this point. . . . The night that would forever change my life came in September 1994. I was twenty-one years old. I was sitting in a packed theater to watch Quentin Tarantino's tour-de-force, *Pulp Fiction*. After having watched only about two minutes of the film, I experienced a feeling unlike anything I had ever known before; it was that feeling that dreamers dream about, singers sing about, and poets write about. I immediately realized two things: (1) I had fallen passionately in love with both *Pulp Fiction* and the medium of film, and (2) that I would never look at film in the same way.

From that single seed grew a continuing love affair with film. A decade has passed and I'm now divorced from the woman who attended that screening with me. (It's no coincidence, either.) But my love for film remains (at least) as strong and passionate as it was then. In fact, it remains the single most rewarding relationship I've experienced to date.

In any relationship, one must come to know as much about the object of one's affections as humanly possible. The only way to fully understand and appreciate that person is to learn their past. There can be no doubt that each of us—for better or worse—have become who and what we are today because of all that we've lived through. This is also true of cinema; it is surely the landmark happenings in its past that have made cinema all that it is today.

It was from this simple observation that *Turning Points in Film History* was born. This book was not conceived as a definitive history of the medium (a great many volumes could be devoted to that), but rather an in-depth look at the people and events that have had the most significant impact upon it.

In structuring this book, I first had to determine what constitutes a turning point. After much debate, I concluded that a turning point should be defined as anything that has significantly changed the way films were created and/or perceived. Isolating these events would prove to be far more difficult than I had first anticipated. Throughout the relatively short history of the cinema, many film movements have taken place around the globe. But how important were these movements in the grand scheme of things? This was a question I had to answer. To help me determine the single most important events in the history of film, I sought the counsel of various scholars, professors, critics, and filmmakers.

It should be noted that the greater number of these turning points involve what is at first glance primarily American cinema. However, considering that Hollywood has, since its earliest days, heavily inspired and influenced the film output of other nations, it must be concluded that the most significant events in the history of American film have ultimately affected world cinema in one way or another.

In an effort to craft something a little bit different from the average film history book, I've chosen a few turning points that are frequently overlooked in scholarly studies. Here you'll find not only the mainstays, such as Eisenstein and Griffith, but also chapters dealing with blaxploitation, American International Pictures (AIP), and *Toy Story* (1995).

In many ways, this book is an open love letter. Although I vowed to make this book an academic study on the history of the cinema, it was written with all the love and passion one might possess when writing such a letter. If you love movies—whether it's the highbrow fare of Bergman and Fellini, or lowbrow "trash" like *Biker Zombies from Detroit* (2001)—this book was written for you. Here, you'll be presented with a history that may not be entirely familiar to you, one that's as funny, sad, rich, and exciting as the movies we all love. So, as Margo Channing proclaims in *All About Eve* (1950): "Fasten your seat belts, it's going to be a bumpy night!"

# Chronology

1646    Athanasius Kircher invents the Magia Catoptrica ("the Magic Lantern").

1826    Joseph Antoine Ferdinand Plateau invents the Thaumatrope.

1834    Plateau invents the Phenakistascope.

       William George Horner unveils the Zoetrope.

1869    Clerk Maxwell improves upon the Zoetrope.

1877    Thomas Alva Edison develops the Phonograph.

1878    California senator Leland Stanford hires Edweard Muybridge to photograph a galloping horse to determine whether all four of its legs ever leave the ground simultaneously.

1880    Muybridge projects photographs of a galloping horse in succession with a device known as the Zoogyroscope—later known as the Zoopraxiscope.

1882    Etienne Jules Marey invents the Photographic Gun.

1888    Augustin Le Prince fashions a single-lens motion picture camera and projector.

       Edison files for a patent for a motion picture camera.

1889    Eastman employee Henry M. Reichenbach invents flexible film based upon studies made by J.W. Hyatt, I.S. Hyatt, and Hannibal Goodwin.

       William Friese-Greene receives a patent for a camera capable of producing short motion picture sequences.

       Wordsworth Donisthorpe and W. C. Crofts patent a motion picture camera using film carried by paper.

1890    Donisthorpe shoots a brief motion picture.

        After perfecting his motion camera and projector, La Prince and
        his invention mysteriously disappear from a Paris-bound train.
        He is never seen again.

1891    Edison employee William Kennedy Laurie Dickson invents the
        Kinetograph, which will later be renamed the Kinetoscope.

1893    Edison unveils "his" new invention at the World's Fair in
        Chicago.

        Edison is contracted to manufacture Kinetoscopes for Raff
        & Gammon for $200 apiece.

1894    Dickson records a short film, *Fred Ott's Sneeze*, which depicts an
        Edison mechanic sneezing.

        The first Kinetoscope Parlor is opened at 1155 Broadway in
        New York City.

1895    Dickson resigns from the Edison Company and goes to work
        for the American Mutoscope Company.

        The Eidoloscope, developed by Dickson, Eugene Lauste, and
        Enoch Rector, is demonstrated for members of the press at
        35 Frankfort Street in New York City.

        Max Skladanowsky projects moving pictures using the Bioscop
        in Berlin, Germany.

        Auguste and Louis Lumière patent and later demonstrate the
        Cinematographe in Paris, France. Georges Méliès is in atten-
        dance.

        Méliès purchases an English-made projector known as the
        Theatrograph.

1896    Méliès produces his first film, *Une Partie de Cartes*, which lasts
        one minute.

        Méliès develops stop-motion photography.

        Charles Pathé and Oskar Messter experiment with the combina-
        tion of the Cinematographe and a Gramophone.

1899    Vladimir Poulsen conceives the idea of magnetic storage.

1900    Méliès utilizes prearranged scenes in his film *Cendrillon*
        (*Cinderella*).

        Méliès makes *L'Homme orchestra* (*The One Man Band*), which
        features seven versions of himself performing music together.

**1902**    Méliès produces his 400th film, *Le Voyage dans la lune* (*A Trip to the Moon*), featuring a linear narrative.

Edwin S. Porter produces *The Life of an American Fireman*.

**1903**    Porter produces *The Great Train Robbery*.

**1904**    The Warwick Company unveils a device known as the Cinephone, which is immediately replaced by Cecil Hepworth's Vivaphone.

**1906**    Lauste patents a device capable of recording sound on film.

**1907**    Porter casts D. W. Griffith in his film *Rescued from an Eagle's Nest*.

**1908**    Nine manufacturers form the cartel known as the Motion Picture Patents Company.

Edison unveils the Cinemaphone.

**1913**    Edison announces the invention of the Kinetophone.

**1915**    Griffith directs *The Birth of a Nation*, which introduces a number of innovations.

The U.S. government finds the Motion Picture Patents Company guilty of restricting trade and monopolizing the motion picture industry.

**1919**    Robert Weine's *Das Kabinett des Doktor Caligari* (*The Cabinet of Dr. Caligari*) is released, and ushers in the German Expressionist movement.

**1921**    Orland E. Kellum devises the Photokinema.

Actress Virginia Rappe dies at a party thrown by Roscoe "Fatty" Arbuckle.

Griffith's film *Dream Street*, which utilizes the Photokinema, is released.

The Motion Picture Producers and Distributors of America (MPPDA) is established, and former postmaster general Will Hays is named as its president.

**1922**    Robert J. Flaherty's *Nanook of the North* is released.

The Hays Code is implemented by the year-old MPPDA.

**1924**    Sergei Eisenstein invents and experiments with montage in his film *Strike!*.

**1925**   Eisenstein masters the art of montage in his groundbreaking film *Battleship Potemkin*.

**1926**   Bell Laboratory scientists unveil the Vitaphone, to which Sam Warner purchases the rights.

   *Don Juan*, a feature film featuring a musical soundtrack throughout, is released.

**1927**   *The Jazz Singer*, which features several minutes of music and dialogue, is released to great acclaim.

   The Academy of Motion Picture Arts and Sciences is founded.

   The MPPDA writes its list of "Don'ts and Be Carefuls."

**1928**   The first all-talking feature film, *Lights of New York*, is released.

**1930**   The Motion Picture Production Code (dubbed the "Hays Code" by the media) is adopted.

**1934**   Joseph I. Breen is named as the director of the Production Code Administration (PCA).

**1937**   Walt Disney's feature-length animated film *Snow White and the Seven Dwarfs* is released.

**1939**   The television is introduced to the world at the New York World's Fair.

**1941**   Orson Welles's *Citizen Kane*, is released.

   *The Maltese Falcon* ushers in the "film noir" cycle.

**1945**   Roberto Rossellini's *Roma, città aperta* (*Rome, Open City*) ushers in the Italian Neorealism movement.

**1947**   The House Un-American Activities Committee (HUAC) begins investigating communism in the motion picture industry.

**1948**   The U.S. government finds the five major motion picture studios guilty of restricting trade and monopolizing the industry. This will become known as "the Paramount Decision."

**1950**   André Bazin (along with Jacques Doinol-Valcroz) establishes *Cahiers du Cinéma*, for which future *nouvelle vague* directors François Truffaut, Jean-Luc Godard, Claude Chabrol, Eric Rohmer, and Jacques Rivette will write under his tutelage.

**1951**   HUAC begins second series of hearings investigating communism in the motion picture industry.

**1954**   James H. Nicholson and Samuel Z. Arkoff establish American Releasing Company, which will later become American International Pictures (AIP).

**1956**   Ampex develops the first video recorder.

**1958**   Claude Chabrol's *Le Beau Serge* is released, ushering in *la nouvelle vague*.

**1967**   Sony introduces the Video Tape Recorder.

**1968**   Motion Picture Association of America President Jack Valenti announces the implementation of a new voluntary ratings system.

**1969**   Dennis Hopper's *Easy Rider* is released. This begins Hollywood's "new wave."

**1971**   Melvin Van Peebles's *Sweet Sweetback's Baadasssss Song* introduces the blaxploitation cycle.

**1972**   AVCO introduces a video player known as Cartrivision. In addition, they begin renting videocassettes of popular movies.

**1975**   Sony unveils the Betamax.

Steven Spielberg's *Jaws* is released to great acclaim, beginning the blockbuster craze.

**1976**   RCA introduces the VHS videocassette player.

**1977**   George Lucas's *Star Wars* becomes a huge hit, reinforcing the blockbuster craze that began with *Jaws*.

André Blay establishes the first video distribution company in Detroit, Michigan.

**1982**   Disney releases *Tron*, a film utilizing more computer-generated imagery than any film to date.

**1983**   George Atkinson opens the first independently owned video rental business in Los Angeles, California.

**1995**   *Toy Story*, the first fully computer-animated feature film, is released.

Lars von Trier announces the Dogme 95 collective and introduces its manifesto.

# TURNING POINTS
## IN
# *Film History*

## Chapter 1

# The Birth of Film

PHOTOFEST

Auguste and Louis Lumière were not the fathers of the medium, as historians have erroneously purported. Nevertheless, they were responsible for introducing the medium to much of the world.

BEFORE THERE WAS a "turning point," there had to be a starting point; therefore, the first significant event in film history was the birth of the medium. That, however, cannot be isolated to a single event because a number of important scientific discoveries and inventions, spanning three centuries, resulted eventually in the birth of the film.

The first seeds were planted as early as 1646. A German Jesuit named Athanasius Kircher was hard at work devising an instrument he called *Magia Catoptrica* ("the Magic Lantern"). Although it is now widely speculated that the device had been invented—on paper, at

1

least—years earlier by a Dutch scientist named Christian Huygens, Kircher is credited with the invention because he was the first to write about it publicly. The Magic Lantern, which Kircher detailed in his book *Ars Magna Lucis et Ombrae*, was an early slide projector consisting of four parts. First was a light-proof box that contains a light source (such as a candle or a lamp). A condensing lens at the front of the box was used to direct the beam of light from its source onto a slide, that held the image. Then, a second lens, set in front of the slide, was used to sharpen the slide image that was projected on a "screen" (usually a wall or a bed sheet).

The next significant work to ultimately play a role in the birth of the motion picture would not occur for almost another two centuries. The year was 1826. A blind Belgian scientist named Joseph Antoine Ferdinand Plateau, working to achieve his doctorate at the University of Liege, had been studying the phenomenon known as "persistence of vision." (If an observer watches an object that suddenly disappears, the image of the object will remain on the retina for approximately one tenth of a second.) During his studies, Plateau made a breakthrough with the creation of a device he called the Thaumatrope. The Thaumatrope—now believed to be a more advanced version of a mechanical device created by the Chinese as early as 200 B.C.—was a disk with an image on both sides, suspended by two strings. When the disk was spun on the strings, the images appeared to merge. For instance, if one side depicted a bird and the other an empty birdcage, the two images would combine when the disk was spun to present a single image of the bird "inside" the cage.

The following year, the results of Plateau's research were published in *Correspondence Mathématique et Physique*. In April 1829, Plateau delivered a thesis entitled "Certain Properties of the Impressions Produced by Light upon the Organ of Sight." This thesis would be an invaluable stepping stone toward the realization of the modern motion picture.

In his book *Magic Shadows: The Story of the Origin of Motion Pictures*, historian Martin Quigley, Jr., details Plateau's findings and their importance:

The chief points—all of importance in building motion pictures—of the Plateau thesis dated April 24, 1829, were: First, the sensation (result of the picture presented to the eye) must stay for a time to form completely—this hinted definitely at the necessity of intermittent movement for a really successful and practical motion picture machine. Second, the sensations do not disappear immediately but gradually dim—this makes motion pictures possible. If each image disappeared all at once, only individual still pictures would be recognized. The gradual dimming makes possible fusion of one image with the next which results in the appearance of motion. The third point covered was the relative effect on the eye of various colors. Plateau concluded that the intensity of the chief colors decreased from white, yellow, red, blue—in that order. He also announced results of perception of various colors at different angles, studies made in the shade and in the light. It was further pointed out that two colors—as two images—changed rapidly result in only one sensation or image.

Plateau would improve upon the Thaumatrope in late 1829. Plateau himself described the instrument:

Two small copper pulleys, (a) and (b), drive by means of an endless cord a large wooden wheel, (c), which has a double groove; the diameters of the small pulleys are such that the two *a* cords are equally taut and the system is placed in movement by means of the handle, (d), the speed of one pulley being an exact multiple of the other; the axes terminate in form of a vise and are devised in such a way that you can attach to them by little screws the drawings or cartoons with which you wish to experiment. The pulleys are held by iron supports, (f) and (g), which slide in two grooves practically parallel with the stand or base (hk), and are held in position by means of thumbscrews.

With this simple mechanical device, Plateau had fashioned the first instrument that made pictures move; the first true motion picture machine. Not one to rest on his laurels, Plateau sought to improve his invention.

In 1834, Plateau unveiled a new invention he called the Phenakistascope (or the Fantascope) at the Royal Academy of Belgium. This device, based heavily on the studies of Austrian mathematician Simon Ritter von Stampfer (who himself had fashioned a nearly identical device, which he called a Stroboscope), was a disk with a series of radial slots placed around its circumference. Between each slot was a picture, each one slightly different from the next. The observer would then stand before a mirror and look through a slot while spinning the disk. This would create the illusion of movement.

That these discoveries would be instrumental in the creation of the motion picture is ironic considering that Plateau himself was blind. Interestingly, Ohio inventor Thomas Edison, who was almost completely deaf, made equally important contributions to the science of recording and reproducing sound four decades later.

The next significant event in the development of cinema came later in 1834, in the form of a child's toy. The toy, known as the Zoetrope (also known as the "Wheel of the Devil" because the first images made to appear on it were that of the devil), was invented by an Englishman named William George Horner. The device consisted of a metal drum with slits through which a viewer could look at a series of drawings on a disk, which appeared to move as the drum rotated. The Zoetrope was later improved upon by a number of inventors and manufactured by Milton Bradley in 1860. In 1869, a scientist named Clerk Maxwell improved the popular device yet again when he suggested the installation of concave lenses rather than mere slots.

A number of important events occurred around the globe in 1878. Among them, Edison developed the electric light, and California senator Leland Stanford proposed a $25,000 wager to a fellow sportsman. Did all four legs of a galloping horse ever leave the ground simultaneously? This bet, which hardly seems important more than a century later, ultimately led to the first motion pictures. After seeing photographer Edweard Muybridge's acclaimed photographs of Yosemite, Stanford approached Muybridge and asked him whether he could somehow settle the wager. Although initially he believed it impossible, Muybridge accepted the challenge. Muybridge's earliest attempts to answer the question resulted in failure. After five years, Muybridge succeeded only after hiring an engineer named John D. Isaacs, who set up a battery of cameras, each placed one foot apart, and triggered by strings above the ground; when the horse galloping by would trip each string, a different camera would capture its image. Each camera was fitted with a special shutter which the photographer claimed to be less than the "two thousandth part of a second." After taking more than twenty thousand photographs, Muybridge proved that there were indeed moments when all four of the horse's legs were off the ground. But perhaps more important, Muybridge also discovered that, when viewed in rapid succession, the photographs "merged" to create the illusion of movement. In 1879, Muybridge was granted a patent for an "apparatus for photographing objects in motion." The following year Muybridge projected the photographs in succession through a device he called the Zoogyroscope (later known as the Zoopraxiscope) onto a screen at the California School for Fine Arts. Thanks to his work, Muybridge helped his employer win his wager—and inadvertently created the first motion pictures.

In 1882, Etienne Jules Marey created a device he called the Photographic Gun, based upon the principle of the revolver, with each chamber containing photographic plates that recorded images when the trigger was pulled. It should be noted that French astronomer Pierre Jules César had used an apparatus like this when he recorded the passage of Venus across the sun in 1874.

In 1889, Henry M. Reichenbach, an employee of George Eastman, invented the flexible and semitransparent celluloid base upon which images would later be printed. It was Reichenbach and Eastman who first called this material film. Reichenbach's invention drew upon earlier discoveries made by J.W. and I.S. Hyatt in 1865 and Hannibal Goodwin in 1888. The basic components of the new film were a transparent base, an adhesive substrate made from gelatin, and a light-sensitive emulsion. Although more than a century has passed, film's basic components remain unchanged.

Later that same year, an English photographer named William Friese-Greene received a patent for a camera that was capable of producing short sequences of pictures. Shortly thereafter, Wordsworth Donisthorpe and W. C. Crofts patented a primitive motion picture camera that utilized "a sensitive film carried by a roll of paper or other material." With this camera, Donisthorpe shot an extremely brief film of Trafalgar Square in 1890. Despite these advances, Donisthorpe abandond his research due to a lack of financial support.

French inventor Augustin Le Prince, who had already fashioned a single-lens motion picture camera and projector as early as 1888, apparently perfected these mechanisms in 1890. With his camera, Le

Prince is believed to have been the first to move film through the camera by use of sprocket wheels engaging perforations in the film. The problem is, these claims are difficult to substantiate because both Le Prince and his invention disappeared mysteriously in September 1890; Le Prince boarded a train in Dijon bound for Paris, but never reached his destination.

Many film historians, including University of Nebraska Film Studies professor Wheeler Winston Dixon, consider Le Prince the true father of the motion picture. "Without a doubt, Augustin Le Prince, who shot the first films in 1888, made the most significant breakthroughs of his time. Both the Lumières and Edison eventually used ideas that Le Prince originated, and he was also arguably the first person to publicly project films. His influence is enormous, and yet his contributions have been all but ignored."

The next individual to help pave the way for the motion picture was the prolific Thomas Edison, who would ultimately patent 1,093 inventions in his lifetime. When Edison invented the "talking" phonograph in 1877, writer Alfred Hopkins of *The Scientific American* concluded that this creation would one day prove valuable as a means of assisting the visual presentation of photographs. Edison found himself in agreement and soon began studying the

### Did You Know?

In his book *The Missing Reel,* film historian Christopher Rawlence suggests that the true inventor of the motion picture, Augustin Le Prince, may have been killed by someone intent on cashing in on his invention.

work of his predecessors. (Some historians believe Edison had quietly begun tinkering with the motion picture camera as early as 1888. That year Edison had met with Edweard Muybridge about his Zoopraxiscope and then filed for a patent on October 17, 1888, for a device that would "do for the eye what the phonograph does for the ear"—record and reproduce images.) Edison, however, saw the possibility of the motion picture as little more than a tool in support of the phonograph rather than as a viable medium in itself. Edison's earliest film devices worked in a similar way to his phonograph, with pictures recorded onto a wax cylinder. Edison soon tired of these experiments and delegated the research to his assistant, William Kennedy Laurie Dickson. Dickson saw things differently than his mentor, and immediately began experimenting with a camera that would use 35mm celluloid film. He called this camera the Kinetograph.

David Robinson describes the device in his book *From Peep Show to Palace*:

> It consisted of an upright wooden cabinet, 18 in. x 27 in. x 4 ft. high, with a peephole with magnifying lenses on top . . . Inside the box, the film, in a continuous band of approximately 50 feet, was arranged around a series of spools. A large, electrically driven sprocket wheel at the top of the box engaged corresponding sprocket holes punched in the edges of the film, which was thus drawn under the lens at a continuous rate. Beneath the film was an electric lamp, and between the lamp and the film a revolving shutter with a narrow slit. As each frame passed under the lens, the shutter permitted a flash of light so brief that the frame appeared to be frozen. This rapid series of apparently still frames appeared, thanks to the persistence of vision phenomenon, as a moving image.

The Kinetograph weighed nearly one ton and showed forty-six photographs per minute.

Edison's first film was directed and photographed by Dickson. The short film *Fred Ott's Sneeze* (1894) depicted a mechanic employed by Edison sneezing. While the subject might seem less than spectacular, *Fred Ott's Sneeze* is significant as it is recognized as the first motion picture.

Because Dickson was employed at his company—a collective— Edison would ultimately take sole credit for the invention despite his having had little to do with its creation beyond the initiation and supervision of the project. (This lack of recognition may explain Dickson's resignation from Edison's company in spring 1895 when he jumped ship to work for the rival American Mutoscope Company.) Edison unveiled this new device at the 1893 World's Fair in Chicago. That same year, Edison was contracted to manufacture these single-viewer Kinetoscopes for a company called Raff & Gammon. For each Kinetoscope produced, Edison received $200, and Raff & Gammon would retail the machine for about $350. On April 14, 1894, Andrew

M. Holland opened the first Kinetoscope parlor at 1155 Broadway in New York City. The converted shoe store featured ten Kinetoscopes, each of which showed a different film.

After Edison balked at a $150 fee for overseas patents, rights to the Kinetoscope were left unprotected in Europe. While Edison himself saw little commercial value in the Kinetoscope, its potential was not lost upon Englishman Robert W. Paul, who began manufacturing them. Paul sold approximately sixty machines, making himself a handsome profit.

Meanwhile, Dickson, having first developed a method of projecting images (Edison had seen no future in projection) began work on a projector, which would allow moving images to be screened for entire groups of people rather than just one. Dickson, Eugene Lauste, and Enoch Rector—in the employ of former Confederate officer Woodville Latham—developed a device they called the Eidoloscope (also known as the Pantoptikon). This device, which utilized 50mm film rather than the now-standard 35mm, was demonstrated for members of the New York press on April 21, 1895, at 35 Frankfort Street. Although this screening was largely forgotten in the years that followed, it is now believed to have been the first public exhibition of motion pictures in the world—preceding by eight months the famed December 28, 1895, public display by Auguste and Louis Lumière. (The Lumières' display was also preceded by Max Skladanowsky's Bioscop projections in Berlin in November 1895.)

> ### *Cinematic Firsts*
>
> The first film projected before a paying audience was the four-minute-long *Young Griffo vs. "Battling" Charles Barnett.* This occurred in New York City in May 1895.

The Lumière brothers hailed from Lyon, France, where they worked in a photographic factory operated by their father. Inspired by the Kinetoscope, the brothers went to work on their own motion picture camera. The Lumières filed their first patent on February 13, 1895, for a camera they called the Cinématographe. The camera the Lumière brothers perfected was far superior to that of Edison and Dickson because it could be used to capture moving images on film as well as to project them before an audience. The films shot by the Lumière brothers were approximately fifty minutes in length. The first Lumière film screened to an audience depicted workers exiting the Lumière photographic factory in Lyon. Although this screening was *not* the first time the public saw a motion picture, it remains significant because of the impact the event had on the rest of the world. Earlier screenings by Dickson and Skladanowsky had not been heavily publicized and thus failed to have significant repercussions.

## Chapter 2

# Georges Méliès and the
# Artificially Arranged Scene

This photograph from Georges Méliès's 1902 production *Le Voyage dans la lune* (*A Trip to the Moon*) has become one of the most famous pieces of cinematic iconography from the earliest years of the medium.

GEORGES MÉLIÈS WAS born to Louis and Catherine Méliès in Paris, France, on the night of December 8, 1861. Georges was the couple's third child. Having opened and operated several Paris shoemaking factories, the Méliès were wealthy. As a child Georges attended classes at the Lycée Impérial, which was located just outside Paris. When Georges was nine years old, the school was bombed during the Franco-Prussian War and he was relocated to a school within the city. The right-brained Georges was an average pupil who earned mediocre marks, but he displayed a fascination and talent for all facets of the arts. He found himself frequently in trouble after sketching caricatures of his instructors during classes. The young Georges conducted his own puppet shows, acted on stage, painted, and began studying magic. After graduation, Georges enlisted in the army.

After his military discharge, Georges, now 23, traveled to London where he studied English. Unbeknownst to his father, Georges studied magic and attended numerous London magic shows. Georges dreamed of working as a professional magician, but his father had more practical ideas. Georges, it was decided, would work as a manager at one of his shoemaking factories. Filled with despair, Georges returned to Paris and began toiling in his father's factory. In 1888, his father announced his retirement and handed the reins of his business operation over to Georges and his older brothers, Henri and Gaston. Seeing an opportunity to finally break away, Georges promptly sold his share of the business to his siblings, and used the money to purchase a theater which had belonged to the late magician Robert Houdin. Georges then reopened the theater, showcasing his own illusions.

Georges's life took a turn at four P.M. on December 28, 1895, when he attended the Lumière brothers' famed motion picture screening, which was held in the café beneath his theater. It is interesting that only thirty-three spectators were in attendance that day (and no news reporters), but Méliès—who was soon to make the next significant contributions to the newborn medium—was. Inspired by what he'd seen, Méliès purchased an English projector known as the Theatrograph and began screening Edison Company shorts in his theater. (Méliès would go on to develop and patent his own motion picture camera.)

In 1896 Méliès began producing his own films. *Une Partie de Cartes* (1896), a one-minute short depicting Méliès playing cards, was the first of approximately eighty films he produced in that first year. These early films had little in common thematically as Méliès roamed the streets of Paris filming virtually everything he came into contact with. While turning his camera on these mundane events, Méliès made an important discovery. One day his camera jammed while filming passing traffic. Méliès cleared the aperture gate, readjusted the film, and resumed filming. It was not until he projected the footage that Méliès made his discovery. He had been filming a bus when the camera had jammed. After correcting this problem, Méliès resumed filming a passing hearse. As fate would have it, both the bus and the hearse were traveling in the same direction, at the same speed, and in the exact same location in the street; thus, when projected, the bus seemingly transformed magically into a hearse! For Méliès, so enamored of creating illusions, this occurrence was fascinating. Through this chance incident, Méliès discovered the trick effect of stop-motion photography.

This revelation led Méliès to produce *Escamotage d'une dame* (*The Vanishing Lady*) (1896), in which a woman seemingly was transformed into a skeleton. This, of course, shocked audiences, who had never seen such a thing. Méliès enjoyed watching the crowds react and continued making motion pictures designed to frighten viewers. These films depicted giant insects, ghostly apparitions, possessed clothing, mad scientists, and bloodthirsty vampires on the loose. (Méliès himself made more than twenty appearances as Satan in these productions.) Because of this it can be said that Méliès was a pioneer not only by dint of his technological and artistic innovations but as the originator of the horror film.

## Cinematic Firsts

The first theatrical trailers were projected by George Méliès in 1898 above the entrance to his theater. With these clips which he'd cut from the films himself, Méliès hoped to give people an idea of what they would see inside.

Through experimentation Méliès began perfecting a number of camera tricks, including masks, double exposures, fades, dissolves, animation, and, of course, stop-motion photography. Despite his discoveries, which were still miles ahead of every other filmmaker on the planet, Méliès was not content to rest on his laurels. The ambitious filmmaker then began working on what he called "artificially arranged scenes"; this meant the construction of a storyline rather than simply catching real-life events on camera. Today this sounds rather obvious and primitive, but at the time it was unprecedented and highly innovative.

Méliès's first film to utilize prearranged scenes was his 1899 production of *Cendrillon* (*Cinderella*). The film featured twenty scenes arranged chronologically. Below is Méliès's outline of *Cendrillon*:

1. Cinderella in the Kitchen
2. The Fairy
3. The Transformation of the Rat
4. The Pumpkin Changes to a Carriage
5. The Ball at the King's Palace
6. The Hour of Midnight
7. The Bedroom of Cinderella
8. The Dance of the Clocks
9. The Prince and the Slipper
10. The Godmother of Cinderella
11. The Prince and Cinderella
12. The Arrival at the Church
13. The Wedding
14. Cinderella's Sisters
15. The King
16. The Nuptial Cortege
17. The Bride's Ballet
18. The Celestial Spheres
19. The Transformation
20. The Triumph of Cinderella

With *Cendrillon* Méliès introduced not only narrative to the medium, but also the trappings of stage productions; among these were costumes and elaborate scenery. In 1900 Méliès produced another groundbreaking film, *L'Homme-orchestre* (*The One-Man Band*), which depicted a seven-piece ensemble performing together. What makes this interesting is that all seven performers were played by Méliès himself and all seven characters interacted and appeared on-screen together at once. This trick was done with multiple exposure and was later duplicated in many other films (most notably Buster Keaton's 1921 *The Playhouse*).

In 1902, Méliès produced *L'Homme à la tête en caoutchouc* (*The Man with the Rubber Head*). In this humorous film Méliès shows his head being pumped full of air, growing larger and larger like a balloon. That same year Méliès crafted a number of films in which his head was removed or a number of heads—all his—fought each other. In the 1904 film *Le Bourreau turc* (*The Terrible Turkish Executioner*), Méliès again revisited this theme; this time, after several prisoners are decapitated, their still-living heads reattach themselves to their bodies and then kill their executioner.

In 1902, Méliès produced his four hundredth and most famous film, *Le Voyage dans la lune* (*A Trip to the Moon*), for which he is most often remembered today. This ambitious project took more than three months to film and cost Méliès ten thousand francs—a then unheard of amount for a motion picture budget. The film was more than eight hundred feet in length, making it twice the size of *Cendrillon*, and far longer than any other film produced at that time. Modeled loosely around Jules Verne's *From the Earth to the Moon and Around the Moon*, this light-hearted, silly film poked fun at science. In it, a group of astronomers travel to the moon in a spacecraft. From the catalogue of an American company that illegally pirated *Voyage* comes this description of the film's most memorable scene:

> In the midst of the clouds the moon is visible at a distance. The shell [spacecraft] coming closer every minute, the moon magnifies rapidly until finally it attains colossal dimensions. It gradually assumes the shape of a living, grotesque face, smiling sanctimoniously. Suddenly, the shell arrives with the rapidity of lightning, and pierces the eye of the moon. The face at once makes horrible grimaces, whilst enormous tears flow from the wound.

The film's thirty scenes are outlined in the catalogue for Méliès's Star Films:

1. The Scientific Congress at the Astronomic Club
2. Planning the Trip. Appointing the Explorers and Servants. Farewell.
3. The Workshops Constructing the Projectile.
4. The Foundries. The Chimney-stack. The Casting of the Monster Gun.
5. The Astronomers Enter the Shell.
6. Loading the Gun.
7. The Monster Gun. March Past the Gunners. Fire!!!! Saluting the Flag.
8. The Flight Through Space. Approaching the Moon.
9. Landed Right in the Eye!!!!

10. Flight of the Shell into the Moon. Appearance of the Earth from the Moon.
11. The Plain of Craters. Volcanic Eruption.
12. The Dream (the Bolies, the Great Bear, Phoebus, the Twin Stars, Saturn).
13. The Snowstorm.
14. 40 Degrees Below Zero. Descending a Lunar Crater.
15. In the Interior of the Moon. The Giant Mushroom Grotto.
16. Encounter with the Selenites. Homeric Flight.
17. Prisoners!!
18. The Kingdom of the Moon. The Selenite Army.
19. The Flight.
20. Wild Pursuit.
21. The Astronomers Find the Shell again. Departure from the Moon.
22. Vertical Drop into Space.
23. Splashing into the Open Sea.
24. At the Bottom of the Ocean.
25. The Rescue. Return to Port.
26. Great Fete. Triumphal March Past.
27. Crowning and Decorating the Heroes of the Trip.
28. Procession of Marines and Fire Brigade.
29. Inauguration of the Commemorative Statue by the Mayor and Council.
30. Public Rejoicings.

This extraordinary film captured the attention and imagination of viewers and filmmakers around the globe. Soon, a number of filmmakers began imitating Méliès's work and passing it off as their own. Méliès addressed this problem in his 1903 catalogue:

Georges Méliès, a proprietor and manager of the Theatre Robert Houdin, Paris, is the originator of the class of cinematographic films which are made from artificially arranged scenes, the creation of which has given new life to the trade at a time when it was dying out. He conceived the idea of portraying magical and mystical views, and his creations have been imitated without success ever since. A great number of French, English, and American manufacturers of film who are searching for novelties, but lack the ingenuity to produce them, have found it easier and more economical to advertise their poor copies, that is, duplicate prints of Méliès's original film, as their own original conceptions. This accounts for the simultaneous appearance in several issues of a well-known New York newspaper of advertisements of the celebrated *A Trip to the Moon* by four or five different concerns, each pretending to be its creator. All these pretensions are false.

In 1904 Méliès produced his most ambitious work yet, *Le Voyage à travers l'impossible* (*The Impossible Voyage*). This film, like *A Trip to the Moon*, lampooned science. This time, however, Méliès's explorers travel to a number of different locations throughout the solar system. (In a scene quite similar to that most famous one from *A Trip to the Moon*, the explorers' locomotive is eaten and then spit out by the caricatured face of the Sun.) Elizabeth Ezra, author of *Georges Méliès* sees a number of parallels between the filmmaker and his film. "*The Impossible Voyage* is colorful, farfetched, ambitious yet playful, at once reassuringly familiar and unlike anything that had been seen before," Ezra observes. "It serves as an apt metaphor for Méliès's own career."

While most believe *The Impossible Voyage* to have been Méliès's masterpiece, the film was overshadowed at the time of its release by Edwin S. Porter's *The Great Train Robbery* (1902). While Porter's film owed a tremendous debt to Méliès, its simple subject matter drawn from the real world was quite a change for audiences who had grown accustomed to Méliès's fantastical creations by now. Méliès's techniques had been years ahead of his competition, but times were changing, and he would soon find himself a step behind his American competition. Restricting himself to the use of a static camera, Méliès enabled those willing to experiment to surpass him. (In fact, in more than five hundred films produced during his prolific career, Méliès never moved the camera once.)

At the end of his career Méliès inked a deal to have his films distributed by Pathé Pictures. This deal came to an end, however, when his 1912 version of *Cendrillon* (a remake of his earlier film) was butchered before its release—the 2,000-foot feature ended up released at approximately 900 feet. Business troubles coupled with Méliès's inability to grow and keep abreast of the newest technological advancements effectively ended his career in 1913. From there on things only got worse for Méliès. His studio was, for a time, overtaken and commandeered by the government because of the war. Now destitute, Méliès sold the theater. (Ironically, it was remodeled into a cinema.) Now at his lowest point, Méliès was forced to sell off his films and moviemaking equipment to a junk dealer just to survive. In 1928, a newspaper reporter recognized Méliès on a Paris street corner; the once-respected innovator had fallen, at the age of sixty-seven, from the highest plateau yet afforded by the motion picture industry to peddling newspapers.

Méliès is remembered today as a pioneer. He introduced a number of important special effects and camera tricks to the industry. His "artificially arranged scenes" introduced narrative to the motion picture; no longer would films be dull "realistic" depictions of passing events. Méliès, in essence, brought a sense of the theater and all its trappings before the motion picture

> ### Did You Know?
> Although Méliès made nearly 500 films in his lifetime, less than 150 exist today.

camera. With this, he also became the first filmmaker to organize rehearsals of scenes. (Many film historians have wrongly credited D. W. Griffith with this.) The imaginative filmmaker also introduced the horror genre, and is recognized today as the first true artist to work within the medium. He can also be seen as the originator of the special effects field; many of his innovations—such as stop-motion photography—are still in use. His work was championed by the innovative filmmakers who would follow him, such as Porter and Griffith, and it can be argued that Méliès had the most significant impact of any one man in the history of the cinema.

"Méliès was the first cinematic auteur, writing, producing, designing, directing, and starring in virtually all of his own films," Elizabeth Ezra concludes. "He introduced many 'special' effects that soon became part of the standard vocabulary of cinema, and to which filmmakers today are heavily indebted. He was no primitive, but a sophisticated filmmaker who had to negotiate uncharted terrain, and who brought a remarkable energy and wry sense of humor to everything he made. He was a true pioneer."

# Chapter 3

# Edwin S. Porter
# and the Principle of Editing

PHOTOFEST

An outlaw (George Barnes) fires at the screen in Edwin S. Porter's *The Great Train Robbery* (1903). Although the scene had little to do with the storyline, it became so popular that some exhibitors played it at the beginning of the film and again at the end.

EDWIN STANTON PORTER was born in Connellsville, Pennsylvania, on April 21, 1869. Porter spent his formative years in a variety of occupations, such as tailor, professional skater, and telegraph operator. In 1895, he enlisted in the United States Navy, where he displayed a talent for improving upon electrical communications devices. Shortly after his release from the Navy in 1898, Porter went to work for Raff & Gammon, promoters and distributors for Edison's Vitascope, in New York City as a projectionist. Lured by a more attractive offer, Porter left them to work as an international exhibitor for motion pictures developed for a rival projector, the Projectorscope.

During this period, American audiences were becoming bored with the motion picture, which had failed to evolve significantly beyond the short non-narrative films such as those Thomas Edison and company had begun crafting for the Kinetoscope in 1894. This lack of creative and artistic growth can be attributed partially to Edison's numerous legal attacks on his competitors for patent infringement, effectively putting many of them out of business. In his book *A Million and One Nights*, author Terry Ramsaye elaborates:

> The public was weary of pictures of prize fights, snatches of acrobatics, freaks and tricks on the screen. The picture had nothing new to say. What with the depressing effect of the patent wars, inhibiting initiative that might have come to freer minds, and the falling off of patronage, it appeared probable the films would disappear even from the screens of the vaudeville houses where they were used to mark the end of the show and clear the house.

Edison had become distraught and had given serious consideration to selling his interests in the fledgling motion picture industry to his competitors, but he decided to continue. Because he was busy with other endeavors and had grown bored with filmmaking, he persuaded Porter to return to work for him in November 1900; this time Porter was hired as head of production for the Edison Manufacturing Company's motion picture division.

Porter soon assumed the role of director, cinematographer, and editor. (Editing was still in his earliest stages in 1900, and consisted of little more than trimming.) At this early point, most filmmakers weren't concerned with editing. Films consisted of several tableaux, or individual scenes that could function by themselves as self-contained films. When a number of these tableaux were pieced together by the exhibitor, they could be fashioned into a much longer film. Since films were as yet non-narrative, they relied largely on the audience's knowledge of events. In this respect, a short one-scene film like *Cripple Creek Barroom* (1899), which consisted of nothing more than a barroom brawl, was effective only because the audience recognized it as such. Because of this, non-narrative films functioned as stories because viewers relied upon their own perceptions of what took place leading up to the events shown. When filmmakers crafted lengthier five- to ten-minute films, made up of between four to ten tableaux, they would provide the exhibitor with the "proper" order in which the scenes were to be shown. Despite this, many exhibitors either projected the scenes in whatever order they chose or tacked them together with as many as ten to twenty other short films to provide longer entertainment.

Porter and scenic designer George S. Fleming comprised the whole of the Edison Manufacturing Company's motion picture production team. One of Porter's first films was *Kansas Saloon Smashers* (1901), which poked fun at prohibitionist Carrie Nation. In the film, Nation and her cohorts were portrayed by men in drag. When the film proved to be a success, Porter fashioned a sequel entitled *Why Mr. Nation Wants a Divorce* (1901). Other early Porter films include *Terrible Teddy, the Grizzly King* (1901), which lampooned President Theodore Roosevelt, and a parody of an earlier Edison production, *The Finish of Bridget McKeen* (1901), which jokingly emulated Edison's popular *How Bridget Made the Fire* (1900). In Porter's film, the Irish girl who had made the fire in the original film accidentally catches fire to herself and dies.

In late 1902, Porter made his first "important" film, *The Life of an American Fireman*. With this film, Porter sought to tell a story. Porter was obviously influenced by the fairy-tale films of Georges Méliès, which the Edison Company was duplicating and selling to the U.S. market. Another apparent influence was the work of two Englishmen, G. A. Smith and James Williamson, who had begun experimenting with parallel editing by cutting from an exterior shot to an interior shot and then back to an exterior shot. While Porter never credited these British filmmakers, one can easily make an argument that *The Life of an American Fireman* is an imitation of Williamson's *Fire!* (1901). (Film historian Barry Salt made this assertion in his 1978 essay "Film Form, 1900–1906," published in *Sight and Sound*.)

Porter would later explain, "From laboratory examination of some of the popular films of the French pioneer director, Georges Méliès— trick films like *A Trip to the Moon*—I came to the conclusion that a picture telling a story in continuity form might draw the customers back to theaters . . ." With his next two films, *The Life of an American Fireman* and *The Great Train Robbery* (1903), Porter would improve upon Méliès's idea of narrative. It is significant to note that Porter was afforded an opportunity in the presentation of a narrative film that his predecessors did not enjoy; because the length of the average film had grown from fifty to six hundred feet between 1902 and 1903, he now had more time to present his story. Porter believed he could piece together a narrative by assembling scenes in a certain order. It was through this simple insight that Porter discovered the principle of editing.

Once Porter had gathered and arranged his footage, he quickly realized he would need to shoot a number of transitional scenes. For the contrived story about firemen saving a damsel in distress from a burning house (which just happened to be the home of the fire chief), an Edison Company executive named James H. White was enlisted to appear in the lead role. When the film was completed and screened for Edison general manager W. E. Gilmore, the manager decided that it was inappropriate for an Edison executive to appear in the film. Gilmore then ordered Porter to cut all scenes featuring White and reshoot them with a different actor.

The resulting film is approximately 378 feet long with a running time of six minutes. In the second scene, Porter employs the cinema's first close-up used to advance a story. Also extremely important is the film's final scene, which is comprised of three separate shots; by cross-cutting, Porter became the first filmmaker to alternate rapidly between two or more perspectives. *The Life of an American Fireman* is primitive, sloppy, and redundant, but is significant because it was the first American narrative film, as well as the first *realistic* narrative film (as opposed to the fantasies of Méliès), and marked clear progress in editing. Film historian A. R. Fulton expounds upon this in *Motion Pictures*:

> [T]he film turned out to be not so much a joining together of motion pictures that Porter had found in the Edison collection but scenes filmed expressly to tell the story and then joined together somewhat in the manner of *A Trip to the Moon* and similar films by Méliès. There is, however, in Porter's film, a difference in the joining. Whereas Méliès's films of arranged scenes are narrative in the way Hogarth's paintings *Marriage à la Mode* and *The Rake's Progress* are narrative, *The Life of an American Fireman* implies . . . a different kind of narration. The scene is not presented in a single shot but is broken down into three shots. *The Life of an American Fireman* represents a step toward the principle of editing, which is the basis of motion-picture art.

*The Life of an American Fireman* was the first film to arouse emotion in viewers. Prior to this, audiences had only seen footage of events, a single act of physical comedy, or the fantasies of Méliès. Here, the viewer found that he or she could easily relate to the characters and their situations. This greatly enhanced the viewing experience, making the viewer more of a participant rather than a passive observer.

### Did You Know?

Edwin S. Porter's *The Life of an American Fireman* was lost until 1944, when the Museum of Modern Art uncovered a 35mm print of the film.

Porter then worked on a number of lesser projects, including *Uncle Tom's Cabin* and *The Road to Anthracite* (both 1903). The latter, which featured photographic model Marie Murray as Phoebe Snow, took place on a Delaware, Lackawanna & Western Railroad car. While shooting this film, Porter made invaluable contacts with the railroad officials—a very important advantage for Porter's next, and most important, project.

In searching for a subject for his next film, it was suggested that Porter adapt a popular stage production of the time entitled *The Great*

*Train Robbery*. The title alone thrilled Porter, who immediately fashioned an outline for a story that bore little if any resemblance to the
original play. In 1903, American transportation was in a transitional
stage. While the newfangled horseless carriage was beginning to dominate the roads and technology seemed to be changing society at every
turn, it was still common for trains traveling through the western
states to be held up by cowboys. With his film, Porter hoped to cash
in on the sensational stories of daring robberies, frequently reported in
newspapers. Calling on his contacts at Delaware, Lackawanna & Western, Porter was granted access to a train and a stretch of railroad track
near Paterson, New Jersey.

Porter began casting the film. His first selection was Frank Hanaway, who had previously served in the U.S. cavalry. Hanaway
appealed to Porter because of his exceptional horse-riding skills. In
addition, Hanaway could perform various stunts such as falling from
a running horse without injuring himself. Porter then hired a vaudeville player named George Barnes for the role of the coldblooded
robber. It was at this stage in casting that Porter met Max Anderson,
who, under the stage name Bronco Billy, would ultimately become
the first star of the Western genre. Porter thought Anderson had the
right look to be a cowboy, but he wanted to know whether Anderson
could ride a horse. According to popular legend the conversation went
something like this:

"Do you have any horse-riding experience?" Porter asked.

"Are you kidding?" Anderson boasted. "I'm from Missouri. I was
born on a horse!"

This made Porter grin. "Good. You're now a train robber."

What Anderson failed to mention was that he was a "city slicker,"
raised in St. Louis and not in a rural setting. When the day of shooting arrived, Anderson revealed an unparalleled ignorance of horses.
Before he could demonstrate his inability to ride, he found even
mounting the steed a difficult task unto itself. Once filming began, he
fell from his horse and missed part of the shoot. Once Porter realized
Anderson was gone, there was no time to hold up the production;
time was money, and producer Edison was not one to waste money.
With no one else around to enlist, Porter doubled for the actor and
finished the shoot.

The resulting film was 740 feet in length and ran approximately twelve minutes. It consisted of fourteen shots and ten tableaux. It also offered exhibitors something different: a close-up of George Barnes's villain firing directly at the audience. The scene, however, had nothing to do with the story, and in this regard, Porter had undermined his efforts to sustain a narrative storyline. Authors George N. Fenin and William K. Everson comment on this scene in their book *The Western: From Silents to the Seventies*:

> *The Great Train Robbery* may be notable for its use of a close-up, but that close-up was so meaningless and ambiguous that the Edison publicity at the time informed exhibitors that they could use it at either the beginning or the end of the film. Porter realized that the scene . . . had both dramatic and shock effect, but he seemed to flounder when deciding what to do with it.

Despite its poor execution, there can be no dispute as to the inventiveness of the scene. At the time of the film's release, Porter, Edison, and the exhibitors were gratified by the effectiveness of the scene. Audiences, unconcerned about artistic intentions or narrative, simply loved it. Each time it played, audiences reacted wildly. In fact, some exhibitors played the scene twice, using it as both prologue and conclusion.

This scene, however, was one of the lesser innovations the film offered. Far more significant was Porter's continuity in editing. There is no intercutting *within* scenes in *The Great Train Robbery*, but Porter cut *between* the scenes. More important, he did this without fading, dissolving, or allowing the scene to play out to its conclusion. David A. Cook explains the value of this in *A History of Narrative Film*:

> [T]his was the beginning of a truly cinematic narrative language, because it posited that the basic signifying unit of film—the basic unit of cinematic meaning—was not the *scene*, as in Méliès, and not the continuous unedited film strip, as in the earlier Edison and Lumiére shorts, but rather the *shot*, of which, as Griffith would later demonstrate, there may be a virtually limitless number within any given scene.

With his discovery that cinematic storytelling is based upon a continuity of shots rather than a series of scenes, Porter made a major discovery. It can be said that all developments in the medium since Porter's discovery owe a tremendous debt to the principle of editing.

With *The Great Train Robbery*, Porter made a number of other significant contributions to the medium. In the film's opening interior scene, the train's arrival can be seen through a window in the railroad station. This was done through the use of rear projection, where the image of the train was projected against a screen outside the window. This was one of the earliest effective uses of rear projection, which later became a staple of American cinema through the 1960s. The film also features two sophisticated panning shots, the most impressive appearing in shot nine. Porter's camera placement in many exterior shots was also quite original for its time. Porter's choreography is also worth noting; in shot six, an actor travels diagonally across the frame rather than from side to side—elementary today, it was then revolutionary. In shot ten there is a cut which, as in *The Life of an American Fireman*, can be seen as a primitive method of parallel editing (also known as parallel cutting or cross-cutting, this is when scenes or sequences are intercut to imply they are taking place simultaneously).

*The Great Train Robbery* is often credited incorrectly as the first narrative Western film (*Kit Carson* claimed that distinction in October 1903, a full two months before Porter's film was released). *The Great Train Robbery* does, however, serve as a blueprint for virtually every Western released since, as it depicts such classic events as the shootout, a dramatic chase, and robbers shooting at the feet of a tenderfoot to make him "dance."

The film is also significant as a commercial watershed moment in the American film industry. *The Great Train Robbery* was a wild success, single-handedly bringing viewers back to the motion picture. This increased popularity led to the opening of movie houses across the country. So tremendous was its popularity that rival filmmakers immediately began producing imitations. One rival even went so far as to produce a ripoff the following year, using the same storyline and title as Porter's landmark film.

Yale Professor Charles Musser, author of *Before the Nickelodeon:*

### *Cinematic Firsts*

Edwin S. Porter's *The Great Train Robbery* is credited as the first narrative Western-themed film. His boss, Thomas A. Edison, had produced the first non-narrative Western films in 1895, which recorded living legends like Wild Bill Cody in action.

*Edwin S. Porter and the Edison Manufacturing Company*, believes Porter was America's first significant moviemaker, "one of the key innovators in the centralization of production and what we now call postproduction within the film company." Musser expounds further:

> In the 1890s, Porter was an exhibitor who often constructed complex programs out of short, one-shot films. In short the projectionist was in control of the editorial process and the telling of the story. Creative responsibilities were in some sense divided between the production company and the exhibitor. Porter was one of a handful of people who moved from exhibition into production around 1900 and took the skills he had developed as an exhibitor and integrated them into creative processes of the production company. This allowed for a new way of telling stories on film, which Porter explored in a variety of ways. This centralization of creative control in the film company created the figure of the "filmmaker." Before that there were really only producers and cinematographers on one hand and exhibitors on the other. This is why we can think of Porter as America's first important filmmaker.

Porter later made two more important contributions to the medium. With his film *The Ex-Convict* (1904), Porter utilized comparative editing, cutting back and forth between the lifestyles of two characters to show the contrast. Porter's next contribution came with *The Kleptomaniac* (1905), where Porter experimented with, and improved upon, parallel editing.

Porter continued working in the film industry for another few years, but failed to expand artistically or technically beyond his earlier innovations. In 1906, he crafted an impressive display of stop-motion work in *The Dream of a Rarebit Fiend* (1906) that was qualitatively better than similar works of Méliès, but the film offered little in the way of artistic or technical discovery. Porter's decline can be attributed in part to his employer, Edison, who was more interested in churning out formulaic motion pictures than experimenting or advancing an art form. Still, even Porter's later work for Adolph Zukor's Famous Players Company showed little in the way of innovation.

Porter did, however, provide another invaluable contribution to the medium, although he did so indirectly. In casting the lead actor for his film *Rescued from an Eagle's Nest* (1907), Porter discovered D.W. Griffith, who would ultimately make the next significant break-throughs in the evolution of filmmaking.

## Chapter 4

# "The Birth of a Nation" (1915)

Director D. W. Griffith claimed he had no idea *The Birth of a Nation* (1915) would be considered racist.

A NUMBER OF significant events occurred around the world in 1914: Carl Jung made significant breakthroughs in the study of human psychology and the unconscious; Edgar Rice Burroughs published *Tarzan of the Apes*; World War I broke out in Europe; Robert Goddard began his groundbreaking work in rocketry; and Charles Chaplin's beloved character, the "Little Tramp," made his debut. Early in that same year, scenario writer Frank Woods advised noted filmmaker D. W. Griffith to read Thomas W. Dixon's Civil War novel *The Clansman*. Woods had been associated with an earlier aborted effort to film Dixon's novel by Kinemacolor Pictures. Despite these setbacks, Woods still believed *The Clansman* held potential for an entertaining motion picture. Griffith, who had already directed more than 500 films, read the novel, began researching the Reconstruction period, and decided that *The Clansman* would indeed be his next picture. For the option to his novel *The Clansman*, as well as his stage play of the same title, Dixon was paid $2,500 with the understanding that he would be paid an additional $7,500 after the film was completed. Griffith and producer Harry Aitken projected the film's budget to be $40,000.

Griffith quietly assembled a group of actors that included Lillian Gish, Mae Marsh, Henry B. Walthall, Miriam Cooper, Spottiswoode Aiken, among others. This film, he informed them, would tell the "truth" about the American Civil War, adding that the history books were false. (His sense of truth was likely instilled by his father, a Confederate veteran who died when Griffith was a young boy.) Griffith swore his cast to complete secrecy to keep rivals from producing similar films to compete with his. In his book *D. W. Griffith: His Life and Work* film historian Robert M. Henderson writes:

> Griffith's relationships with his actors were cemented through his sharing of confidences. He would take each aside and seemingly make that person the recipient of some private confidence binding the actor to him in a much stronger fashion than even money and legal contracts.

In the end, it would seem that Griffith didn't really need Dixon's book. The story that emerged would be largely his own. According to Billy Bitzer, Griffith's director of photography, Griffith's approach toward filmmaking changed with this project. "*The Birth of a Nation* changed D. W. Griffith's personality entirely," Bitzer once said. "Where heretofore he was wont to refer in starting on a new picture as 'grinding out another sausage' and go at it lightly, his attitude in beginning on this one was all eagerness. He acted like here we have something worthwhile . . ."

Griffith was determined that every aspect of *The Clansman* would be authentic. To ensure that his sets had the proper look, he consulted a number of historical references, including *Civil War Photographs* by Mathew Brady and several biographies of Abraham Lincoln. Planning to emulate the scenes depicted in some of these photographs, Griffith cast actors who strongly resembled such historical figures as Lincoln and Ulysses S. Grant. Griffith also used the photographs to construct sets that were exact replicas of original locations, such as the Ford Theater where Lincoln met his demise. The photographs also allowed Griffith to copy hair and clothing styles of the time.

## Cinematic Firsts

D. W. Griffith's *Ramona* (1910) marked the first time a filmmaker paid for the rights to adapt a novel to the screen. Publisher Little, Brown & Co., who published Helen Hunt Jackson's novel, were paid $100 for the film rights.

Filming began on July 4, 1914, in Los Angeles. Despite being a far lengthier, and more ambitious undertaking than his earlier films, Griffith filmed *The Clansman* just as he had those films: he and his company went by little more than a structural outline, relying heavily on improvisation. There was, it is believed, no actual screenplay. Because of their intensive rehearsal process, however, most of the dialogue was established before the cameras had begun rolling.

The elaborate battle scenes, shot in the San Fernando Valley, were the first scenes filmed, and were meticulously planned and prepared for both authenticity and safety. In *D. W. Griffith: An American Life* scholar Richard Schickel writes:

> Munitions were a particular hazard on this film, many of the techniques later used to simulate warfare on screen not yet having been fully developed. Incredible as it may seem, live cannon rounds were actually employed in order that shots could be seen to land and explode fairly near the soldiery—the technique of planting charges to imitate explosions not having been invented. Elaborate warnings were signaled when these rounds were used . . .

Despite such dangers, not a single cast or crew member was killed while making the film. Injuries did occur, however; an assistant named Tom Wilson nearly lost his hand in a grenade accident. In the event of accidents, Griffith kept a number of medical personnel on hand at all times. While filming, Griffith served as general to his squad of extras, barking orders through a bullhorn. Some five hundred extras were skillfully made to appear as thousands, portraying soldiers on both sides. (A number of them, however, loyal to the army of their fathers or grandfathers, refused to wear the uniforms of the opposing side, whether Union or Confederacy, and resigned immediately.) Another unique problem presented itself during filming: while Griffith envisioned thousands of horses filling the screen during some scenes, he found this an impossibility. With the world on the verge of war, Griffith discovered there was a shortage of steeds. (Richard Schickel explains that the first World War was a "war everyone imagined would require cavalry just as the wars of the nineteenth century had.") Nevertheless, Griffith was given access to nearly every horse in Hollywood. Western productions were shut down until after Griffith had shot the ride sequences, and even more horses were flown in from Arizona. (Humorously, the horses were transported on a passenger plane.)

More troubles soon arose. Midway through the shoot Griffith found himself in financial straits. His commitment to accuracy had been costly; he had already spent the entire $40,000. Griffith managed to squeeze another $20,000 from his producers, but still needed more. He then stumbled across the idea of convincing businessmen and other individuals to invest smaller amounts. Eventually the film's budget soared to $110,000, an astounding figure in its day.

For *The Birth of a Nation*, Griffith sought many strange new shots, such as close-ups of the galloping horses' feet. Bitzer accomplished this by lying in a ditch near the running horses. His camera was kicked in by the horses' hooves but he managed to walk away unscathed and with the shot in hand. Virtually every scene was filmed from a number of different angles, which was unheard of at the time. Assistant cameraman Karl Brown would later reveal his own confusion at the time of filming in his book *Adventures with D. W. Griffith*:

I saw every scene as it was being shot. I had to, for it was an essential part of my job to keep a record of the action and the scene numbers in my notebook. And yet nothing seemed to go together, nothing seemed to fit. Oh, there were a few sequences that made sense, like the assassination of Abraham Lincoln in Ford's Theater, but this all took so long to shoot, with so many individual shots from so many different angles, that I couldn't see how they could possibly be put together in anything much better than a series of set pieces, like the old-style panoramas during which one man turned the crank to reveal the pictures, one after another, while a second man delivered the lecture.

Despite Brown's doubts, the resulting film would be the most spectacular, epic motion picture ever produced. Clocking in at nearly three hours, *The Birth of a Nation* (as *The Clansman* was later retitled) was also the lengthiest film made to date.

Upon its release, the film stunned audiences everywhere. Griffith charged audiences two dollars per ticket, and although two dollars was a hefty sum to watch a motion picture at that time, audiences flocked to see it again and again. While no exact figures are available, *The Birth of a Nation* is believed to be one of the highest grossing films of the silent film era, if not *the* top moneymaker.

The film's release was also accompanied by controversy. Griffith's film, like the racist novel it was based upon, glorified the Ku Klux Klan as heroes and depicted blacks as being ignorant rapists. Adding to the offensiveness of the film, Griffith, who had gone to great lengths to ensure authenticity if not accuracy, had not hired black actors; instead, blacks were played by whites in blackface. When novelist Dixon convinced his old college chum Woodrow Wilson to screen the film at the White House, Wilson reportedly remarked that the film was "like writing history with lightning. My only regret is that it is all true."

---

### Did You Know?

One particularly racist scene excised from *The Birth of a Nation* depicted Jesus Christ happily watching over blacks being shipped back to Africa by the boatload.

National Association for the Advancement of Colored People head Roy Wilkins would assess the film's impact on society nearly five decades later:

> Since the film appeared fifty years ago, Negroes have made many a breakthrough. But all the Duke Ellingtons, Marian Andersons, Ira Aldridges, Jackie Robinsons, Bert Williamses, Fritz Pollards, the Olympic heroes and the heroes of two world wars, the scientists, the scholars, technicians, political figures, poets, playwrights, entertainers, and diplomats have not succeeded in erasing the vicious image etched by the Griffith racial epic.

Strangely enough, all of the controversy seemed to shock Griffith, who seemed to have no comprehension that his film was misguided. Relying upon the "truths" that had been instilled in him as a son of the South, Griffith naively believed that he was not a racist. Years later, actress Lillian Gish insisted that none of the film's participants had any idea the film would be seen as racist. However, many, such as *Focus on D. W. Griffith* editor Harry M. Geduld, don't buy this claim. "Well, of course, I wasn't privy to the private thoughts of Griffith—so I can't be absolutely certain," Geduld explains. "However, consider (1) that the film was based on two novels by Thomas Dixon that had been widely attacked for being racist; (2) the film avoids any explicit condemnation of slavery. Indeed, Stoneman (Elsie's father) is shown to be paternalistically kind to his slaves; (3) The post-War scenes in the South Carolina Legislature and the would-be rape and miscegenation episodes are patently anti-Black; (4) The film is obviously pro-Klan. Nevertheless, I think that D. W. Griffith would have said that querying the racism of his film was to obscure its main objective: to underscore the theme of Union. In this regard, the movie pivots on two intertitles. At the beginning we are told: 'The seeds of disunion were sown when the Black Man was brought to the New World.' Near the end of the film (during the siege of the cabin) we are told: 'The North and South united at last in defense of their Aryan heritage.' That's why Griffith altered the title of the film from *The Clansman* to *The Birth of a Nation*. Just prior to the film's New York premiere, Griffith explained to a reporter that the title indicated that in his opinion the nation was just being born! This would probably have been clearer to the film's first audiences who saw footage of the film that has long since disappeared. Part of this lost footage showed Blacks being transported to Africa."

While the film's content may be questionable, there is no denying its many technical achievements. Like *Citizen Kane* twenty-five years later, Griffith's film can be seen as a compendium of innovative techniques. Make no mistake: most of the innovations *The Birth of a Nation* is known for did not originate with Griffith. "The 'father of film technique' was not an innovator," historian David Parkinson writes in *History of Film*. "Instead, he was an intuitive refiner and extender of existing cinematic methods."

The film's innovations include:

- **Color tinting.** Griffith extensively utilized tinting to convey dramatic or psychological effect.

- **Panning.** Griffith's film introduced moving camera tracking shots.

- **Close-ups.** While Griffith was not the first filmmaker to use total screen close-ups, he used them to great effect in *The Birth of a Nation*. By using them to emphasize certain details or emotions, Griffith managed to enhance this technique. It can be argued that this is the film that brought the close-up to the forefront of Hollywood consciousness.

- **The "iris" effect.** One of the many innovations found in this film was the technique of the camera "iris" effect, which means the contracting or expanding of circular masks to start or finish a scene.

- **Camera angles.** While Griffith would later improve upon this in films such as *Intolerance*, his camera placement in *The Birth of a Nation* was highly innovative. In this film, he frequently used panoramic long shots and high-angle shots.

- **Long shots.** Many filmmakers had been experimenting with long shots by this time. Griffith, however, mastered this technique in *The Birth of a Nation*.

- **Pre-montage.** Griffith's depiction of parallel events through cross-cutting can be seen as a precursor to Sergei Eisenstein's "montage of attractions."

- **Fade-outs.** Griffith's film utilized some of the earliest examples of fade-outs in screen history.

- **Night photography.** Griffith's use of night photography in the film is believed to have been the first time this was ever done. Griffith achieved this by using magnesium flares to illuminate his subjects.

- **Costumes.** The costumes made specially for the film were among the most elaborate ever created at that time.

- **Lap dissolve.** The lap dissolve is when one image dissolves into another, rather than by the traditional direct cutting. This had originated with Georges Méliès as a trick effect. Griffith, however, used it for dramatic reasons, becoming one of the first filmmakers to do so.

- **Authenticity.** More effort was put into ensuring the appearance of authenticity in *The Birth of a Nation* than in virtually any other film produced previously.

- **Original score.** Griffith's film was the first to feature its own original music score. (Other films still relied on the theater's house musicians playing their own selections, which often contradicted the intended atmosphere of scenes.)

- **Length.** *The Birth of a Nation* is significant for its length (twelve reels) and its 1,544 separate shots, both of which were unprecedented.

- **The still shot.** Griffith and others had used the still shot previously, but it was still a relatively new device when the film was produced.

*The Birth of a Nation* is also significant because of Griffith's experimentation with shot compositions and his usage of the "cameo-profile," which is a combination of the medium close-up against a blurred background. In *The Emergence of Film Art*, Lewis Jacobs observes another technique Griffith introduced in the film: "This was the editing of certain blocks of imagery to coincide with, and thus intensify, the rhythm and emotional build-up of certain passages of classical music, planned as symphonic orchestration for these scenes."

Today the film is remembered primarily for its cruel, vilifying depiction of blacks and for its artistry—the vast number of technical innovations it either introduced or brought to the forefront of the film industry's awareness. While Griffith's depiction of blacks foaming at the mouth and raping white women is surely one of the vilest sins committed in the name of art, there is no denying that the film is a technical and artistic landmark.

# Chapter 5

# The Edison Monopoly Decision

Thomas Alva Edison, the driving force behind the cartel known as the Motion Picture Patents Company.

IN THE EARLY 1900s, a number of production companies were making a handsome profit from the motion picture industry. When these newly established companies found opposition from the Edison Company on the grounds of patent violations, some began using motion picture cameras and projectors patented and manufactured by other inventors. Others simply bought and sold illegal reproductions of raw stock, equipment, and completed films on the black market. This angered Edison, who viewed anyone making motion pictures outside his own company, as well as the inventors of similar cameras and projectors—some of which were developed before or at the same time as those of the Edison Company—as violating his patents. He went to great lengths to track down as many offenders as possible, engaging in legal disputes with all of them. Nevertheless, most bootleggers continued to operate; they simply moved from location to location, hoping to evade the law. The larger manufacturers, however, did not have this luxury. Most of them had suffered through the industry's decline just as the Edison Company had, and were forced to battle Edison in court. For them, it was all or nothing; if they won, Edison would be off their backs; if they lost, most of them would be forced out of business because of the exorbitant damages they would have to pay. Also, should the Edison Company win, these manufacturers would be forced to obtain licenses from Edison.

The basis for these battles was that each major studio held the rights to their own patents; while these patents might have been similar to those of the Edison Company, each believed their patents entitled them to function without the permission of the Edison Company or anyone else. Although very few of these companies had substantial claims, they were allowed to continue functioning until the Supreme Court could rule on the issue.

> **Did You Know?**
>
> The first film studio was Thomas Edison's Black Maria, which was built in West Orange, New Jersey, in 1893.

Benjamin B. Hampton describes this turbulent period in his book *History of the American Film Industry*:

> The larger manufacturers, in addition to fighting against Edison, fought the crooks, and fought bitterly and constantly among themselves. A fourth of a producer's time and thought went to the making of pictures, and three fourths were absorbed by legal battles with big and little competitors who sought to imitate his inventions or averred that he was stealing theirs. Every minor appliance and improvement became

the subject of bitter controversy and litigation. The studios were turning out at least as many damage suits as movies. For a dozen years the industry was a battle ground, filled with intense hatreds and constant guerrilla warfare, and the mass of movie litigation grew to be so great that a regiment of lawyers was needed to follow its intricacies through the courts. The business itself was prosperous—people were anxious to see pictures—but inventors, producers, distributors and exhibitors were so inflamed with enmities and bewildered with strife that administration of the industry became almost impossible.

Finally fed up and unable to take it any longer, George Kleine, a prominent Chicago importer of motion picture equipment, suggested that the major companies involved with motion pictures combine to form a trust. This suggestion led to months of discussion before all parties agreed to pool their collective patents under one umbrella. In December 1908, nine manufacturers—Edison, Biograph, Vitagraph, Pathé Pictures, Star Pictures, Essanay, Sigmund Lubin, William Selig, and the Kalem Company—combined with Kleine to form the Motion Picture Patents Company. By combining their interests, these leaders sought to control the industry through legal monopoly. The newly formed trust then issued licenses to each of the ten parties involved. Although there were many other studios operating when the trust was established, none of them would be issued licenses under any circumstances. When these companies continued operating, the trust went after them through litigation. By effectively shutting down most of their competition, members of the trust were then able to raise the rental prices of their films. Because of this, exhibitors were forced to raise admission prices to survive.

During this time, a number of independent studios continued operating without licenses from the Motion Picture Patents Company. To combat these independent studios, the trust formed a subsidiary called the General Film Company. The sole purpose for the General Film Company's existence was to stamp out these non-licensed independents by any means necessary. The General Film Company began confiscating and/or destroying unlicensed equipment and prosecuting and sometimes jailing those who owned it. The next order of business for the General Film Company was the refusal of products to any exhibitor caught showing films made by the independents; this was done through the issuing of licenses—through the trust, of course, for a fee of two dollars per week. Anyone not obeying the rules of the trust would then find their license revoked. Theaters were then classified and motion picture rental rates were standardized accordingly, ranging from $15 to $125 per week. The unethical business practices of the General Film Company were taken up another notch when they began purchasing all the licensed film exchange centers around the United States. This was achieved through threats; if the exchange refused to sell,

> ### *Cinematic Firsts*
>
> Maverick producer Carl Laemmle struck a blow to Thomas Edison's company in 1909 when his most popular actress, Florence Lawrence, who had become known as the "Biograph Girl," signed with Laemmle's IMP (Independent Motion Picture Corporation of America). Lawrence's defection would lead to the "star system," in which actors started to receive on-screen credit for their work.

their license would be revoked. This left them only two choices: take what money they could get from the trust or be put out of business. (The General Film Company would ultimately control every film exchange in the United States except one, which was owned by William Fox.)

These tactics resulted in more opposition; when exhibitors found themselves without films to show, many of them began producing their own films. The independents began making longer "feature" films as opposed to the customary one-reelers produced by the trust in an effort to distinguish their films. The independent producers soon began to relocate in the hopes of outrunning the strong arm of the trust. In *The Rise of the American Film: A Critical History* author Lewis Jacobs explains how this effort to flee the trust would ultimately lead to the relocation of the entire film industry:

> The establishment of Hollywood as the production center of the industry was prompted by the independents' desire to

avoid the attacks of the trust. Independents fled from New York, the center of production activity, to Cuba, Florida, San Francisco, Los Angeles. Cuba proved to be disease-ridden; Florida, too warm; San Francisco, too far from the Mexican border. The safest refuge was Los Angeles, from which it was only a hop-skip-and-jump to the Mexican border and escape from injunctions and subpoenas. Other advantages soon showed this location to be even more desirable than New York: good all-year-round weather, cheap labor, a rich variety of topography, and the ready cooperation of business and real estate interests in the community. Independent companies were soon flocking to Los Angeles, and the bigger licensed companies, too, began to settle there. By 1913 a suburb of Los Angeles was so developed as the home of motion picture making that it was separated from Los Angeles proper and given the legal name of Hollywood.

As the number of independents continued to increase daily, the trust soon found that this was the least of its concerns. Despite having been assured of the trust's legality by a team of lawyers, the Motion Picture Patents Company was slapped with antitrust charges by the United States government. In October 1915, it was determined that the Motion Picture Patents Company and its subsidiary, the General Film Company, constituted a monopoly in its efforts to control and restrict trade. The trust was ordered to pay more than $20 million in damages, and the government would later call for the trust to be disbanded.

"Though the strong-arm tactics of the Trust was largely ineffectual," observes J.A. Aberdeen, author of *The Hollywood Renegades*, "the perceived threat and discriminatory stance gave the independent movement an impetus for survival which probably enabled the 'outlaws' to achieve greater success than the Trust companies. By the time the government caught up with Edison, the Patents Trust had already been an outmaneuvered dinosaur."

The struggle between the independent "outlaws" and the Motion Picture Patents Company ultimately marked a turning point in film history for two reasons: first, the battle led to the production of feature-length films; second, Hollywood became the center of the film industry in the United States. With Hollywood effectively colonized by the industry, this centralization of talent made the production of motion pictures easier, and ultimately led to higher-quality productions. With every aspect of production immediately at their disposal, filmmakers could produce pictures more efficiently and with more regularity. This colonization also afforded producers more talent in regards to actors, effectively increasing the overall performance level of American films.

## Chapter 6

# The Hollywood Studio System

Paramount was one of the studios to rise in Hollywood as the "studio system" was established.

DUE IN PART to the Motion Picture Patents Company (see page 39 for more information), a number of film companies began operating in the Los Angeles suburb of Hollywood around 1910. This area quickly became the central hub of the American motion picture industry. These studios, which had begun as maverick independents battling the MPPA, would soon grow into the most dominant studios in the business, first by making feature-length films (films that are a minimum of ninety minutes long) instead of the traditional shorts, and later by streamlining production into efficient motion picture factories. These companies (and eventually others) developed the Hollywood studio system.

During the period that became known as the studio era (1930–1949), eight major motion picture studios dominated production, distribution, and exhibition: Famous Players–Lasky (Paramount), Loew's, Inc. (Metro-Goldwyn-Mayer); Warner Bros., 20th-Century Fox, RKO, Universal, United Artists, and Columbia, five of which (RKO, Warner Bros., Famous Players–Lasky, Fox, and Loew's) were fully integrated in all three aspects of the industry.

Producer Thomas Ince—most famous today because of the controversy surrounding his death, which may or may not have been at the hands of William Randolph Hearst—played a major role in the development of the factory production system. In 1913, while working at Mutual, Ince devised the hierarchy that would ultimately become the standard. This included the studio boss, the producer, and the film's director. Soon, each specific function in the filmmaking process was divided into its own specialized position.

### Cinematic Firsts

The first studio to be established in Hollywood was the Nestor Studio in 1911.

Famous Players-Lasky (Paramount) was the first studio to develop the "three-part strategy" that enabled the studios to dominate their competition just as the MPPC had previously done to them. In *The Hollywood Studio System*, Douglas Gomery defines the strategy as thus: (1) differentiating its products; (2) distributing both nationally and internationally; (3) dominating exhibition through ownership of theaters. Of differentiating products Gomery writes:

For production, Famous Players differentiated its films using stars. Gone were the days of films being sold by the foot. Each motion picture had become a unique good. Early producers (including the MPPC) did not exploit actors' and actresses' images. In contrast, Famous Players heralded certain players who seemed to guarantee high box office revenues. One of the most successful was Mary Pickford, a "superstar" to her adoring fans, who ascended the salary ladder from $100 per week to $15,000 per week in less than one decade. By 1920, Famous Players (and its competitors) had regularized the issuance of features with stars. Famous Players, true to its name, raided the legitimate stage for potential "kings and queens" of the screen. Other studios attempted to create indigenous stars by testing potential luminaries in cheaper productions or shorts. Studios linked stars to exclusive, long-term contracts so that the player could not seek a higher salary from a rival company. Fans may not have known they were going to see a Famous Players product, but they would stand in line for hours to see a vehicle with Mary Pickford or Douglas Fairbanks, two of the studio's most popular attractions.

The second aspect of the three-part strategy (worldwide distribution) speaks for itself. In regards to the purchasing and operation of venues of exhibition, Famous Players–Lasky acquired several first- and second-run houses in every major city. Soon, Famous Players's competitors followed suit and began purchasing theaters. By 1920, these 2,000 studio-owned theaters accounted for three quarters of all revenue from the average film. By 1930, Famous Players alone owned more than 1,000 exhibition houses. Later, when Famous Players became Paramount Pictures, it would become the first studio to exclusively distribute its feature-length films.

The studios soon developed another technique that aided them in monopolizing the industry: "block-booking," an arrangement whereby the studios stipulated that exhibitors had to purchase less-desirable films in order to obtain their "A" films. Although this tactic angered exhibitors, they had little choice but to comply.

Over the years, the studios would continue to refine their methods of assembly-line production so that films could be made economically with as little risk as possible. In her 1950 survey *Hollywood, the*

*Dream Factory: An Anthropologist Looks at the Movie-Makers,* Hortense Powdermaker observed:

> A feature of all mass production is the uniformity of the man-ufactured product. Hollywood has tried to achieve this by seeking formulas that it hopes will work for all movies and insure their success . . . The common denominators of pan-tomime, slapstick and romance could be understood and enjoyed by uncritical audiences all over the world. Since all members of the human species have the same basic needs and have some characteristics in common, there are certain simple forms of entertainment to which they can all respond . . . The formulas for pictures have been a series of constantly changing *do's* and *don'ts,* such as, "You cannot make an A picture about a prize fight," "No picture with any kind of message can make money," "The love story must be the most important part of an A picture." Each one of these formulas has been success-fully broken and shown to be false at one time or another through a box office success. This was accomplished by some-one with imagination, courage and faith in his own judgment, usually a director or producer with sufficient prestige to get his own way. But each time anyone departs from the formula and meets with success, the departure then becomes another formula.

Eventually, the screenplays from which films were made became for-mulaic as well. Characters were driven by explicit motivations, and storylines involved clear examples of cause and effect. Audiences were given classic protagonists to root for, and most films concluded with happy endings.

During the studio era, competitors were constantly changing their methods to imitate the most successful techniques of their rivals. The studio system was quite effective in maximizing profits and restricting the trade of competitors. In fact, the studio system was so effective that the motion picture industry accounted for three quarters of all money spent on entertainment in the United States in 1937. As this factory-like industry was effective at home and abroad for American studios, foreign film companies began to copy the Hollywood studio structure.

The late 1940s saw the decline of the studio system for a number of reasons, most notably damaging antitrust charges (the Paramount Decision) similar to those which had been levied against the MPPA and had been instrumental in the development of the studio system. While a number of artists have managed to create works of art from within this system, the American motion picture industry would forever be seen as essentially that—an industry.

### Did You Know?

Irvin Thalberg began his career working as Carl Laemmle's secretary at Universal Pictures and later became vice president and head of production at Metro-Goldwyn-Mayer.

# Chapter 7

# "Das Kabinett des Doktor Caligari" (1919) and German Expressionist Cinema

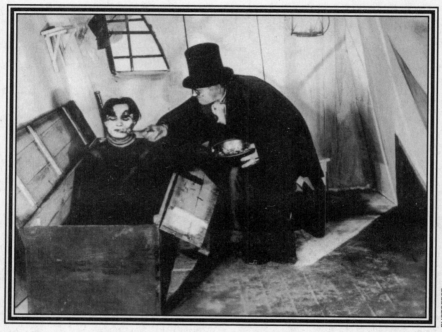

A scene from Robert Weine's 1920 film *Das Kabinett des Doktor Caligari* (*The Cabinet of Dr. Caligari*), which launched the Expressionist cinema movement.

EXPRESSIONISM began in Europe around 1906 as a style of painting and theater that was a reaction to the realist works of the previous century. This style of art and drama was especially embraced in Germany, where it flourished. While Expressionist artists each had their own distinctive styles, their work shared some characteristics: the world depicted in Expressionist art was an unrealistic, stylized one. In these works, buildings and structures were distorted so that they appeared to sag or lean to the side. The ground was often uneven, and human figures were contorted grotesquely. Why, questioned the Expressionists, should one duplicate the real world when it already exists for everyone to see? Although this style of art became quite popular, no attempts to produce Expressionist works of cinema were made until *Das Kabinett des Doktor Caligari* (*The Cabinet of Dr. Caligari*).

> ### Did You Know?
> Germany's "Golden Age" of cinema is sometimes referred to as the "Weimar Cinema" because Germany from 1919 to 1933 was known as the Weimar Republic. This name is derived from the city of Weimar, where a national assembly convened to produce a new constitution after Germany's defeat in World War I. The term "Weimar Cinema" is sometimes used indiscriminately to describe German Expressionism but it refers actually to all types of film produced in Germany during this period.

Also significant at this time was Germany's loss of World War I. This national feeling of displacement created the atmosphere for a like-minded national cinema. In his study *Profoundly Disturbing: Shocking Movies That Changed History*, Joe Bob Briggs writes:

> In the midst of this gloom there appeared two angry, bitter ex-soldiers, Hans Janowitz and Carl Mayer, who wrote a screenplay that they didn't regard as a horror story at all. *The Cabinet of Dr. Caligari* was intended as a political allegory about the way powerful men hypnotized helpless millions into doing their bidding, even if it meant turning them into killers and then murdering them. It was a revolutionary film about totalitarianism, directed at Kaiser Wilhelm but eerily prophetic of Hitler.

In 1918, an Austrian artist named Carl Mayer and a Czechoslovakian poet named Hans Janowitz presented a treatment for *Das Kabinett des Doktor Caligari* to DECLA-Bioscop producer Erich Pommer. After reading their story about a somnambulist who becomes an unwitting pawn in a mental asylum, Pommer agreed to finance the film. (While many historians have stated that Pommer accepted the project because he desired to improve the artistry of his company's films, this is now believed to be inaccurate. Today it's widely accepted that Pommer's reason for making the film had nothing to do with art and everything to do with money.) Pommer then hired the now-legendary filmmaker Fritz Lang to helm *Caligari*. Lang, however, was removed from the project because his most recent film, *Die Spinnen* (*The Spiders*) (1919) was so successful. "Erich Pommer gave me *The Cabinet of Dr Caligari* to direct, but the theater owners had made so much money with the first part of *The Spiders* that (DECLA-Bioscop) wanted to have the second part immediately," Lang recalled to Peter Bogdanovich in *Who the Devil Made It?*. "Pommer was forced to take me off *Caligari* so that I could finish the series." Pommer then replaced Lang with Robert Weine.

Over the many decades that have passed since the film was produced, there has been much debate over whose idea it was to film *Das Kabinett des Doktor Caligari* in an Expressionistic manner. Virtually every crew member offered an explanation that contradicts those given by others.

According to Pommer, it was Mayer and Janowitz who first conceived the idea of doing *Caligari* in an Expressionistic style. Mayer and Janowitz then suggested filming the entire movie on one set with stylishly painted canvas backdrops. Pommer considered this suggestion for several days, and ultimately agreed. After all, what could be more economic than filming on one set against painted backdrops? Mayer and Janowitz then made another suggestion: Why not commission noted designer Alfred Kubin to create the film's landscape? This time Pommer said no. The first suggestion made economic sense, this one did not; an artist of Kubin's stature would be costly. Therefore, Kubin was never contacted.

Set designer Hermann Warm offers a different story regarding the film's Expressionist origins. According to Warm, *he* suggested to Pommer the idea of fashioning *Caligari* in the manner of Expressionist painters. Warm says he conceived this after consulting with painters Walter Rohrig and Walter Reimann. "We spent a whole day and part of the night reading through this very curious script," Warm contends. "We realized that a subject like this needed something out of the ordinary in the way of sets. Reimann, whose painting in those days had Expressionist tendencies, suggested doing the sets Expressionistically."

Not surprisingly, filmmaker Robert Weine remembers things differently. According to him, it was *he* who conceived the idea of giving the film its Expressionist look. In the end, it's not really that important who's responsible (although it does serve as an interesting example of how the passage of time can alter one's memory). What is important here is simply that the film as ultimately produced turned out to be a a masterwork of Expressionism.

Interestingly, the prologue and epilogue of the film were shot in a more conventional manner than the body of the film they bracket. Carl Mayer later explained that these sequences were conceived by Janowitz and himself, although these sequences do not appear in Mayer and Janowitz's original treatment. Lang, however, who was attached to the project for only the briefest of periods, contends that he initiated a realistic style for these sequences. Lang tells Bogdanovich:

> The whole story had been written, and the only contribution I made was that I said to Pommer, "Look, if the Expressionistic sets stand for the world of the insane, and you use them from the beginning, it doesn't mean anything. Why don't you, instead, make the prologue and epilogue of the picture normal?" So the film begins in the garden of an asylum and is told normally; when the story is told from the viewpoint of one of the inmates, it becomes Expressionistic; and at the end it becomes normal again and we see the villain of the picture, Dr. Caligari, is the doctor of the asylum.

As in Expressionist paintings, the buildings in *Caligari* have a slanted appearance. Despite their being mere paintings on canvas, *Caligari*'s sets give an appearance of depth. In her seminal 1952 study of expressionism *The Haunted Screen*, Lotte H. Eisner observes:

> The depth comes from deliberately distorted perspectives and from narrow, slanting streets which cut across each other at unexpected angles. Sometimes also it is enhanced by a back-

cloth which extends the streets into sinuous lines. The three-dimensional effect is reinforced by the inclined cubes of dilap-idated houses. Oblique, curving, or rectilinear lines converge across an undefined expanse towards the background; a wall skirted by the silhouette of Cesare the somnambulist, the slim ridge of the roof he darts along bearing his prey, and the steep paths he scales in his flight.

Weine's film offered a blueprint for the Expressionist films to follow. Utilizing dramatic chiaroscuro lighting, it was filmed entirely in the studio (making it somewhat stagy at times), featured exaggerated sur-realist settings, psychological probing, a moving camera, uncompli-cated editing, and heavily stylized acting. Expressionist films offered dark, nightmarish realms which were, in essence, everything Holly-wood's slick and stylish settings were not. Through severely distorted visuals and experimental lighting, the film allowed the viewer to see the world through the eyes of a madman. Just as the French Impressionist cinema—which emerged at roughly the same time—would discard the notion of an objective camera to convey charac-ters' emotions, German Expressionist cinema would use the camera to convey the depraved psychological states of its tortured subjects. As film historian David A. Cook explains, Expressionist filmmakers attempted to "discuss interior realities through the means of exterior realities."

In his 1930 study *The Film Till Now*, author Paul Rotha explains:

> *The Cabinet of Dr. Caligari* was the first significant attempt at the expression of a creative mind in the new medium of cin-ematography. It broke with realism on the screen; it suggested that a film, instead of being a reality, might be a possible real-ity; and it brought into play the mental psychology of the audience. There has been a tendency of late to look back with disdain at the theatrical character of Weine's film. It has been objected that *The Cabinet of Dr. Caligari*, in its structural coordi-nation of light, design, and players, in its cubist-expressionist architecture, was pure stage presentation. It needs but little intelligence to utter this profound criticism, but it must be realized that *The Cabinet of Dr. Caligari* was produced under extraordinary circumstances. It is simple to look back now and

diagnose the crudities of Wiene's work, with the most recent progress of the Soviet film and the American "compound" cinema fresh in mind, but in 1919 all theory of cinema was extremely raw. It is only through the experiments as that of Weine . . . that advance has been at all possible . . . Without the creation of *The Cabinet of Dr. Caligari*, much that is admired in the cinema today would be nonexistent. It bore in it a suggestion of the fantasy that was to be the prominent characteristic of the art film.

Filmed in 1919, *Das Kabinett des Doktor Caligari* was released on February 27, 1920, and German Expressionist cinema was born. The film was met with great acclaim and became an enormous hit. Noted film scholar Lewis Jacobs contends that *Caligari* was "the most widely discussed film" of its time. Certainly, the resulting Expressionist movement tends to overshadow the French Impressionist movement of the same period. Viewers today might guess that *Caligari* was so unconventional that it shocked its initial audiences, catching them off guard. This, however, was not the case as most German audiences in 1920 were already quite familiar with Expressionism, even if it had not previously appeared on film. Also, German audiences had not had access to American films produced from 1914 through 1919. Because these audiences had been able to view only German films, which tended to be somewhat darker than their American counterparts, the contrast between Hollywood films and *Caligari* might not have been as apparent. Unconventional as it might have been even in comparison to their own films, *Caligari's* sensibility is one which is distinctly German.

It seems doubtful that *Caligari* would have led to an entire movement had it been less effective. (The film remains one of the better Expressionistic films that emerged from the movement, which lasted through 1927.) So successful was *Caligari* that it holds up even today. "[The film] is such an apt use of the medium as it existed in the first quarter of the twentieth century that it is difficult to imagine the film done better with the benefit of sound, color, or any innovation since," praises BBC film writer Nick Hilditch.

*Caligari* galvanized the German film industry, and soon many more Expressionistic films were in production. Like *Caligari*, most of these productions were shot on dark, abstract sets, with heavy shadows and chiaroscuro lighting, emphasizing composition and atmosphere. Although a few Expressionist films took place in contemporary settings, most dealt with fantastical subjects and took place in distant times, a such as F. W. Murnau's *Nosferatu, eine Symphonie des Grauens* (1922) and Lang's *Metropolis* (1927), which is generally considered the last of the Expressionist films.

> ## Cinematic Firsts
>
> F. W. Murnau's *Nosferatu, eine Symphonie des Grauens* (1922) is often credited as being the first "monster movie." The success of *Nosferatu* and the similarly-minded projects that followed would eventually inspire (and greatly influence) the Universal horror cycle of the 1930s, which included *Dracula* (1931), *Frankenstein* (1931), and *The Mummy* (1932).

As is the case with most artistic film cycles, German Expressionism died out as a result of its being insufficiently commercial. Because an enormous emphasis was placed upon cinematic export, German producers and filmmakers began to imitate the styles of Hollywood, a trend evident even among the Expressionist films; note the contrast between the simplicity of *Caligari* and the flamboyance of *Metropolis*.

Although *Das Kabinett des Doktor Caligari* and the Expressionist films it spawned did not make an immediate impact upon world cinema, its influence became apparent only a few years later when a similar wave of Expressionism emerged in Japan. In Hollywood, German Expressionist films also influenced the Universal horror cycle of the thirties (largely because many of the Universal pictures were directed by German filmmakers). The single most important legacy of Expressionist cinema, however, is its unmistakable influence on the American film noir.

# Chapter 8

# "Nanook of the North" (1922)

Under the direction of Robert Flaherty, Nanook throws his harpoon at his prey.

FILM HISTORIANS love to dub innovators of the medium "fathers" of their creations. Depending on who you're talking to, Thomas Edison, the Lumières, or Augustin Le Prince are referred to as "the father of the motion picture", and Edwin S. Porter is often called "the father of the narrative motion picture." Similarly, Robert J. Flaherty is often called "the father of the documentary film."

Flaherty was born in Iron Mountain, Michigan, in 1884. His father was the manager of a gold mine, and enjoyed a good living. However, he wanted a better life for his son, and enrolled him in college. After stints at Upper Canada College and Michigan College of Mines, Robert Flaherty gave up on higher learning, earning a living mining for both copper and gold before taking a job with the Canadian Northern Railroad in 1910. As a railroad employee, Flaherty was sent on a series of iron ore expeditions "along the East Coast of Hudson Bay, through the barren lands of the hitherto unexplored peninsula of Ungava, along the west coast of Ungava Bay, and along the southern coast of Baffin Land." Carrying a Bell and Howell motion picture camera with him, Flaherty shot 70,000 feet of film. After returning to Toronto, he began editing the film with the hope of selling it and making a living as a travelogue director. The film, however, was destroyed by a fire shortly after its completion. Despite receiving compliments on the surviving work print, perfectionist Flaherty found the film problematic, an assessment that would lead him to craft *Nanook of the North*. Flaherty explains this revelation in Roger Manvell's *Cinema 1950*:

> **Did You Know?**
>
> Filmmaker Orson Welles often compared *Nanook* director Robert J. Flaherty to Henry David Thoreau and Walt Whitman, and considered him one of the greatest men ever to work in film.

My wife and I thought it over for a long time. At last we realized why the film was bad, and we began to get a glimmer that perhaps if I went back to the North, where I had lived for eight years and knew the people intimately, I could make a film that this time would go. Why not take, we said to each other, a typical Eskimo and his family and make a biography of their lives through the year! What biography of any man could be more interesting? Here is a man who has less resources than any other man in the world. He lives in a desolation that no other race could possibly survive. His life is a constant fight against starvation. Nothing grows; he must depend utterly on what he can kill; and all of this against the most terrifying of tyrants—the bitter climate of the North, the bitterest climate in the world. Surely this story could be interesting!

Flaherty then began meeting with potential investors, but no one expressed any interest. In 1920, Flaherty convinced the French fur company Revillon Frères to finance his next film. Thierry Mallot, with whom he'd made this deal, along with two other fur company employees, embarked upon the arduous journey with Flaherty. They set up base at a fur post at Cape Dufferin.

Inside his hut, Flaherty set up a makeshift photography lab. His printer, an old English Williamson, proved to be tempermental because the light it produced fluctuated. The ingenious filmmaker then devised a method of printing by utilizing carefully projected rays of sunlight. He controlled the light that streamed through the inlet by adding or removing layers of muslin. Washing and drying the film in the freezing arctic air proved to be a task, as well. Despite his previous misfortune with fire and film, Flaherty was forced to dry his film near a coal-burning stove.

Flaherty selected a dozen Eskimos as his subjects. He then chose one named Nanook to be his chief on the project. The Eskimos were entranced by the many strange items Flaherty brought with him. When shown photographs of themselves, they turned them upside down because the only image they had ever seen of each other was their reflection in water. The charismatic Nanook was so pleased with Flaherty's portable gramophone that he attempted to eat one of his records. The Eskimos also enjoyed hearing Flaherty play the violin. After spending time explaining what he wanted from them, Flaherty gained their respect and friendship.

The first scenes Flaherty shot depicted the Eskimos hunting a walrus on Walrus Island, located twenty-five miles from shore. Before making their way to the island by whale boat and kayak, Flaherty explained to the Eskimos that this hunt would be different from those they had previously experienced; this time, killing the walrus would come second to obtaining footage. The Eskimos agreed to hold their harpoons until they were given a sign by Flaherty. Flaherty and the hunters then traveled to the shore, where they were forced to wait three days for suitable sailing weather. Once they were able to make the trip to Walrus Island, it took Flaherty and the hunters several days to locate a walrus herd on land.

Flaherty recounted the hunt in his 1922 essay "How I Filmed *Nanook of the North*":

> Behind the rise, I mounted the camera and Nanook, stringing his harpoon, began slowly snaking over the crest. From the crest to where they lay was less than fifty feet and, until Nanook crawled to within half that distance toward them, none of them took any alarm. For the rest of the way, whenever the sentinel of the herd slowly raised his head to look around, Nanook lay motionless on the ground. Then when his head drooped in sleep, once more Nanook wormed his way slowly on. I might mention here that the walrus has little range of vision on land. For protection he depends upon his nose and so long as the wind is favorable one can stalk right into them . . . Nanook picked out the biggest bull, rose quickly and with all his strength landed his harpoon. The wounded bull, bellowing in rage, his enormous bulk diving and thrashing the sea (he weighed more than 2,000 pounds), the yells of the men straining for their lives in their attempt to hold him, the battle cry of the herd that hovered near, the wounded bull's mate which swam in, locked tusks—in an attempt to rescue—was the greatest fight I have ever seen. For a long time it was nip and tuck—repeatedly the crew called to me to use the gun—but the camera crank was my only interest then and I pretended not to understand. Finally Nanook worked the quarry toward the surf where he was pounded by the heavy seas and unable to get a purchase in the water. For at least twenty minutes that tug-o'-war kept on. I say twenty minutes advisedly for I ground out 1,200 feet of film.

After returning to the post, Flaherty screened the footage of the hunt for the Eskimos inside his hut. As this was the first motion picture they'd ever seen, the Eskimos became quite excited. The jubilant (but concerned) Eskimos yelled warnings and words of advice as they watched their own images participating in the hunt. News of the *aggie* (the Inuit word for Flaherty's film) quickly spread along the coast and new Eskimos arrived at the post daily; each of them begged to view the footage.

The next obstacle Flaherty had to overcome was the filming of interiors. Because the average igloo was far too small to film in, Flaherty asked the Eskimos to construct an igloo twice as large solely for this purpose. To assist him with this task, the ever-helpful Nanook recruited a handful of men, women, and children. After two full days of building, the Eskimos attempted to cut insets for the windows. However, this weakened the dome and the igloo caved in. This didn't bother Nanook, however, who insisted that he could successfully build the igloo Flaherty wanted. It took two more attempts before Nanook succeeded, only for Flaherty to discover that there still wasn't enough light inside the igloo to film. The Eskimos then cut away half of the igloo to shoot the interiors.

On January 17, 1921, Flaherty, Nanook, and three other Eskimos left the post to film a bear hunt. The men journeyed more than six hundred miles and the trip lasted two months. Temperatures reached forty below zero, and starvation claimed the lives of two sled dogs. In the end, however, the trip proved a failure; the men could not locate a single bear.

Flaherty concluded the shoot after sixteen months, and returned home. Once the film was fully edited, Flaherty began showing it to distributors. Paramount Pictures called Nanook "a film that just couldn't be shown to the public" and execs at First National refused to accept Flaherty's calls after screening the film. *Nanook of the North* was finally picked up by Pathé Pictures, which released it in 1922 to great commercial and critical acclaim.

"*Nanook* had little impact initially on the nonfiction world," explains *Robert J. Flaherty: A Biography* editor Jay Ruby. "It was only after [cinema vérité pioneer] Jean Rouch began to talk about Flaherty's participatory methods that the documentary and ethnographic film world began to appreciate him. *Nanook*'s immediate impact was in Hollywood." On the heels of *Nanook*, dozens of "real-life" native dramas were attempted. However, none of them caught the public's interest the way *Nanook* had.

*Nanook of the North* is significant because with it Flaherty single-handedly created the narrative nonfiction genre. At the time of *Nanook*'s release Flaherty explained:

> Plenty of pictures have been made of the life of savages in various parts of the world, especially the tropics. The difficulty is that such pictures are usually episodic, showing unrelated scenes with little to hold the wandering attention of one who has not a scientific interest in the lives of primitive people.

While Flaherty has been criticized for reconstructing events rather than filming them spontaneously, it is precisely this reconstruction which ultimately made *Nanook of the North* a turning point in film history. *Nanook* is also significant because Flaherty shot the film using a third-person perspective rather than including himself in its action as had those before him. The film, however, is more than a historical footnote. *Nanook of the North* is similar to *The Birth of a Nation* and *Battleship Potemkin* in that it remains a well-crafted, entertaining, and enduring film more than eight decades later.

### Cinematic Firsts

The first sound documentary is believed to have been the 1923 German film *Life in a Village*.

Two years after Flaherty finished *Nanook*, its "star" died of starvation on a hunting expedition. Apparently impressed more with *Nanook*'s commercial success than with the film itself, Paramount approached Flaherty to make another. This film, *Moana*, depicted Samoan life, but unlike *Nanook*, *Moana* was not a success. Before his death in 1951, Flaherty crafted several more documentaries, none of which repeated the success of *Nanook of the North*.

## Chapter 9

# The Hays Code: Protecting the World from Indecency

PHOTOFEST

It was said that Mae West "even managed to make clean lines sound dirty." It was this suggestiveness that brought most of her films under fire from the Hays Code.

By 1921, several religious organizations had begun to blame the film industry for promoting sex, crime, and immoral activity. These conservative Bible-thumpers believed viewers would imitate any actions they saw on-screen, whether they were those of cowboys, clowns, or Roman soldiers. As Gary Morris observes in his *Bright Lights Film Journal* essay "Public Enemy: Warner Bros. in the Pre-Code Era," Hollywood provided naysayers with plenty to complain about:

> Conventional wisdom says that before the taboo-bursting '60s, all deviance in American filmmaking was suppressed. No cursing, no whores, no queers. Anyone who's looked a little harder at film history knows this is far from true. [In the early Thirties] Hollywood films were rife with left-wing sentiments, anticapitalist rhetoric, images of the politicized poor, crime, sex, drugs, nudity, deviances of every description, and—yes—even the words "damn!" and "hell!" . . . [In films of this era] fetishes abound—everything from naked women and men, foul language, drugs, homosexuality, sadomasochism, transvestism, and child abuse.

Films of the early 1930s were also guilty of depicting premarital sex, unflattering depictions of organized religion, infidelity, alcohol abuse, death by machine gun, lust, and—perhaps worst in the eyes of Hollywood's critics—sinners who did not repent and faced no moral consequences.

During this period a number of scandals involving film personalities rocked Hollywood, which only fueled the perception that motion pictures = sin.

The most publicized of these scandals was that of comic actor Roscoe "Fatty" Arbuckle. The 266-pound Arbuckle, who first rose to prominence as one of Mack Sennett's Keystone Kops, was now one of the most popular actors in Hollywood. The trouble for Arbuckle began on September 5, 1921, in San Francisco, California, when twenty-five-year-old starlet Virginia Rappe fell ill and died at a party he hosted. Based on information given by Bambina Maude Delmont, who was also in attendance at the party, the San Francisco Police Department charged Arbuckle with rape and murder. Newspapers across the country immediately ran sensational stories about Arbuckle's plight. "The newspapers had proved in less than a week that the public got a much greater thrill out of watching stars fall than out of watching them shine," actress Gloria Swanson would later write. "One day Fatty had been their most beloved comedian next to Chaplin; the next day they were screaming for his head." In his book *Hollywood Babylon*, Kenneth Anger comments:

> As headlines screamed, the rumors flew of a hideously unnatural rape: Arbuckle, enraged at his drunken impotence, had ravaged Virginia with a Coca-Cola bottle, *or* a champagne bottle, then had repeated the act with a jagged piece of ice . . . *or*, wasn't it common knowledge that Arbuckle was exceptionally well-endowed? . . . *or*, was it just a question of 266-pounds-too-much of Fatty flattening Virginia in a flying leap? What was certain *was* a leap in circulation; the tabloids had a field day printing insinuations about Arbuckle's "bottle party."

Arbuckle was ultimately tried three times for Rappe's death. The result of each trial was the same: Arbuckle was found not guilty. After the third trial, the jury issued a statement: "Acquittal is not enough for Roscoe Arbuckle. We feel a grave injustice has been done him and there was not the slightest proof to connect him in any way with the commission of any crime." Despite his innocence, Arbuckle's career was finished. Where the tabloids had splashed innuendo-filled stories of murder and rape by Arbuckle across their front pages, news of his third acquittal was buried on the back pages.

After the Arbuckle case, religious groups increased their scrutiny of Hollywood, which they viewed more than ever as the new Babylon. It made no difference to them that Arbuckle—the personification of all the wrong they perceived in Hollywood—had been proven not guilty, not once but three times. If anything, it made them only more determined. In *Censorship of the Movies* Richard S. Randall writes:

> In spite of the extreme claims of some of the agitators, it is doubtful that the movies can be called the cause of the supposed "moral indifference" of the postwar years. If they were even a kind of early accomplice of the Jazz Age, it was probably only through coincidence. The medium already had a well

established reputation for excess, and in the postwar years it found a permissive climate in which this vice could flower. Whether the movies reinforced the new morality and how much so if they did remains an interesting, if unanswered, question. Many of their detractors were willing to believe they were a prime mover. Their defenders countered that movies merely reflected their times. Actually, any established guilt lay somewhere in between—movies reflected and exaggerated the new age. Yet for many of the jury, this alone was enough to convict for the greater crime of causation.

Two key events occurred in 1921 which played an important role in the establishment of the Motion Picture Producers and Distributors of America (MPPDA). The first was the establishment of a motion picture licensing system in the state of New York. The second was the government's rejection of a request by the National Association of the Motion Picture Industry for a one-year grace period during which the industry could reform itself. The potential ramifications of these events were not lost upon the studio moguls; if they didn't act quickly, the government would step in to regulate the production of motion pictures. Of course, this would be a clear violation of the First Amendment, but, nonetheless, there were whispers that the government was considering such regulation.

Taking a page from organized baseball's decision to hire Kenesaw M. Landis as all-powerful "Czar" following the Black Sox scandal of 1919, the motion picture industry decided to hire their own squeaky-clean Czar. Their selection was Will Hays, who had served as Warren Harding's postmaster general and campaign manager. (Irony of ironies: Mr. Squeaky Clean later admitted to having accepted $250,000 in political "gifts.") Hays, it was announced, would preside over a newly formed organization known as the Motion Picture Producers and Distributors of America (later renamed the Motion Picture Association of America, or MPAA). Hays's earliest efforts to clean up the motion picture industry included the establishment of the "morals clause" in film contracts, investigations into the personal lives of screen artists, the drafting of a so-called "Doom Book" listing the names of actors who should not be employed due to their off-screen activities, and a lifetime ban of Roscoe Arbuckle from the motion picture industry. (Hays later rescinded the ban.)

In 1924, Hays presented a plan to the MPPDA board of directors labeled "the Formula." Under this plan—Hays's first attempt at self-regulation—the studios would send all scripts and source materials to his office for clearance before cameras could begin rolling. He then drafted a list of taboo subjects and scenarios known as the "Don'ts and Be Carefuls." However, these had little effect on the film industry as studios chose to turn a blind eye on films that did not comply.

In 1929, the Catholic Church became involved with the MPPDA's attempts to self-regulate motion pictures. After a group of prominent church leaders agreed that a Catholic production code should be enacted, Jesuit priest Daniel Lord was selected to draft it. The highly repressive code he drafted severely restricted a variety of "immoral" subjects, including crime, sex,

> ### Cinematic Firsts
> The first production Seal granted by the Hays Office was given to John Ford's *The World Moves On* (1934).

and nudity, deemed suitable for the movies. In his book *Hollywood Censored: Morality Codes, Catholics, and the Movies*, Gregory D. Black writes:

> Lord and his colleagues shared a common objective with Protestant film reformers: they all wanted entertainment films to emphasize that the church, the government, and the family were the cornerstones of an orderly society; that success and happiness resulted from respecting and working within this system. Entertainment films, they felt, should reinforce religious teachings that deviant behavior, whether criminal or sexual, cost violators the love and comforts of home, the intimacy of family, the solace of religion, and the protection of law. Films should be twentieth-century morality plays that illustrated proper behavior to the masses.

When this code was presented to Hays, he proclaimed that "this was the very thing I had been looking for," and worked closely with Lord to fashion an official code based on Lord's earlier draft. On February 10, 1930, Hays and Lord proposed the Motion Picture Production Code (also known as the "Hays Code") to the motion picture chieftains, who accepted it. Among the restrictions of the Production Code were:

- "No picture shall be produced which will lower the moral standards of those who see it. Hence, the sympathy of the audience shall never be thrown to the side of crime, wrong-doing, evil or sin."

- "Action showing the taking of human life is to be held to the minimum. Its frequent presentation tends to lessen regard for the sacredness of human life."

- "Revenge in modern times shall not be justified."

- "Stories on the kidnapping or illegal abduction of children are acceptable under the Code only . . . (if) the child is returned unharmed."

- "Correct standards of life . . . shall be presented."

- "The subject of abortion shall be discouraged, shall never be more than suggested, and when referred to shall be condemned."

- "Vulgar expressions and double meanings having the same effect are forbidden."

One of the biggest problems with the Production Code was that it left considerable room for interpretation. In his book *The Face on the Cutting Room Floor*, Murray Schumach writes:

Who shall say whether a movie about crime will "inspire others with desire for imitation"? A classic example is on file at the offices of the movie censors. There one can find a clipping about a youth who murdered his teenaged date while they were necking in a car shortly after seeing a movie. The film was Walt Disney's *Snow White and the Seven Dwarfs*. The censors shudder at what might have been the public reaction if the picture had been something like *Anatomy of a Murder*, in which both rape and murder figured so prominently.

Eventually, filmmakers began devising ways to get around the code. Raoul Walsh had previously circumvented Hays by filming W. Somerset Maugham's expressly forbidden play *Rain* as *Sadie Thompson* (1928). Likewise Paramount Pictures would bring William Faulkner's controversial novel *Sanctuary* to the screen under the title *The Story of Temple Drake* (1933). Another highly visible thorn in Hays's side was playwright/actress Mae West, whose highly controversial films *She Done Him Wrong* and *I'm No Angel* (both 1933) pushed the boundaries far beyond what had been deemed inappropriate by the MPPDA.

In 1934, Hays named Joseph I. Breen as the director of a new organization called the Production Code Administration (PCA). Under the guidelines of the PCA, no studio belonging to the MPPDA could produce or distribute a film that was not sanctioned. Filmmakers were now forced to show married couples sleeping in separate beds, religion and government could not be mocked, and films about crime would be allowed only if they featured condemnatory, moralistic endings. "Tacked-on moralistic endings make perfect sense

> ### *Did You Know?*
>
> In his notorious book *Hollywood Babylon*, writer/director Kenneth Anger describes Will H. Hays as being "a prim-faced, bat-eared, mealy-mouthed political chiseler."

if you take a reductive view of creative works—that is, if you see no difference between art and propaganda," explains Marjorie Heins, author of *Not in Front of the Children: Indecency, Censorship, and the Innocence of Youth* and *Sex, Sin, and Blasphemy: A Guide to America's Censorship Wars*.

The enforcers of the Production Code thought corrective moral lessons at the end of gangster films were necessary because they mistakenly assumed that audiences will imitate the fictions that they see. It is only when we understand creative art as a healthy outlet for fantasies and vicarious pleasures, and as a means of confronting horrors and consorting with forbidden behaviors, that the perceived need for censorship will fall away.

One positive result of the code was the "screwball comedy." In his book *Key Moments in Cinema*, Geoffrey Macnab writes:

An intricate new game was played by the filmmakers and the censors. The former would submit their scripts to the Production office, where Breen and his boys were liberal with their use of the red pen. The trick was to hoodwink the censors—to smuggle in action and dialogue that had a completely different meaning (or at least subtext) from what Breen imagined.

For the next thirty years the Production Code kept the film industry as repressed as the Catholic clergymen who had originally conceived it. There can be little doubt that these restrictions limited Hollywood's artistic growth, forever altering the course of the film industry.

# Chapter 10

# Sergei Eisenstein and the Use of Montage

An advertising poster for Sergei Eisenstein's groundbreaking *Battleship Potemkin* (1925)

SERGEI MIKHAILOVICH EISENSTEIN was born in Riga, Latvia, on January 23, 1898. His father was an architect and city engineer. As a child, Eisenstein attended science classes at Realschule to prepare him for engineering school. Eisenstein proved himself to be a genius with an uncanny artistic talent. (Eisenstein biographer Ivor Montagu calls him an "almost Picasso-level infant prodigy.") Eisenstein's interest in art was not confined to drawing; he established a children's theater troupe, in which he also performed. His father, a practical man, who had no interest in creative pursuits, insisted that Sergei attend the Institute of Civil Engineering in Petrograd despite his flourishing artistic talents. During this period Eisenstein began studying art and attending theater productions. After the 1917 revolution, Eisenstein enlisted in the Red Army as an engineer, where he spent two years building bridges and other structures. While he was in the military, Eisenstein also managed to stage a number of theatrical productions, functioning in various capacities, including actor, costume designer, and set designer.

> ## Cinematic Firsts
>
> A. P. Fedesky's *The Religious Procession* (1896) was the first motion picture produced in Russia.

In 1920, Eisenstein joined the Moscow Proletkult Theatre as a scene designer. There he studied under the likes of Konstantin Stanislavsky, Vladimir Mayakovsky, and Vsevolod Meyerhold. The latter had the most impact; Meyerhold's stance against internalized method acting would influence Eisenstein so much that he would later refer to him as his "artistic father." David A. Cook explains Meyerhold's influence in *A History of Narrative Film*:

> What Eisenstein learned from Meyerhold was, essentially, the possibility of mixing two ostensibly contradictory artistic approaches—that of rigorous systematization and spontaneous improvisation. Under Meyerhold's method for acting, which he called "bio-mechanics," spontaneity was systematically conditioned. . . . Eisenstein's encounter with bio-mechanics marks

the beginning of his lifelong theoretical concern with the psychological effects of the aesthetic experience: specifically, the question of what combination of aesthetic stimuli will produce what responses in the perceiver under what conditions.

In 1922, Eisenstein began directing avant-garde theatrical productions. His first production was an adaptation of Alexander Ostrovsky's *Enough Simplicity for Every Wise Man*. This enterprise was marked by Eisenstein's unorthodox approach: rather than dividing it into acts, Eisenstein chose to arrange them in what he called a "montage of attractions." With this, Eisenstein sought to evoke responses from the audience by exploding fireworks under their seats, enacting satirical sketches, and by screening a short film. This film, which parodied newsreels of the time, is significant because it was Eisenstein's first cinematic work. Another memorable Eisenstein production was his version of Tretyakov's *Gas Masks*, which he held in the Moscow gas works. Eisenstein would later explain (in "How I Became a Film Director") that his revolutionary methods were a product of revolutionary times:

> All around was the insistent demand to destroy art, substitute materials and documents for the chief element of art—the image, do away with its content, put constructivism in the place of organic unity, replace art itself with practical and real construction of life without any fiction or fable.

Eisenstein came to believe he needed a new canvas on which to create; he had pushed the artistic boundaries of theater as far as they could be pushed. Having closely studied the films of Griffith and the German Expressionists, he was fascinated with the cinema. In 1924, the Proletkult announced that it would sponsor a series of Goskino films to be collectively titled *Toward the Dictatorship of the Proletariat*. (Although several films were planned, Eisenstein's contribution to the series would be the only one released.) When Proletkult director Valeri Plentyov was assigned writing duties on one of these films, he invited Eisenstein to direct. The result was *Strike*.

Eisenstein knew little about the technical aspects of motion pictures. Just as Griffith before him and Orson Welles fifteen years later, the naive beginner teamed up with a seasoned cinematographer (Eduard Tisse), who would ultimately provide on-the-job training. With *Strike*, which told the story of a labor action that leads to the slaughter of workers, Eisenstein began to experiment with an editing technique he would later dub "montage," a "mounting of shots." This means that contrasting shots are edited together quickly to provide a brief impression of character, place, or time. By juxtaposing images, time and space may be manipulated so that metaphorical meanings are established. Although Eisenstein was the first filmmaker to use this device, it is in fact a combination of techniques developed by Griffith and Lev Kuleshov. In his essay "Methods of Montage," Eisenstein would later conclude that there are five types of montages: (1) the metric montage, (2) the rhythmic montage, (3) the tonal montage, (4) the overtonal montage, and (5) the intellectual montage. Cutting within the metric montage was determined solely by the lengths of shots. With the rhythmic montage the cutting rate was based upon the rhythm of movement that occurs within the shots. With the tonal montage, cutting was determined by the emotional tone of the shots. The overtonal montage was simply a combination of the three aforementioned montages. It was, however, the intellectual montage that most fascinated Eisenstein. Cutting in this style was determined by the "conflict-juxtaposition of accompanying intellectual affects."

Thomas W. Bohn and Richard L. Stromgren expound upon the innovative cutting of *Strike* in *Light and Shadows*:

> With his shots—and through the editing of those shots—he produced his own documents, his own arguments much as a historian does with selected facts and selected words. When in *Strike* shots of butchers killing a bull were combined with Czarist cavalry cutting down the masses, the simile was crystal clear. This was anything but the smoothly edited matching action material, the passivity-inducing Hollywood product. This editing idea agitated, shocked, and compelled the viewer into participation. Of course, it is a highly manipulative method, one which allows only for one deductive meaning: the filmmaker's.

In his efforts to expand and create the boundaries of art by breaking the accepted conventions of the medium, Eisenstein chose to follow the masses rather than an individual protagonist. He had no interest in the individual or his problems, an emphasis that derived, perhaps, from Eisenstein's loyal Communist beliefs, which focused on "community" rather than the individual. Eisenstein also used what he called "typage," a preference for casting non-actors rather than professional actors, based on their physical characteristics. Eisenstein had a painter's eye for composition; just as a painter composes a picture from various individual objects, Eisenstein composed his frames from individual objects and people that were meant to be seen as a whole.

In recognition of his groundbreaking achievements, the Central Committee of the Communist Party commissioned Eisenstein to produce a film. This propagandistic project was to be based on the unsuccessful revolution of 1905, and would be released in 1925 on the twentieth anniversary of the uprising. The film, conceived as eight separate episodes, was initially titled *Year 1905*. Eisenstein began filming in Leningrad in March 1925, and continued until August, when the weather proved unsuitable for filmmaking. He and his crew then traveled to the port of Odessa to begin filming one of the eight episodes, "Potemkin." When Eisenstein stood at the massive Odessa steps where citizens had been slaughtered by Cossacks two decades before, he began to envision a completely different film, one that would focus solely on the mutiny of the battleship *Potemkin* and the massacre that followed.

The *Potemkin* was still being used as a training ship. Eisenstein asked for and received permission to use the ship and its crew in his historical reenactment. (It should be noted that there has been some controversy over whether Eisenstein actually filmed on the *Potemkin*; some records indicate that shooting actually took place on the cruisers *Komintern* and *Twelve Apostles*.) By studying sketches made by a witness of the Odessa steps massacre and interviewing survivors who had seen the slaughter firsthand, Eisenstein started crafting the new scenario. He structured the film in five acts: (1) "Men and Maggots," (2) "Drama on the Quarterdeck," (3) "An Appeal from the Dead," (4) "The Odessa Steps," and (5) "Meeting the Squadron." (In his book *The Cinema of Eisenstein* David Bordwell suggests that the translated title of the first act should actually be "Men and Worms" in order to properly reflect a metaphorical meaning.) Once Eisenstein had completed the scenario, he began filming. The shoot would last ten weeks in all. The famed Odessa steps sequence was filmed in just under one week.

While the film would come to be one of the greatest ever created, and arguably the finest example of film art produced before *Citizen Kane*, Eisenstein's goal was primarily to craft an effective piece of propaganda. It was out of this utilitarian desire to move the masses that Eisenstein's creatively manipulative (and highly innovative) editing techniques were born. In *Sergei M. Eisenstein: A Life* biographer Marie Seton writes:

> To Sergei Mikhailovich, the most important thing was to affect the spectator. By its portrayal of revolutionary heroism, *Potemkin* must electrify the masses, inspire them in their effort to build a new society. His attitude was that of a scientist. As he later explained: "The cinema can make a far bigger contribution and a far stronger impression by projecting matter and bodies than feelings. We photograph and echo the rat-tat-tat of a machine gun. The impression is physiological. Our psychological approach is on the one hand that of the great Russian scholar, Pavlov, with his principles of reflexology, and on the other, that of the Austrian Freud—the principle of psychoanalysis. Take the scene in *Potemkin* where the Cossacks slowly, deliberately, walk down the Odessa steps firing into the masses. By consciously combining the elements of legs, steps, blood, people, we produce an impression. Of what kind? The spectator does not imagine himself at the Odessa wharf in 1905. But as the soldiers's boots press forward he physically recoils. He tries to get out of the range of the bullets. As the baby carriage goes over the side of the mole he holds on to his cinema chair. He does not want to fall into the water.

It now became apparent that, with his first feature, *Strike*, Eisenstein had only scratched the surface regarding the montage. With *Battleship Potemkin*, he was able to fully define and master the aesthetic principles of this device. "In *Battleship Potemkin*, Eisenstein applied to cinematic language his theory of Montage of Attractions," explains Harry M. Geduld, author of *Sergei Eisenstein and Upton Sinclair: The Making and Unmaking of* Que Viva Mexico. "In essence, he replaced the conventional logic of dramatic action by images arbitrarily chosen to create the maximum psychological impact on the audience." In some sequences, Eisenstein uses montage to compress time. In others, such as the Odessa Steps sequence, the montage is used to expand time. The technique is also used to maximize tension in one scene in which the Marines hesitate when ordered to shoot their crew mates. In this instance, Eisenstein uses nearly sixty separate shots to convey an action which, in reality, would have lasted mere seconds. The most significant example of montage in the film is, of course, the Odessa Steps sequence. Here, the civilians greet the mutinous sailors with cheers. As they do so, Cossacks approach on the steps above. A title card consisting of a single word—"Suddenly"—provides transition between the joyous greeting and the massacre that ensues. The audience is then presented one long montage of the massacre, expressions of shock and dismay, acts of violence, a baby carriage rolling down the steps toward the sea, gunships firing from the harbor, and, lastly, symbolic shots of a stone lion awakened from slumber.

It has been suggested that Eisenstein's innovations were motivated by reasons of practicality. In *Living Images* Stanley Kauffmann writes:

> Commentators have pointed out that both the montage in *Potemkin* and its five-part structure had their origins at least partly in practical considerations. Raw film stock was in very short supply in the early Soviet days. Most of what was available was in relatively short snippets, so directors had to work in short takes. Eisenstein developed the aesthetics of montage out of exigency. Also, most Soviet film theaters at the time had only one projector; there was a pause when one reel ended and another reel had to be put on the machine. The five parts of *Potemkin* are on five reels, so the pauses come at reasonably appropriate moments. But, as is so often true in the history of art, the practical needs were not constrictive but stimulating.

The resulting film would prove to be as revolutionary as its subject. While noted for its editing, *Battleship Potemkin* is an extraordinary film in nearly every aspect. The film received acclaim around the world, and Eisenstein's experiments in montage had a lasting effect on the medium. Within a few years, each of the major Hollywood studios would employ "montage directors," who were separate from the films' primary directors, to produce montage sequences. The film has been listed on many critical and popular all-time top-ten lists, and it remains one of the most influential films in the history of cinema. The Odessa Steps sequence alone has been imitated and reconstructed in a number of films, including *Brazil* (1985) and *The Untouchables* (1987).

After *Battleship Potemkin*, Eisenstein continued working, but his output was sporadic, at best. (He completed only seven films during his twenty-five year career.) The best of his later works were *October* (1928) and the two-part film *Ivan the Terrible* (1945; 1958). However, Eisenstein's true contribution to the medium was the montage, developed in tandem with his first two features.

The montage changed the way filmmakers approached the medium; no longer restricted and forced to tell stories in a straight-forward manner, filmmakers were able to manipluate time. While the montage is rarely used today—except as a stylistic device—its legacy lives on through the non-linear approaches of films such as *Pulp Fiction* (1994) and *21 Grams* (2003).

### Did You Know?

Sergei Eisenstein once stated that Walt Disney's *Snow White and the Seven Dwarfs* (1937) was the greatest motion picture ever made.

It can be said that any film which uses editing to manipulate time in any way owes a tremendous debt to Eisenstein. D. W. Griffith and Eisenstein have often been called the two most influential filmmakers in the history of the medium; there can be little doubt that these two filmmakers were largely responsible for creating the language of cinema within which all films have since been created.

# Chapter 11

# The Movies Learn to Speak

*The Jazz Singer* (1927) proved to be so successful that it almost single-handedly ended the silent film era.

"THE EYE, which is called the window of the soul, is the chief means whereby the understanding may most fully and abundantly appreciate the infinite works of nature," Leonardo da Vinci once observed. "The ear is the second, inasmuch as it acquires its importance from the fact that it hears the things which the eye has seen." While da Vinci's observation seems more obvious than particularly profound, there was a time when many motion picture insiders believed sound and image did not go hand in hand. For the generations that have matured since the advent of the talking picture, silent films generally hold little interest. For them it may be difficult to believe that the motion picture begrudgingly came to accept the talking film only because it had no choice. Studio moguls and film critics once believed sound could only result in the end of the medium, and few were able to envision a film in which the actors could speak. A fact that may be of even greater shock: audiences were, at one time, completely uninterested in the idea of talking films. Thomas Edison himself predicted that "the talking motion picture will not supplant the regular silent motion picture."

Ironically, it was Edison who made the first significant contributions toward the development of talking pictures. In 1877, Edison discovered a method by which to record and reproduce sound with his invention of the Phonograph. In 1891, Edison invented the Kinetoscope. This peepshow device made it possible for an audience of one to view moving pictures. Edison then combined these two inventions to make the crude Kinetophane. In 1896, Frenchman Charles Pathé and German scientist Oskar Messter began studying the possible combination of the Cinematograph with Berliner's Gramophone. Twelve years later, England's Warwick Company introduced Cinephone, which was quickly replaced by Cecil Hepworth's Vivaphone and Leon Gaumont's Chronophone. All three devices, however, posed problems, as they relied upon the Phonograph. As Ernest Lindgren points out in *The Art of Film*, two limitations restricted these devices from becoming "anything more than novelty": the insufficient level of sound produced by the Gramophone and the still-flawed methods of synchronization they employed. In 1906, an English researcher named Eugene Lauste patented a system that recorded sound onto the film itself, which meant the synchronization between the sound and the images would be perfect. In 1908, Edison returned with a device known as the Cinemaphone. This device adjusted the speed of a motion picture to match that of a Phonograph. This led to the Kinetophone (introduced in 1913) on which Edison himself made a number of early "talking" films. The *New York Times* reviewed one of these shorts, noting that "the prophecy that the talkies soon will supplant grand opera or the legitimate drama seems fantastical."

In 1921, Orland E. Kellum devised another device to marry sight and sound. This was called the Photokinema. D. W. Griffith's film *Dream Street* featured a sound sequence which utilized Kellum's contraption. However, both the synchronization and the sound levels left much to be desired and the scene was excised from the film after its first showing. (*Dream Street* is still recognized by film scholars as the first feature film to use sound.)

In 1926, scientists employed by Bell Laboratories announced a new synchronization process called Vitaphone, by which sound could be mechanically reproduced onto a disc and then synchronized to projected film images. The scientists shopped their invention to the major studios in the hopes that they might purchase the patents, but much to Bell's chagrin, the studios were not interested. Sensing that sound may very well figure the future of the motion picture, Hungarian-American movie mogul William Fox (founder of Fox Studios, which later merged with Daryl Zanuck's Twentieth Century Pictures to become Twentieth Century-Fox) hired his own team of scientists to begin the development of a similar process.

At this time Warner Bros. was struggling financially. Taking an extraordinary gamble, Sam Warner convinced his brothers to purchase the Vitaphone patents. This proved to be costly, and most banks were hesitant to grant the studio a loan. It should be noted that Warner's earliest interest in sound was not to make "talkies," but films that would feature musical soundtracks. Warner believed exhibitors would embrace these films because they would allow them to save money by dismissing their house musicians. Exhibitors, however, had no interest in this idea. While it initially cost no more than a few hundred dollars to equip sound booths to project Vitaphone films, exhibitors nevertheless complained about the expenditure. Film critics, trade newspapers, and purists also condemned the impending arrival of sound. Warner Bros., however, had two things going for them: the ever-increasing popularity of radio, and the emergence of William Fox's similar process, which was known as Movietone (a system that recorded sound on film alongside the image, rather than on a separate disk that required synchronization with the film). When inventions so similar in nature emerge at roughly the same time, they often tend to undermine each other's cause; this, however, was not the case with

Vitaphone and Movietone. In fact, Fox's widespread campaign for the acceptance and utilization of sound technology ultimately aided Warner's efforts.

The first Warner Bros. Vitaphone feature, *Don Juan*, was released on August 6, 1926. *Don Juan* was, in truth, a silent film; the first Vitaphone film had no spoken dialogue but featured a musical score by the New York Philharmonic. This film led to a series of Warner Bros. Vitaphone shorts featuring the likes of Marion Talley and Anna Case. In May 1927, Fox introduced the Movietone Newsreel. These small projects set the stage for the first significant sound film. Hoping to score a hit and popularize the talkie, Warner Bros. decided to craft a Vitaphone project that would feature the singing of a popular crooner. Samson Raphaelson's play *Day of Atonement* was thought suitable material for such a project. A script was hammered out and the project was titled *The Jazz Singer*. Warner Bros. first offered the lead to Eddie Cantor and then George Jessel, who had originated the role on stage. When both declined the offer, Al Jolson was cast. While the film is remembered by and large as the first talkie, this is inaccurate. In *A Song in the Dark: The Birth of a Musical Film*, film historian Richard Barrios writes:

> Popular history always seems to crave the convenience of significant events that can be labeled "THE FIRST." Unfortunately, there are not many major incidences that are worthy of this designation; history seldom permits such tidy corners. Since the drive persists, folklore has passed off *The Jazz Singer* as various firsts in the history of film: The First Sound Film, The First Talking Film, The First Movie Musical. It was none of these; it was not even Al Jolson's first film.

"Most of the film has silent movie intertitles and synchronized incidental music," explains Harry M. Geduld, author of *The Birth of the Talkies: From Edison to Jolson*.

> Jolson sings, of course, and his songs are heard by the audience. At one point, in a night club scene, Jolson interpolates his songs with spontaneous spoken dialogue; in another scene, with his mother, Jolson interpolates some more spoken dia-

logue. This was also spontaneous and is not found in the film's shooting script. Alan Crosland, the film's director, liked the spontaneous dialogue passages and decided to leave them in the film.

*The Jazz Singer* was released on October 6, 1927, and was a huge hit, the lucrative film revitalizing the fledgling Warner Bros. studio. Success, however, did not come without personal cost; due to the stress involved with the project, Sam Warner fell ill and passed away the day before the film's premiere. *The Jazz Singer* was not the first sound film, but it played a

> ### Cinematic Firsts
>
> The first hit song from a talking movie was Al Jolson's "Sonny Boy," which he performed in the film *The Singing Fool* (1928).

key role in the public acceptance of the technology. The demand for talking films soon became so great that by late 1929 the silent film died out completely. It should be noted that Warner Bros. released *Lights of New York* (1928), the first full-length "all talkie" Vitaphone film, the following year.

The emergence of the talking film had a tremendous impact on the film industry. The most significant changes brought about as a result of the talking motion picture were:

- **Made the motion picture accessible to the visually impaired.** This most obvious of all contributions made by the sound film is rarely, if ever, noted. Talking pictures introduced a whole new audience to the motion picture.

- **Caused Paramount to lose its stranglehold on the industry.** Both Fox and Warner Bros.'s work in the talking film led to increased revenue for those studios. Paramount had been the first studio offered the Vitaphone technology, but had turned it down. Paramount owned a large chain of motion picture theaters and quickly installed projectors to screen talking films.

- **Warner Bros. becomes a dominant force.** Prior to the Vitaphone, the studio had been quite close to going under. The triumph of *The Jazz Singer* led to a windfall of money with which Warner Bros. purchased longtime Paramount competitor First National Pictures.

- **Put many independent studios out of business.** Once the public had developed an insatiable desire for talking films, the independents found themselves unable to meet this demand due to the high costs of producing such films. By 1929, most American films were produced by the four major studios: Warner Bros., Paramount, Fox, and Metro-Goldwyn-Mayer.

- **Gave birth to the musical genre.** Musical films could not be made without a soundtrack. Sound film was directly responsible for the origination of this genre, which would blossom in the 1930s.

- **Changed the style of motion picture acting.** Actors were now able to convey attitudes and intentions through vocal inflections. This led to more subtle, naturalistic approaches.

- **Ended the careers of many, many actors.** It's difficult to say just how many actors who had prospered during the silent era saw their careers cut short as a result of the talkie. This generally occurred for one or more of three reasons: actors who had never before been heard by the public had irritating or unacceptable voices; actors' voices didn't match the public's image of them; or actors failed to adapt to the new acting style needed for the talking film.

- **Led character actors to receive recognition.** In the era of the silent film, only stars were recognized and treated as royalty. With the advent of the talkie, the individual personalities and styles of character actors and supporting players became recognized.

- **Led to the acceptance of educational films.** While some educational films had been produced prior to the introduction of sound, they were few and far between. An exorbitant amount of information needed to be conveyed, and because title cards were unable to hold more than a few words and still maintain viewer interest, silent educational films were impractical. Educational leaders of the time immediately took interest in the talking film. Dr. George F. Zook, president of the American Council of Education, is quoted in John W. Oliver's *The History of American Technology*: "The sound motion picture is potentially the most revolutionary instrument introduced in education in this generation."

- **Led to the censorship of newsreels.** This unfortunate side-effect is documented in the 1938 book *The History of Motion Pictures* by Iris Barry, Maurice Bardeche, and Robert Brasillach:

It may be all very well to see a dictator or a riot, but it becomes dangerous to hear them as well. Censorship, whether official or officious (in France, by some admirable hypocrisy, censorship is theoretically not supposed to apply to newsreels), got its claws on the producers of newsreels. So it came about that while the world was being shaken by catastrophes, the screen showed us only dull boxing or tennis matches, bicycle races, the cultivation of the grape in California, harvesting in Denmark and—in every country in the world—local beauty contests at the seashore, local dog shows, but never the truth.

The earliest talking films were, by and large, primitive. Most of them contained more dialogue than the stories called for; because of this, directors used a lot of close-up shots of the characters speaking, which resulted in a static camera. Some theaters were slow to convert, and

### Did You Know?

Following the success of *The Jazz Singer* (1927), Al Jolson enjoyed a period of tremendous success, but by the mid-1930s his film career had stalled. In 1945, Jolson tried out for a part he believed himself perfect for: the role of himself in *The Jolson Story* (1946). The part went to Larry Parks, who also appeared in the sequel, *Jolson Sings Again* (1949).

silent versions of talking films were sometimes exhibited. Even legendary actor/director Charles Chaplin was hesitant to adapt. His first
sound film, *City Lights* (1931), featured synchronized sound effects
and music, but absolutely no spoken dialogue. Eventually, those who
resisted the talkie found it futile to stand in the way of progress.

The talking film forever changed the way we experience motion
pictures. There can be little doubt that the advent of the talking film
was one of the most significant turning points in the history of
cinema. Whereas most of the turning points charted in this book
altered only certain aspects of the motion picture industry, sound
transformed nearly everything in its wake.

# Chapter 12

# The Academy Awards

The Oscar remains Hollywood's most sought-after prize.

METRO-GOLDWYN-MAYER PRODUCTION head Louis B. Mayer conceived the Academy of Motion Picture Arts and Sciences in 1927. Its official mission was to advance motion pictures as an art form, but this wasn't its true purpose; in reality, Mayer saw the Academy as an organization that would combat the impending threat of the labor unions. "The original impetus behind the Academy of Motion Picture Arts and Sciences was to create a body for arbitrating labor disputes within the movie industry," explains Damien Bona, author of *Inside Oscar* and *Inside Oscar 2*. "Louis B. Mayer and his cohorts had an agenda, though. As one of the major powers in the film industry and an archconservative, Mayer was strongly anti-union and his intention was that this new organization would consistently and firmly come down on the side of management. The founding fathers of the Academy maintained that it would be a fair and impartial body, and they also declared that the organization would be the equivalent of a literary salon where Hollywood's best and brightest could come together and engage in a rewarding exchange of ideas; they also promised the Academy would be involved in such noble endeavors as ridding the screen of immoral content and promoting technical advances in movies. For Mayer and the other poobahs, these were secondary in importance to the control the Academy would have over industry workers."

On May 4, 1927, a group of thirty-six prominent individuals representing every branch of the industry was assembled. On that day they established the Academy as a nonprofit organization under California law. The original thirty-six founders were:

*Actors*
Richard Barthelmess
Douglas Fairbanks
Jack Holt
Harold Lloyd
Conrad Nagel
Milton Sills

*Directors*
Cecil B. DeMille
Henry King
Frank Lloyd
Fred Niblo
John M. Stahl
Raoul Walsh

*Producers*
Fred Beetson
Charles H. Christie

*Writers*
Joseph Farnham
Benjamin F. Glazer
Jeanie MacPherson
Bess Meredyth
Carey Wilson
Frank Woods

*Technicians*
J. Arthur Ball
Cedric Gibbons
Roy J. Pomeroy

*Lawyers*
George W. Cohen
Edwin Loeb

Sid Grauman
Milton E. Hoffman

| *Producers* | Harry Rapf |
|---|---|
| Jesse L. Lasky | Joseph M. Schenck |
| M. C. Levee | Irving G. Thalberg |
| Louis B. Mayer | Harry Warner |
| Mary Pickford | Jack Warner |

The group also elected its first officers at the meeting. Because of his immense popularity and charisma, Douglas Fairbanks was elected president. His vice president was Fred Niblo, M. C. Levee was elected as treasurer, and Frank Woods as secretary. One week later, the newly-founded Academy held a banquet in the ballroom of the Biltmore Hotel. It was there that Fairbanks publicly announced the organization's establishment and goals. In his book *Academy Awards Illustrated*, Robert Osborne quotes Fairbanks as explaining, "Our purpose is positive, not negative. We are formed to do, not undo."

The Academy would ultimately fail in its attempts to stop the unionization of Hollywood. In the end, the organization accomplished little beyond establishing what we now know as the Academy Awards. (The Academy has, however, assembled a substantial library of research material on film history and produces a newsletter for its members.) The Academy's committee on merit awards selected a dozen categories in which they would present an annual award. It was then decided that films released between the first of September of one year and the first of September of the next year would be eligible. Initially, there was no Best Picture award. Instead, the Academy would present two separate Distinction Awards; one would be given on the basis of production and the other for artistic merit. After the first year of the awards, in which *Wings* (1927) won the award for production and *Sunrise* (1927) won for artistry, this policy was changed; the Academy decided to adopt a single Best Picture award, as had other awards programs that predated the Academy Awards. In his book *An Evening's Entertainment: The Age of the Silent Feature Picture 1915–1928*, Richard Koszarski explains:

> There are a number of reasonable explanations for this, including the greater economic impact that a single award carries, and the ego problem with designating one group of nominees as "not so artistic." In tracing the lineage of the current Best Picture category, however, official histories approved by the

Academy consciously elevate *Wings* at the expense of *Sunrise*. One such volume not only discounts the "artistic quality of production" award, lumping it with the minor technical citations and special awards, but retroactively changes the name of the award given to *Wings* to Best Picture.

Considering that producers outnumbered other types of members within the Academy in those early years, perhaps it's not so strange that the Academy chose to elevate the award for production over that of artistry.

The award itself—a little gold statuette of a man holding a sword and standing atop a reel of film—was designed by Academy founder and MGM art director Cedric Gibbons, and crafted by sculptor George Stanley for $500. As cast by Alex Smith, each statuette cost almost $100 to produce due to the amount of bronze and gold required for its production.

The Academy realized almost immediately that other awards beyond those for the basic categories would be needed. In its first year the Academy presented two such awards: one to Charles Chaplin for writing, directing, producing, and starring in *The Circus* (1928); the second to Warner Bros. for producing *The Jazz Singer* (1927). (It was the Academy's view that silent films could not compete against talkies. Because of this, the Academy deemed *The Jazz Singer* ineligible for competition.)

The first awards ceremony was held on May 16, 1929 at the Hollywood Roosevelt Hotel. Just under 250 people attended and tickets were sold to the general public for $10 each. Ceremonies were held variously in the Ambassador and Biltmore Hotels until 1942, when the Academy discontinued the banquet. The awards have since been presented in locations that have included Grauman's Chinese Theater, the RKO Pantages Theatre, and the Dorothy Chandler Pavilion. In 2002, a permanent home, known as the Kodak Theatre, was constructed solely for the Academy Awards.

From 1929 through 1940, the Academy announced the names of winners in press releases prior to the ceremony, so that the news would be ready for publication in the late edition. This system would be changed because of a journalistic blunder—the *Los Angeles Times* published the list of winners before the ceremony. Thus, the sealed-envelope system was implemented in 1941.

Today the Academy Awards are also known as the Oscars. Although the name was adopted officially after appearing in a 1934 article by Hollywood columnist Sidney Skolsky, its origins are unclear. One popular legend finds Academy librarian (and later executive director) Margaret Herrick remarking that the man on the statuette resembled her uncle Oscar. After this, the staff apparently began referring to the statuette as Oscar. Another rumor is

> ### *Cinematic Firsts*
> The Oscars were first broadcast in color in 1966.

that Skolsky overheard someone say that the figure resembled *their* uncle Oscar, and that he incorporated the story into the article. Both accounts are unlikely, but provide color to the organization's history.

Today there are nearly 6,000 voting members of the Academy. According to Academy bylaw, one must be "active in the film business" to be a member. In his essay "What Do the Oscars Really Mean?" filmmaker Josh Becker questions this:

[S]ince the greater percentage of Academy members are older than sixty-five years of age, we might assume most of them are retired or nearing retirement. Thus, there are at least two distinct factions of Academy members—the old and the young. This is what undoubtedly caused *Midnight Cowboy* to win Best Picture in 1969 and John Wayne to win Best Actor in the same year; the younger faction must have canceled each other out by splitting their votes between Dustin Hoffman and Jon Voight.

In retrospect, the Academy has made its fair share of mistakes. In fact, *Citizen Kane* (1941)—the film almost everyone seems to agree upon as being the greatest film in the history of the American cinema—failed to win Best Picture in its respective year. (It was bested by *How Green Was My Valley*, 1941.) Oscar-winning actor Richard Dreyfuss once lamented, "We've all participated in two rituals: one is watching the

Academy Awards, and the other is putting down the Academy Awards. Both are very sacred and traditional American events." That most film buffs disagree with most of the Academy's selection only seems to increase their curiosity. (It is estimated that the Oscars are viewed by more than a billion viewers each year.)

Oscar expert Robert Osborne believes oversights and mistakes are simply a result of human nature:

> The little statue is ruled, and voted, by human beings who are sometimes blinded by color and razzmatazz. These people are conscientious and try to rule with their heads, but they are human and sometimes rule with their emotions.

In his introduction to Paul Michael's *The Academy Awards: A Pictorial History*, legendary producer David O. Selznick expressed a similar sentiment:

> [I]t is no doubt true that in other cases there has been inadequately expressed appreciation by an electorate influenced unduly by transient tastes, by commercial success, by studio log-rolling, and by personal popularity in the community of Hollywood.

"The bottom line is that the Academy Awards simply reflect the opinions of roughly 5,800 people who work—or have worked—in some capacity in the film industry," Damien Bona explains. "These are people with middlebrow taste and fairly liberal politics, and while most are undoubtedly sincerely voting for what they feel is the best, they are susceptible to such influences as advertising campaigns, box-office grosses, and personal prejudices. And since they are mostly part of the Hollywood establishment, their proclivities are for safe, conventional filmmaking. If you [instead sampled] roughly 5,800 cinephiles, you'd come up with much more interesting and credible results."

Academy voters, it would seem, frequently vote for the films they believe have the most important messages of the year. Films that deal with anti-Semitism or historical injustice, or anti-drug or alcohol messages are frequently award winners.

There can be no doubt that the advent of the Academy Awards was a turning point for the film industry. Today studios spend exorbitant amounts of money to campaign for awards. The prestige an Oscar brings can transform a film that earned very little money into an asset in the eyes of studio executives, most of whom generally look at little beyond the bottom line. Oscars can rejuvenate stalled careers, if for no other reason than the fact that producers love being able to print "starring Academy Award-winning (insert performer's name here)" on posters and advertisements for their films. The prestige an Oscar brings a performer is a conundrum; everyone talks about the Academy's lack of good judgment, yet those who win the statuettes become instant royalty. The ceremony draws attention to the industry, gains publicity for those performers who attend or are nominated, and often

> **Did You Know?**
>
> The person who has received the most Oscar nominations is Walt Disney, with a whopping sixty-four. Disney has also won more statuettes than anyone else: an impressive twenty-six.

creates an audience for films which may have otherwise been swept beneath the rug. Sometimes films with little chance of making any money are produced with the hope of winning an award thanks to the prestige they bring the studios. Such films are generally referred to as "Oscar bait." As the poor response to *The Shipping News* (2001) suggested, for example, Academy voters can be turned off by films they feel have been made simply to entice them.

In the aforementioned essay, Becker concludes:

I think the Oscars are meaningful to help people keep going in a heartless industry. There's something to hope for. I might have given up long ago if it had not been for the hope of hitting big, which is inextricably tied up with winning an Oscar. Sure many people who deserve it never got it, sure there's a slight smell of corruption, sure it's the industry patting itself on the back, sure it's all egotism, but who cares? It's not real anyway; it's movies.

Damien Bona observes, "The Academy Awards provide a good deal of enjoyment because of the silliness, intrigue, self-importance, suspense, and attendant froth, and they do have an undeniable significance as a piece of popular culture and American social history. But in terms of providing any sort of aesthetic standard, they should in no way be taken seriously."

Oscar remains the elusive dream for the tens of thousands of would-be actors and actresses who travel to the city of angels each year only to wind up waitressing or working in video stores. The studios and producers who win the awards gain bargaining power, and the salaries of Oscar-winning actors skyrocket. Moguls, studio execs, and performers have come and gone since 1927, but Oscar continues to wield the most power of anyone in Hollywood.

# Chapter 13

# "Snow White and the Seven Dwarfs" (1937)

A scene from Walt Disney's landmark animated feature *Snow White and the Seven Dwarfs* (1937).

WALT DISNEY had long envisioned a feature-length animated film. His first attempt, in 1931, was an adaptation of Lewis Carroll's *Alice's Adventures in Wonderland*, which he aborted during preproduction when Commonwealth Pictures released a live-action version. In 1933, Disney again considered producing a feature based upon Carroll's novel, this time a combination of live action and animation with

93

Mary Pickford as Alice. Pickford, who was one of the cofounders of
United Artists, wanted so badly to work with Disney that she offered
to finance the project out of her own pocket. Disney must have felt a
sense of *déjà vu* when he was again forced to pull the plug on the
project after Paramount announced its own live-action version. Disney
then considered another combination of live action and animation,
an adaptation of Washington Irving's *Rip Van Winkle* which would
have starred Will Rogers—abandoned when he learned that Paramount owned the exclusive rights to the story. Disney faced a similar
dilemma over a feature-length animated version of *Babes in Toyland*.

### Cinematic Firsts

The first animated feature film,
according to the Cinematheque
Francaise's definition of a feature
("a commercially made film over
one hour in duration"), was the
Argentinean film *The Apostle*
(1917).

Fully anticipating the
extra workload involved in
making an animated fea-
ture, Disney decided to
strengthen his animation
team. His first step was
the development of an
in-house animation school
where his artists could
refine their craft. He then
augmented his staff, hiring
a number of promising
young artists.

In 1934, Walt Disney Studios experienced a financial windfall
when it received merchandising revenue from the short film *Three
Little Pigs* (1933). With the profits from that film, Disney was able to
negotiate a $1 million line of credit from Bank of America. With this
financing in place, Disney planned to realize the first animated feature. Recalling his own enjoyment as a youth attending a screening of
the 1915 live-action version of *Snow White*, Disney chose this fairy
tale as his subject. In February 1935 Disney held a late night sound-
stage meeting with his animators. Because rumors that Disney was
going out of business had been circulating throughout the studio,
many of the animators feared Disney would announce just that. Marc
Elliot details the meeting in *Walt Disney: Hollywood's Dark Prince*:

> There was . . . a great collective sigh of relief when Walt stood
> in the center of a circle of his employees like a wagon master

awaiting an Indian massacre and announced that he had gathered them all together to proclaim officially the start of production of *Snow White*. After a burst of enthusiastic applause, Walt decided to act out the film's entire scenario for them. He played every character and scene: the young girl, the seven dwarfs she "adopts," the evil queen obsessed with beauty, her seduction of stepdaughter Snow White with the poisoned apple, and the arrival of Prince Charming. Once again Disney amazed his employees with his ability to shift from one portrayal to another. A mood of hushed awe came over his audience as he slowly completed his performance by turning and seeming to actually recede into the happily ever after. A stunned silence followed, until finally one person began to clap. What followed was a thunderous round of applause, which Walt acknowledged with a smile, a nod, and the holding up of one hand, palm out, fingers spread apart.

News of Disney's new project, initially budgeted at $250,000, appeared in newspapers across the country. Although the announcement was, by and large, accepted optimistically by the press, it was met less enthusiastically by the other studios. "The film industry's reaction to the news that Disney was producing a feature-length cartoon ranged from disbelief to cynicism to downright derision," explains animation expert John Canemaker, author of *Walt Disney's Nine Old Men* and *Treasures of Disney Animation Art*. "No one, said the Hollywood pundits, would sit still for over an hour watching drawings move. Why, the fast slapstick action would grow tiresome and the bright colors would hurt audience's eyes, it was said. Furthermore, no one could possibly become emotionally involved with cartoon characters." Within the industry, *Snow White and the Seven Dwarfs* became known as "Disney's Folly." Even Disney's own wife had reservations regarding the project. (She believed there was "something nasty" about the dwarfs.) Nevertheless, the determined Disney pressed forward.

Two obstacles had to be overcome to maintain viewer interest: the bright colors used in animated shorts might indeed become irritating to viewers' eyes after an hour, and flat, one-dimensional, traditional animation would bore viewers after a short while. To combat the first concern, it was decided that the film's colors would be slightly muted. The answer to the second problem came in the form of a new

device known as the multiplane camera. *Chicago Sun-Times* film critic
Roger Ebert explains in his essay "Snow White and the Seven Dwarfs":

> [The multiplane camera] gave the illusion of three dimensions
> by placing several levels of drawing one behind another and
> moving them separately—the ones in front faster than the
> ones behind, so that the background seemed to actually move
> instead of simply unscrolling.

This device, first utilized in a short entitled *The Old Mill* (1937),
received critical acclaim and a special Oscar. It should be noted that
the multiplane camera soon became the standard in animation until
the mid-90s when computer animation began taking over.

At first Disney planned to direct *Snow White and the Seven Dwarfs*
himself, but later reconsidered. (Disney's only personal directorial
effort was the 1935 "Silly Symphonies" short *The Golden Touch*, which
is said to be among the worst of the studio's films. *The Golden Touch*
has never been reissued since its brief theatrical run.) While Disney
himself would still oversee the film, he appointed animator David
Hand as director. Hand may have been the director of record, but all
decisions regarding the film would be Disney's. A common misconception would have it that Disney himself was artistically responsible
for the films he produced; Disney himself never personally con-
tributed to the art. His films were, however, the result of his vision.
Disney didn't know much about art, but he knew what he liked. His
naiveté regarding art is the stuff of legends; he once remarked that
Cézanne didn't know how to draw. "That vase is all crooked," he once
said. Another anecdote finds him referring to Goya as "that Goya
guy." It was perhaps this lack of understanding that limited the artistry
of his films; while he spoke frequently of improving the animation
techniques of the time, he never permitted such development. In
Disney's films, realism and cuteness were often at odds with one
another. (Nowhere is this more evident than in *Bambi*, where the realism of the deer is sharply contrasted by the cuddly cuteness of the
other forest animals.) Disney's unrefined tastes were almost always
reflected in his films through his penchant for crude comedy, cute
characterizations, and overt sentimentality.

In the case of *Snow White and the Seven Dwarfs*, Disney planned to imbue the dwarfs with a cuteness and comical quality that was not present in the Grimms' original fairy tale. In *The Disney Films* Leonard Maltin writes:

> Just as Disney learned that his hero Mickey Mouse was downright dull in comparison with such colorful sidekicks as Pluto and Donald Duck, he quickly discovered that the heroes and heroines of fairy tale stories were frequently the least interesting aspects of those tales. Yet, one couldn't eliminate them or relegate them to supporting roles; the answer was to have their actions intertwined with those of the comedy characters so subtly that it would never seem as it did, for example, in the archetypal Broadway musical comedies of the 1920s and 1930s that two separate and distinct elements were at work.

In Disney's initial story outline the dwarfs were quite different from what ultimately ended up on screen. At first their names were to be Happy, Sleepy, Doc, Bashful, Jumpy, Grumpy, and Deafy. Through numerous creative sessions these characters would evolve into the dwarfs audiences know and love today. The last of these characters to change was Deafy, who became known as Dopey. (In early depictions of this character, Dopey was a bucktoothed buffoon.) Both Disney and David Hand realized the importance that each dwarf have his own distinct character. On November 17, 1936, Hand reportedly challenged the animators: "We are going to lose [the audience] because I haven't enough confidence in you animators to tell the difference between these dwarfs. I have looked at the reel many times, and I don't know what characters are being presented to me."

Initially, Disney envisioned Dopey as a mixture of comics Harry Langdon and Harpo Marx. In the end, comedian Eddie Collins became the basis for his personality. (At one point Disney considered hiring Langdon, but decided against it because of a perceived drinking problem.) Pinto Colvig, who had previously lent his voice to Goofy, was hired to provide vocals for Grumpy. Roy Atwell, then a famous vaudeville comic known for the substitution of the first syllables of consecutive words, was employed to voice Doc. Upon hearing that the studio would be hiring someone to voice a character named Sneezy, comic Billy Gilbert promptly telephoned Walt Disney and engaged in his trademark sneezing routine. Disney reportedly told Gilbert, "You're my man."

Animating and voicing the three human characters would prove to be equally challenging. Disney's original outline of the story had provided only rough descriptions of these characters. Disney had envisioned Snow White as being a fourteen-year-old version of Janet Gaynor, the Prince a younger version of Douglas Fairbanks, Jr., and for the evil Queen, Disney provided no human likeness, referring to her as a "mixture of Lady Macbeth and the Big Bad Wolf." Prior to *Snow White*, only the most basic, caricatured human beings had been animated in Disney films. For *Snow White*, Disney would have his animators draw the human characters through rotoscoping, a process by which live performers act out the characters' scenes before a camera so that their movements could be traced. This, Disney believed, would help the artists achieve a greater sense of realism. In his book *Hollywood Cartoons: American Animation in Its Golden Age*, Michael Barrier explains Disney's view of the rotoscope process:

> [L]ive action could be the servant of animation, helping the animator to enhance what remained a fundamentally animated conception. That conception had to be . . . rooted in an understanding of the acting that successful animation required; if it was, then the use of live action could be, like the endless drawing and redrawing that animation involved, a way of working through to the heart of the character—and no more confining than an easel painter's use of a live model.

However, most of the animators disapproved of this technique. In *Animation: From Script to Screen*, longtime Disney animator Shamus Culhane would later write:

> [A]fter a certain amount of animation on *Snow White* was finished, Walt and his directors should have seen that it was quite possible to create very fine animation without the laborious photography of the actors and the subsequent tracing of their actions. According to Grim Natwick, he animated about a hundred scenes of Snow White, and most of them were done without the aid of the rotoscoped drawings. He merely used

the first and last tracings to be sure that he hooked up to the scenes before and after the one on which he was working. He then flipped through the tracings a few times but he never referred to them while he was animating. It is doubtful that Walt Disney ever became aware that his safeguard against poor animation was being flouted this way.

Disney hired a young dancer named Marjorie Belcher to perform Snow White's movements. (She would later become famous as a dancer under the name Marge Gower.) Disney animator Arthur Babbitt was assigned the task of photographing Belcher in costume. However, Babbitt and Belcher, who was still in high school at the time, would become engaged in a sexual affair. This type of fraternization was forbidden under Disney's well-known "house rules." Although for most Disney employees it would be nearly impossible to be fired as long as they remained loyal to their boss, an affair was the type of policy infraction that Disney refused to ignore. When rumors of the affair began to circulate around the lot, Walt's brother, Roy Disney, urged Babbitt to end things. Babbitt refused. When Walt finally caught wind of the affair, he planned to fire them both, but Babbitt and Belcher quickly got married and Disney spared them their jobs. Babbitt, however, was reassigned to work on the Queen.

Another notable incident that had an impact on the animation of Snow White occurred when animator Grim Natwick transformed the character into a sultry, well-endowed temptress—a depiction clearly at odds with Disney's idea of what the character should be. Natwick was reprimanded, and these depictions were discarded.

A bevy of actresses auditioned for the voice of Snow White. One whom Disney turned down was Deanna Durbin; Disney said she sounded "too old." Finally, Disney heard an innocent, childlike voice which fit perfectly with his conception of the character. The voice belonged to nineteen-year-old Adriana Caselotti, the daughter of a Hollywood vocal coach who had been trained in Italian opera. According to sound editor Sam Slyfield, Caselotti's voice was so petite that it could "scarcely be heard at a distance of three feet."

As the creation of *Snow White and the Seven Dwarfs* moved forward, shifts worked literally around the clock. Disney spent increasingly long hours overseeing the project. With his staff active twenty-four hours a day, Disney felt that it was his responsibility to remain at the studio at all times, and slept on a couch in his office. He told his brother in confidence that he was experiencing the same lack of concentration which had preceded a nervous breakdown he'd suffered in 1931. His smoking increased to three packs a day, he began losing handfuls of hair, developed a facial tic, and was losing weight rapidly. Just as *The Jazz Singer* had killed Sam Warner a decade before, *Snow White* now threatened to take Disney's life. (Disney often joked that the project should have been retitled *Frankenstein* after Mary Shelly's novel about a monster that kills its creator.) To make matters worse, Disney's animators, whom he'd always considered a tightly knit family, were beginning to grumble about the long hours. Disney then found an anonymous note posted on a projection screen that read: STICK TO SHORTS. This infuriated him; it was bad enough he was being ridiculed throughout the industry, but having his own employees—those responsible for crafting the film itself—follow suit was too much. Disney then launched an all-out investigation to find the note's author. The identity of this person was never uncovered, but it has since been suggested that Walt's brother Roy wrote the note himself.

The film's cost was now soaring well beyond what Disney had budgeted (its final budget would be estimated at $1.7 million). The studio owed approximately $1 million in payroll. Joseph Rosenberg, who worked as United Artists' financial advisor and studio liaison at Bank of America, asked to see the unfinished film in its rough form before agreeing to provide any more money for Disney. Although Disney feared showing incomplete footage to him, Rosenberg said prophetically, "That thing is going to make you a hatful of money." (Similar comments were made around this time by the owner of Radio City Music Hall, who booked the film sight unseen.)

Despite his failing health, Disney remained optimistic about *Snow White*. For him, the endeavor was still worthwhile despite all the challenges—not for visionary reasons or because it would make him a fortune, but because he was still as fascinated by the story and characters as when he'd first conceived the project. In *Disney Animation: The Illusion of Life*, Frank Thomas and Ollie Johnston write:

Walt was so immersed in these characters that at times, as he talked and acted out the roles as he saw them, he forgot that we were there. We loved to watch him; his feeling about the characters was contagious.

Disney was a perfectionist. In order to maintain the rhythm of the film, Disney decided to cut four scenes: Snow White's mother dying in childbirth, a sequence featuring the dwarfs eating soup, another sequence in which the dwarfs build a bed for Snow White, and a dream sequence in which Snow White realizes that she's in love with the Prince. This same degree of perfectionism led Disney to consider redoing an entire scene after the film was completed. In that scene, he believed the prince "shimmered." "Real people don't shimmer!" he observed. Roy Disney, the pragmatist of the family, ultimately convinced him that this was not a smart move from a financial standpoint.

Just before the film was completed, Disney and United Artists parted ways over a disagreement concerning the television rights of the Disney backlog. Disney would later admit that he didn't know anything about television, but didn't want to hand over the television rights to the studio's archives. Disney then inked a deal with RKO, who would now be distributing *Snow White and the Seven Dwarfs*. However, RKO executives didn't believe adults would pay to see a fairy tale. Because of this, they suggested that Disney shorten the film's title to *Snow White* so they could emphasize the romantic aspects of the story in advertising. Disney refused. In the end, it didn't matter; Disney was correct to assume that adults would pay to view the film, fairy tale or no.

*Snow White* opened on December 21, 1937, at the Carthay Circle Theater in Los Angeles, California, followed by openings at New York's Radio City Music Hall and in Miami. It quickly became a huge hit, as well as a critical darling. Howard Barnes of the *New York Herald Tribune* raved:

After seeing *Snow White and the Seven Dwarfs* for the third time, I am more certain than ever that it belongs with the few great masterpieces of the screen. It is one of those rare works of inspired artistry that weaves an irresistible spell around the beholder. Walt Disney has created worlds of sheer enchantment before with his animated cartoons, but never has he taken us so completely within their magic bounds. *Snow White and the Seven Dwarfs* is more than a completely satisfying entertainment, more than a perfect moving picture, in the full sense of that term. It offers one a memorable and deeply enriching experience.

John Canemaker agrees with this assessment:

Disney's *Snow White and the Seven Dwarfs* is one of the great cinema masterpieces of all time. It remains a model of film-making craftsmanship and artistry. One admires the succinct storytelling and editing contrasted with the fullness of the personalities (especially the dwarfs) and the lavish art direction and storybook design. There is the subtle interweaving of memorable songs that advance our knowledge of character and plot and move the story briskly along, rather than stopping it dead. There is the perfection of the "personality animation," a form of acting and performance that provides audiences with a range of emotions from laughter to (very rare for animation) tears.

Disney was awarded a second special Oscar, and in 1998 the film would be included in the American Film Institute's "100 Years, 100 Movies" list of the one hundred greatest American films.

---

### Did You Know?

Walt Disney's version of *Snow White* was actually the second animated film based upon the Grimm Brothers' fairy tale. The first was a 1933 short directed by Max Fleischer that featured Fleischer's famous character Betty Boop in the title role.

## Chapter 14

# "Citizen Kane" (1941):
# Mr. Welles Comes to Town

Media mogul Charles Foster Kane (Orson Welles) attempts to buy his way into political office in *Citizen Kane* (1941).

ON JULY 20, 1939, a brash young hotshot arrived in Hollywood. His name was Orson Welles and RKO Pictures had just given him the proverbial keys to the kingdom. Without having ever directed professionally so much as a single frame of a movie, he'd been given a deal most veteran filmmakers would never have dreamed to ask for. This twenty-four-year-old *wunderkind*, who had already conquered both

Broadway and radio, secured a contract unlike anything Hollywood had ever granted before or since (even at this stage Welles was breaking new ground in Tinseltown). He would write, direct, produce, and star in two films. He was given the right to perform his own casting and hire his own crew. He was granted the right to screen the dailies in privacy and edit and complete the films to his own satisfaction. He would be paid $100,000 for his first film and receive 20 percent of the profits. On his second film he would receive $125,000 and 25 percent of the profits. RKO had the right to approve the project or storyline, and could veto any film which exceeded $50,000.

Welles would later explain his reasons for going to Hollywood in *This Is Orson Welles*, coauthored with Peter Bogdanovich:

> [F]or quite a while Hollywood kept making me offers, which, in the natural order of things, kept getting better as I kept turning them down . . . Movies sounded like fun, but I was busy and happy with my own theater and radio show. The more I didn't care, the more they did; and when they gave me the last and wildest of my demands, well, then, of course I gave in happily. Not, believe me, with any sense of vocation, but, rather, in the spirit that I'd become an actor in Ireland and a bullfighter in Spain.

Welles was immediately looked down upon in Hollywood and viewed as an outsider. Who was this young man, and why did he deserve such a contract when he'd done nothing to distinguish himself in film? Welles' contract was viewed with mixed feelings; most believed him a sucker for not holding out for more money—which he would have received had he asked—and all of them were in awe or were jealous regarding the liberties he'd been granted. To many, he was viewed as a legitimate threat. They found Welles' belief that he could simply walk in and become a great filmmaker without any experience offensive. After all, they reasoned, Hollywood was a tough place. It took years of hard work to become a great director. Young Welles could certainly talk the talk, but very few insiders believed he could walk the walk.

In November 1939 it was announced that Welles' first picture would be an adaptation of Joseph Conrad's novella *Heart of Darkness* (which would later serve as the inspiration for Francis Ford Coppola's

1979 Vietnam epic *Apocalypse Now*. Welles had already performed in a radio adaptation of the novella and felt its subject matter would make a suitable directorial debut. Welles went to work on a screenplay, which ended up exceeding two hundred pages. Much to his chagrin, however, RKO decided to pull the plug on the project when it was estimated that it would cost more than $1 million to produce. Welles then bandied about the idea of adapting Nicholas Blake's spy thriller, *The Smiler with a Knife*. Although a screenplay was fashioned, Welles's heart was never really in the project.

In early 1940, Welles and veteran screenwriter Herman J. Mankiewicz conceived a film that would be loosely based upon the life of media mogul William Randolph Hearst. Mankiewicz inked a deal on February 19, 1940, to write the first draft of the project, which he titled *American*. For this endeavor he was to be paid $1,000 per week with a $5,000 bonus payable upon delivery of the script. To ensure secrecy (and, it has been said, to conceal the writer's drinking habit), Mankiewicz went into seclusion in Victorville, California. To oversee the project (read: keep Mankiewicz out of trouble) actor John Houseman accompanied him. Six weeks later, the screenwriter sent Welles his first rough draft, which was 268 pages long. In late May, Welles began rewriting the screenplay. In doing so, he began writing entirely new scenes and threw out others he deemed ineffective. In his rewrites, Welles' primary goal was to present Kane as a somewhat sympathetic character. Out of what Welles has speculated as hatred for Hearst, Mankiewicz opposed this approach. Nevertheless, Welles proceeded to whittle away at Mankiewicz's draft.

On June 14, 1940, RKO estimated that *American* would cost more than $1 million to produce. Again faced with the same dilemma which had led to their decision to shut down *Heart of Darkness*, RKO begrudgingly agreed to okay the film if Welles and Mankiewicz could cut roughly $300,000 in production costs. It was around this time that Welles retitled the project *Citizen Kane*. By July 2, Welles and Mankiewicz had sufficiently trimmed both the size of the script and the production costs, thus keeping the project alive. Once the screenplay was completed, an intense legal battle was waged behind closed doors; Welles, it seems, had intended to take sole screenwriting credit on *Kane*, and less than pleased with the prospect of being humiliated in public, Welles reluctantly gave Mankiewicz credit as his cowriter.

Welles began assembling his crew. First he hired cameraman Gregg Toland, recognized by many as the finest cinematographer working at the time. Although the two men may not have been close friends off the set, Welles and Toland were a collaborative match made in heaven. Both were nonconformists, unafraid to take risks in the name of art, or to share ideas and incorporate those ideas into their work. When initially approached about the project, Toland remarked that it would be nice to work with "an amateur" as opposed to someone who "knew everything." This wasn't a swipe at the young director; to the contrary, Toland was simply expressing his eagerness to work with someone who had not yet accepted as given the standard ways in which to work. Through Welles, Toland saw a chance to experiment with many different types of unconventional shots and methods of lighting.

Welles then began selecting the members of his cast, many of whom—Joseph Cotten, George Coulouris, and Everett Sloane—had been part of Welles' Mercury Theatre group. For the role of Susan Alexander—Kane's love interest—Welles cast a young actress with few credentials named Dorothy Comingore. Composer Bernard Herrmann, who in the years that followed would be responsible for many of the finest scores in cinema history, was hired to write the film's music. Robert Wise, who would one day direct such fine films as *West Side Story* (1961), was hired as editor. RKO veteran Perry Ferguson was hired as art director. Welles' detractors have always been quick to pass off *Kane*'s massive achievements by calling attention to the enormous level of talent that surrounded him at every turn. What they fail to realize is that filmmaking is a collaborative act, something Welles himself was very much aware of. Whether one loves him or hates him, one must credit Welles' decision to surround himself with extraordinary talent.

### Cinematic Firsts

The first feature film to utilize computerized special effects was *The Andromeda Strain* (1971), which was directed by *Citizen Kane*'s editor Robert Wise.

During this period, Welles immersed himself in the cinema; he began studying films he considered masterworks. He screened John Ford's *Stagecoach* (1939) more than forty times. (Because of the many techniques Welles seems to have borrowed from Alfred Hitchcock's *Rebecca* (1940), it's apparent that he screened this film a few times, as well.) In this respect Welles learned filmmaking from the masters; he meticulously studied every frame, taking note of their lighting and composition. Through these studies Welles learned the language of cinema.

Although RKO scheduled the film's official starting date for August 1, 1940, Welles and crew began shooting on July 22; the studio believed Welles and company were conducting last-minute screen tests. Welles worked very long days, and those who were present would later express astonishment at the first-time director's control of the production. However, this was nothing new for Welles; *Kane* might have been his first film, but he had directed many stage productions, some of which boasted as many as 125 cast members. Those who had collaborated with Welles prior to his arrival in Hollywood were not at all surprised by his tenacity and his ability to juggle every facet of the production. Welles was very much at ease in his role as director, and found no difficulty expressing himself to his collaborators. Although he didn't know to what extent he was rocking the boat, Welles was aware that the studio would put up with only so much organized rebellion. This, coupled with his ever-increasing paranoia that spies would report his activities to Hearst, spurred Welles to shut down the production whenever anyone—studio execs or otherwise—came poking around the set. Naturally, this irked the RKO brass, who were not accustomed to being kept in the dark about projects filmed on their own lot. John Ford, who was Welles' hero, was one of the few people permitted to visit the set. When he did, he informed Welles that his first assistant director was an RKO spy.

In August, Welles was faced with a spy of a different sort in gossip columnist Louella Parsons. While it was common practice for directors to be interviewed by Parsons during filming, her intentions regarding Welles were less than professional. Parsons had been asked to investigate rumors that *Citizen Kane* was based, at least to some extent, on her boss, William Randolph Hearst. Over dinner Parsons asked Welles about the rumors, to which the director spun her some flannel that *Kane* was a modern-day retelling of *Faust*, successfully misinforming her. It has been suggested that Parsons was a bit dim, and if this were true, Welles must have had a field day deceiving her.

On *Kane*, Welles shot more film than "anyone in the history of the cinema." In one day Welles reportedly shot more than three thousand meters of film. Welles also broke new ground when he permitted composer Herrmann unlimited access during filming. Composers were normally excluded from productions, but Welles saw Herrmann as yet another collaborator, who in turn became very involved with the dubbing process. The result of this collaboration was a marriage of music, dialogue, and sound effects unlike anything Hollywood had ever heard before.

While the film was in postproduction in November 1940, Mankiewicz, perhaps still angry over his credit dispute with Welles, showed the film's screenplay to his friend Charles Lederer. Since Lederer was the nephew of Hearst's mistress Marion Davies, it didn't take long for the news to reach Hearst. Shortly thereafter, gossip columnist Hedda Hopper—Parsons' rival—attended a press screening of the film. Although the version of the film she saw was incomplete and rough, she saw enough to know who it was about. Hoping to make Parsons look bad, Hopper telephoned Hearst and told him what she'd seen. Making matters worse for both Welles and Parsons, *Friday* magazine ran an article about the film, in which Welles joked about Parsons being a huge fan of his. "Wait until the woman finds out the picture's about her boss," Welles was quoted as saying.

On January 8, 1941, Hearst issued a memo to all his publications stating that there was to be no mention of *Kane* within their pages (beyond Parsons' now daily attacks), and the publications were not to accept advertising for other RKO projects. This signaled that Hearst and his army of lawyers were ready to go to war. RKO executives were threatened with blackmail and ordered to burn the negative. In addition, Hearst's legal team did their best to tie up the film with lawsuits. Publishing mogul Henry Luce, who reportedly served as additional inspiration for the film's storyline, offered to purchase the film from RKO for a reported $1 million. Despite these fiascos, RKO announced that the film would be released as planned. In addition, RKO said, the film's release would be accompanied by one of the largest promotional campaigns the studio had ever launched.

Film critic Pauline Kael describes the climate in Hollywood at the time of *Kane's* release in her essay "Raising Kane":

By then, just about everybody in the industry was scared, or mad, or tired of the whole thing, and though the feared general reprisals against the industry did not take place, RKO was getting bruised. The Hearst papers banned publicity on RKO pictures and dropped an announced serialization of the novel *Kitty Foyle* which had been timed for the release of the RKO film version. Some RKO films didn't get reviewed and others got bad publicity. It was all petty harrassment, of a kind that could be blamed on the overzealous Miss Parsons and other Hearst employees, but it was obviously sanctioned by Hearst, and it was steady enough to keep the industry uneasy.

The film premiered at the Palace in New York City on May 1, 1941, five days before Welles' twenty-sixth birthday. *New York Times* critic Bosley Crowther praised:

> [I]t can safely be stated that suppression of this film would have been a crime. For, in spite of some disconcerting lapses and strange ambiguities in the creation of the principal character, *Citizen Kane* is far and away the most surprising and cinematically exciting motion picture to be seen here in many a moon. As a matter of fact, it comes close to being the most sensational film ever made in Hollywood.

When *Kane* opened in Chicago and Los Angeles the following week, local reviewers echoed Crowther's belief that the film was a masterpiece. *Newsweek*'s John O'Hara called *Kane* the finest film he'd ever seen, and the headline of the *Hollywood Reporter*'s review read: MR. GENIUS COMES THROUGH; "KANE" ASTONISHING PICTURE. Pauline Kael would later conclude that *Kane* was "more highly praised by the American press than any other movie in history." Yet critical acclaim was not enough to make the film a box-office success. Although it's unclear whether exhibitors were threatened by Hearst, RKO did encounter difficulty in getting the film shown; some exhibitors refused to show it, while others booked it but did not play it. When all was said and done, RKO lost more than $150,000 on *Kane*.

The film received an astounding ten Oscar nominations—Best Picture, Best Director, Best Screenplay, Best Actor, Best Cinematography,

Best Art Direction, Best Sound Recording, Best Editing, and Best
Score—but won only one, for its screenplay. (It has been suggested
that the Academy intended this award for journeyman Mankiewicz,
perhaps for putting up with Welles.) It's a telling sign that *Citizen Kane*
won Best Picture honors in many non-industry competitions that
year.

During the sixty-plus years since *Kane* was made, Welles' masterpiece has topped nearly every poll of the finest motion pictures. Those
who question the greatness of *Citizen Kane* fail to realize its impact
upon the language of cinema and its influence on virtually every film
produced in its wake. *Kane* is, in essence, a compendium of groundbreaking filmmaking techniques.

In his book *A History of Narrative Film*, author David A. Cook
assesses:

> *Citizen Kane* was a radically experimental film—fully twenty
> years ahead of its time . . . [I]t stood in the same relationship
> to its medium in 1941 as did *The Birth of a Nation* in 1915 and
> *Potemkin* in 1925—that is, it was an achievement in the devel-
> opment of narrative form, years in advance of its time, which
> significantly influenced most of the important films that fol-
> lowed it.

*Citizen Kane* must be seen as one of the most significant milestones in
the history of cinema because of its many innovative techniques. *Kane*
was not the first film to use many of these techniques, but it brought
them to the forefront of Hollywood's consciousness. In *Kane*, Welles
and Toland had the opportunity to develop or enhance a number of
elements considered unconventional at the time, among them:

**Deep focus photography.** Toland's use of deep focus simultaneously kept the background, middle ground, and foreground all
in sharp focus. According to critic André Bazin, deep focus photography is effective for three reasons: the viewer is brought into
closer contact with the scene than they would experience in reality; deep focus requires more mental participation from the
viewer; and it allows more ambiguity than shallow focus because
the viewer's attention is not guided toward any specific element
within the scene.

Toland had previously experimented with deep focus on the 1937 film *Dead End*. This technique was also utilized in *Rebecca*, released one year prior to *Kane*.

**Experimental lighting.** Toland suggested that interior scenes would appear more realistic if lit from below rather than from above. *Kane*'s introduction of low-key lighting anticipated the "look" of film noir.

**Low-angle shots revealing ceilings.** Ceilings rarely appeared in films because most sets did not have them; this was done so that boom microphones and lights could remain out of sight above the actors' heads. Toland's experimental lighting made it possible to show ceilings because the interior scenes were lit from below. The ceilings were made from muslin, and the microphones were held just above them. This actually allowed the microphones to be placed closer to the actors, which improved the sound and the clarity of the dialogue, and reduced the chances of the camera photographing annoying boom mike shadows in the shot.

Ceilings had appeared previously in a number of British films, as well as in *Stagecoach*, a film Welles studied closely. In a conversation with Peter Bogdanovich, Welles once remarked, "I hope you don't think I ever pretended to be the inventor of the ceiling." Bogdanovich informed him that many people have credited him with this, to which Welles replied, "A lot of people ought to study *Stagecoach*."

Experimentation with low-angle shots in *Kane* resulted also in a number of stunning compositions throughout the film.

**Moving shots used as wipes.** This is a visual effect in which an object or person moving onscreen wipes away one image while presenting another. This effect is often used as a means of transition between shots of life-sized sets and miniature models.

These wipes (film critic Roger Ebert labels them "invisible wipes") appeared previously in both *King Kong* (1933) and *Algiers* (1938).

**Overlapping dialogue.** In most films before *Citizen Kane*, characters took turns speaking; one character would wait until the other was completely finished speaking before saying what they had to say. This annoyed Welles because it wasn't realistic; this wasn't the way real people spoke. So, in *Citizen Kane*, Welles opted to have his characters interrupt each other and sometimes speak simultaneously.

Although Welles wasn't the first filmmaker to utilize the technique, he had been doing this on his radio shows for years. Among films that precede *Kane*, overlapping dialogue is a prominent feature in *His Girl Friday* (1940).

**Long uninterrupted shots.** Welles has been lauded for his use of long uninterrupted shots. This technique is difficult as most films employ a series of editorial cuts in each scene to shape the performance of the actors and the rhythm of the film. The effective use of lengthy takes requires the use of highly skilled actors. As with deep focus cinematography, one of the benefits of unbroken shots is that the viewer is given the choice of looking at whatever he or she chooses in the frame, rather than be guided by the filmmaker. (Bazin once observed that *Kane* "require[s] in the spectator an intellectual alertness incompatible with passivity.")

Again, Hitchcock's *Rebecca* was one of the first pre-*Kane* films to employ extended shots, as was Ernst Lubitsch's *The Shop Around the Corner*, also released in 1940.

Other important techniques used in *Citizen Kane* include the use of flashbacks, nonlinear storytelling, optical illusions, Expressionist photography, creative use of shadows, the subjective camera, carefully layered sound, and characters who age throughout the film. Also, in a clever update of the montage, Welles and editor Wise show the ever-increasing distance between Kane and his wife. In each new shot introduced in the montage, which shows the couple eating dinner together at various points of their lives, the length of the table (and thus the distance between them) is increased. This lengthening of the table to imply distance in a marital relationship was another device that Welles had apparently lifted from Hitchcock's *Rebecca*. However, Welles manages to improve upon this by using a number of cutaways.

Film historian Wheeler Winston Dixon believes Welles' inexperience in the medium accounts for his innovative approach. "Welles, given a free hand for the only time in his career, created a masterpiece through sheer ignorance," observes Dixon. "Not knowing what he couldn't do, he simply tried everything, and with the help of his cinematographer, Gregg Toland, created a film that has lasted as one of the deepest, most tragic films of the American cinema."

### Did You Know?

In 1982 Orson Welles and Oja Kodar penned a screenplay for a film Welles envisioned as a companion piece to *Citizen Kane*. However, Welles was unable to find financing for the project. A decade after Welles' death, director George Hickenlooper revived the project, and with screenwriter F. X. Feeney revised the script. The 1999 Hickenlooper-directed film, *Big Brass Ring*, stars William Hurt, Nigel Hawthorne, and Miranda Richardson.

# Chapter 15

# Murder, Greed, and Betrayal: The Dark Streets of Film Noir

PHOTOFEST

Scheming lovers Phyllis (Barbara Stanwyck) and Walter (Fred MacMurray) try to avoid being seen together in Billy Wilder's *Double Indemnity* (1944).

As is often the case with film cycles, *film noir* is almost impossible to define concisely. No two critics seem to agree on a single definition. In *Dark City: The Film Noir*, Spencer Selby concludes, "The classification of films has always been a tenuous business, and with film noir, which is perhaps the most slippery of all film categories, complications of this type reach a level of almost baffling complexity." Alain Silver, author of numerous books on the subject including *Film Noir Reader* and *Film Noir: An Encyclopedic Reference to the American Style*, explains what he sees as being the primary misunderstanding of noir: "The biggest misconception is that film noir is a genre and not a movement." (Even labeling film noir as a movement is problematic considering that most true film movements were acknowledged as such during the period in which they occurred.) In *Film Noir*, Andrew Spicer calls noir a "contested construction." He writes: "*Film noir* has been defined as a genre, a movement, a visual style, a prevailing mood or tone, a period, or as a transgeneric phenomenon. This uncertainty partly stems from its retrospective status . . ." Equally debated is the precise life span of the cycle, as well as the stylistic traits and themes which distinguish film noir.

> ### *Did You Know?*
> *The Maltese Falcon* (1941), considered by many to be the first film noir, was actually the second adaptation of Dashiell Hammett's novel. The first, produced in 1931, was directed by Roy Del Ruth and featured Ricardo Cortez in the role of gumshoe Sam Spade.

The term "film noir" originated with French critic Frank Nino in 1946. The film most often cited as the first noir picture is John Huston's *The Maltese Falcon* (1941). However, it has also been suggested that *Citizen Kane* (1941), released the same year, was the first noir production. Yet another common theory is that noir began in the 1930s with gangster films like *Scarface* (1932). Although the noir film is uniquely American, it was not recognized as a distinct cinematic style in America until well after its demise. In his study, *In a Lonely Street: Film Noir, Genre, Masculinity*, author Frank Krutnik observes:

> Although the conception of film noir as a new, progressive, strain in both wartime and postwar Hollywood cinema was elaborated further in French criticism . . . it did not figure in Anglo-American criticism until the late 1960s and early 1970s. Since then, not only has film noir become institutionalized as a "set topic" within studies of Hollywood cinema but, like auteurism before it, the term has also circulated beyond critical and academic contexts, becoming increasingly established within more broadly popular discourses on the cinema.

Some film scholars (a minority, to be sure) view certain Westerns, musicals, and comedies as being noir films. However, the most widely accepted position is that noir deals exclusively with urban crime tales similar to those of novelists Raymond Chandler, Dashiell Hammett, and James M. Cain. (Several novels by these authors were adapted famously as noir films.) In a frequently quoted passage, Chandler described the bleak milieu in which noir resides:

> A world gone wrong, a world in which long before the atom bomb, civilization had created the machinery for its own destruction and was learning to use it with all the moronic delight of a gangster trying out his first machine gun. The law was something to be manipulated for profit and power. The streets were dark with something more than night.

The typical protagonists of noir films are male antiheroes, loners with a coldly detached view of life. The noir protagonist is a cynic, and the finest of noir films feature razor-sharp dialogue. The noir storyline typically begins with the protagonist crossing paths with a sexually alluring *femme fatale* who will inevitably lead him to his demise. Almost all action within film noir takes place at night; what doesn't, occurs inside gloom-darkened interiors. The noir film typically centers around one of three characters: the streetwise detective, the hardened criminal, or the naive scapegoat. In *Film Noir: The Dark Side of the Screen*, Foster Hirsch describes the latter:

> "The world is a dangerous place" is one of the axioms of noir—and it is especially so for the man who has lived according to the rules. The solid bourgeois is a prime target, his straight and narrow virtue an invitation to downfall, a thin shield against churning inner dissatisfactions. No one is immune from the temptations of sex and money, noir says— and the seemingly mundane characters, the ones living small, repressed, outwardly conventional lives, like the ripe victims of *Double Indemnity* and *Scarlet Street*, are the most susceptible of all.

In his seminal essay "Notes on *Film Noir*," Paul Schrader states that noir is "not defined . . . by conventions of setting and conflict, but rather by the more subtle qualities of tone and mood." The mood of noir is a grim one, and its tone is repellent. These films are distinguished by low-key lighting. Most noir films have sexual undertones that are both heterosexual and homosexual. Noir films almost always contain first person voice-overs performed by the protagonist. The darkened streets of the city are often slick with rain, adding to the gloomy atmosphere of the films. Noir films frequently use flashbacks to tell their stories. They also utilize the deep focus photography popularized by *Citizen Kane*. With their stylistic usage of chiaroscuro lighting (i.e., a technique that uses strong dark and light contrasts), there is little doubt that film noir is a descendant of German Expressionism. (One reason for this is that many of the filmmakers who directed noir films—Billy Wilder, Otto Preminger, Fritz Lang, among them—were expatriates from Germany and Austria.)

Many of these films feature titles that represent the dark urban themes with which *noir* is generally associated: *The Dark Corner* (1946), *Dark Passage* (1947), *Fear in the Night* (1947), *The Long Night* (1947), *The Naked City* (1948), *Dark City* (1950), *City that Never Sleeps* (1953), and *The Desperate Hours* (1955) are but a few examples. Which films are most representative of noir is the subject of much debate, given the cycle's ambiguous definition. Billy Wilder's *Double Indemnity* (1944), however, is the picture most scholars consider the archetypal noir film. "Perhaps I have become prejudiced from having also

> ### Cinematic Firsts
>
> Eight years after *The Maltese Falcon* (1941) began the film noir cycle, director John Huston and his father, Walter Huston, became the first father and son to be nominated and win Oscars in the same year. Both awards were given for *Treasure of the Sierra Madre* (1948), which John Huston directed and Walter Huston starred in. (It also features *The Maltese Falcon* star Humphrey Bogart.)

cowritten a book about Raymond Chandler," Alain Silvera explains, "but the clear choice for me now (regarding the definitive film noir) is *Double Indemnity*. Why? Many reasons in two categories: (1) The filmmakers: Cain as the source novel; Chandler as the co-scenarist; Billy

Wilder, one of many refugees from Nazi Europe to work in the USA after directing films with a heritage of Expressionism in Germany; superb cinematography by John Seitz, including extensive night location work, and score by Miklos Rozsa; and stars Barbara Stanwyck, Fred MacMurray, and Edward G. Robinson, all cast somewhat against type. (2) The contents: ironic, first person narration; extensive flashbacks organized around that; a femme fatale; greed that leads to murder; as forthright a portrayal of adultery as the Hays Office would permit; a savvy investigator; finally, betrayal and death (actual and implied) for the illicit lovers."

When discussing noir, one must also examine two offshoots: *film gris* and *neo-noir*. The term *film gris* ("gray film"), coined by writer Jon Tuska in his 1984 study *Dark Cinema: American Film Noir in Perspective*, is often applied to films that feature the characteristics of a noir film, yet have a happy ending. (True noir films *never* end happily.) The neo-noir film is simply a noir produced after the "classical" noir period. Although some film scholars have dated the classical noir period as lasting through 1959, the general consensus is that the cycle reached its end with Orson Welles's *Touch of Evil* (1958). In his essay "Kill Me Again" Todd Erickson describes neo-noir as "a new type of noir film, one which effectively incorporates and projects the narrative and stylistic conventions of its progenitor onto a contemporary canvas. Neo-noir is quite simply a contemporary rendering of the film noir sensibility." One major element that differentiates neo-noirs from classic *noir* is that most of them were filmed in color. (True noir films were shot in black-and-white.) *Chinatown* (1974), *Body Heat* (1981), and *L.A. Confidential* (1997) are good examples of neo-noir.

But what makes noir a turning point in the history of film? Prior to film noir, Hollywood films utilized what has been called the "classical" style of filmmaking, which meant that filmmakers employed a standard system of camerawork and editing devices. This system included glamorous high-key lighting, "soft" lights, and lenses used at maximum aperture. Noir films, however, ignored these standardized rules of filmmaking. Where Hollywood previously sought to tell its stories as straightforwardly as possible, noir films frequently attempted to give viewers a feeling of disorientation. This break away from traditional lighting and camerawork, as well as the use of antiheroes, would ultimately change the way films would be made. Noir encouraged filmmakers to discard the old systematic rules and devices. In this light, noir can be said to have directly impacted not only those films with a distinctly noir look, but also any film that didn't subscribe to the conventional standards of filmmaking in most pre–World War II films.

It can also be argued that noir is responsible for the auteur. The auteur theory, which concluded that directors were the "authors" of films and thus were the primary creative forces behind them, was based upon American noir films. It was only with the acceptance of the auteur theory that Hollywood allowed filmmakers the creative freedom to truly become auteurs. This theory served as the primary building block upon which both the French and Hollywood New Wave movements would be established. (It is no coincidence that filmmakers of both movements chose to pay homage to these films. The American "New Hollywood" produced *Chinatown* (1974), and *Taxi Driver* (1976). The French New Wave produced *Breathless* (1959), and *Shoot the Piano Player* (1960).)

# Chapter 16

# Italian Neorealism, 1945–1952

Father (Lamberto Maggiorani) and son (Enzo Staiola) and the bicycle that means their livelihood in Vittorio De Sica's 1947 masterpiece *Ladri di biciclette* (*The Bicycle Thief*).

ITALIAN NEOREALISM refers to a cycle of films that emerged just after the Second World War and lasted from 1945 through 1952 (although some films whose style resembled Neorealism were produced later). This cycle was anticipated in 1941 by filmmakers Mario Alicata and Giuseppe De Santis who said, "We are convinced that one day we will create our most beautiful film following the slow and tired steps of the worker who returns home." The following year screenwriter Cesare Zavattini—often credited as the spiritual father of Neorealism—took this observation a step further. Zavattini challenged Italian filmmakers to discard plot, which he felt was inauthentic, and to work with untrained actors. He urged filmmakers to move out of the studios and film on location, and encouraged them to authenticate their work by improvising and "stealing" dialogue and stories from individuals they encountered on the streets. Zavattini believed that the "ideal film" would follow an average worker in real time through ninety minutes of his life. Through this, he concluded, one might find the beauty in the day-to-day details of life. Zavattini also felt that films should take place in a contemporary setting and suggest that they were happening at the exact moment in time they were viewed. The term Neorealism was coined by critic Umberto Barbaro in 1943—two years before the cycle began.

Luchino Visconti's *Ossessione* (1943) offered the first glimpses of what would become known as Neorealism. "*Ossessione* was a precursor to Neorealism in that it offered an entirely different view of Italy than was generally accepted by the official culture of the times," explains Peter Bondanella, author of *Italian Cinema: From Neorealism to the Present.* "Its protagonist was the opposite of the 'new man' Italian fascist culture wanted to produce—an outsider, a latent homosexual, and a drifter. It is this quality about the film, and not its supposed realism (a goal many fascist directors pursued long before realism became the battlecry of critics after the war) that made the film unique."

### Did You Know?

Luchino Visconti's *Ossessione* (1942) was the first of three adaptations to date of James Cain's novel *The Postman Always Rings Twice,* although Visconti adapted the novel without securing permission from either Cain or his publisher. The second produced in 1946, was directed by Tay Garnett and starred John Garfield and Lana Turner. The third version, produced in 1981, was directed by Bob Rafelson and starred Jack Nicholson and Jessica Lange.

Roberto Rossellini's *Roma, città aperta* (*Open City*) (1945) is generally regarded as the first true Neorealist film. Rossellini began shooting
*Roma, città aperta* in 1944 before the Nazis had left Rome. Written by
Zavattini, the film depicted the resistance of the common man against
the German soldiers. Rossellini was well aware that shooting in the
streets of Rome lended the production a documentary-like quality,
but it was largely for financial reasons that the film was made outside
the studio. Because Rossellini had been given permission by the government to shoot a documentary rather than the fictional feature he
made, he was forced to shoot the film without sound. (Dialogue was
dubbed later.) Arthur Knight details the making of this landmark film
in *The Liveliest Art*:

> What emerged was a film strikingly unlike anything that had
> been seen before. Technically, it was far from flawless. Rossellini
> had been forced to use whatever scraps of film stock he could
> lay his hands on, while the lighting—particularly in those inte-
> riors not taken in a studio—was often too weak for dramatic
> effects or even adequate modeling. Indeed, shooting had to be
> abandoned entirely several times while the director set about
> raising money to continue. But the very passion that had
> inspired the production of *Open City* seemed to create the cen-
> trifugal force that held it all together. Its roughness, its lack of
> finish, became a virtue. And the cumulative power of Rossellini's
> feeling for his subject was translated into a visual intensity that
> made the picture sometimes almost unbearable to watch. Here
> was true realism—the raw life of a tragic era. "This is the way
> things are," said Rossellini in presenting his film. It became the
> credo of the entire Neorealist movement.

*Roma, città aperta* soon became a box-office hit around the world, and
was one of the few Neorealist films to succeed commercially. In Italy,
it quickly became the highest grossing film released since the beginning of the war. The film also won a handful of prizes, including the
prestigious Grand Prix at the 1946 Cannes film festival, and received
an incredible amount of praise throughout the Western world. Nevertheless, it was shunned by critics in its homeland, a fact that had
more to do with the still unbalanced political climate of Italy than the
film itself.

In his book *Italian Cinema: From Neorealism to the Present*, Peter Bondanella lists the general characteristics of the Neorealist film: "realistic treatment, popular setting, social content, historical actuality, and political commitment." These films were, in many ways, more about their form than content. But mainstream audiences found little entertainment in their simple, direct depictions of working class lives. Hence, Neorealist films were perceived as being "art pictures" and most of them weren't successful even in Italy. Many scholars have concluded that this cycle in which artists sought to break free from the restraints of convention was a direct reflection of Italy's breaking free from the restraints of fascism. (*Roma, città aperta* was released the same year dictator Mussolini was put to death.)

The key filmmakers involved in this movement were Rossellini and former matinee idol Vittorio De Sica. Rossellini called Neorealism the "artistic form of the truth." De Sica saw it as "reality transposed into the realm of poetry." Federico Fellini, whose own time would come later, said, "Neorealism is a way of seeing reality without prejudice, without conventions coming between it and myself—facing reality is not just social reality but all there is within a man."

In addition to *Roma, città aperta* several other key Neorealism films (presented chronologically) were:

**Rossellini's *Paisà* (*Paisan*), 1946.** *Paisà* follows *Roma, città aperta* as the second installment in Rossellini's "war trilogy." Presented in six episodes, *Paisà* depicts the Allied invasion of Italy and tells the story of not only the military movement, but of the cultural differences between the Allied forces and the Italian partisans. Rossellini utilized a combination of professional and non-professional actors.

**De Sica's *Sciuscià* (*Shoeshine*), 1946.** The story of two shoeshine boys who save their change and purchase a horse. However, they are caught up in an illegal black-market operation and sent away to a reformatory. *Sciuscià* is thematically similar to De Sica's later film *Ladri di biciclette* (*The Bicycle Thief*) (1948) in that it charts the gradual disintegration of a relationship. While *Sciuscià* was not successful in Italy, it was a major hit in the United States, where the film won a special Oscar.

**Rossellini's *Germania anno zero* (*Germany, Year Zero*), 1947.** This is the third installment of Rossellini's "war trilogy." *Germania anno zero* was shot entirely on location in the bombed-out streets of Berlin, with a cast comprised solely of nonprofessional actors. The protagonist of this bleak film, which was also written by Rossellini, is a young German boy who has been corrupted by the beliefs of the Nazis. Saddened by the news that the Nazis have been defeated, he kills his invalid grandfather before committing suicide. Notable is a lengthy sequence in which the boy wanders toward his own death, a scene that typifies Zavattini's vision of actionless activity depicted in real time.

**De Sica's *Ladri di biciclette*, 1948.** This Zavattini-scripted film tells the story of a common worker who is dependent upon his bicycle. When it is stolen, he and his son embark upon a citywide search. *Ladri di biciclette* focuses on the relationship between the father and son, and the distrust created when the father, in desperation, attempts to steal a bicycle to replace the one he has lost.

**Luchino Visconti's *La terra trema*, 1948.** Visconti's film depicts the uprising of impoverished fishermen against those who exploit them. Although Visconti originally intended *La terra trema* as the first part in a trilogy of films, this was the only film that materialized. Orson Welles remarked that Visconti was the only filmmaker ever to photograph malnourished peasants as a *Vogue* photographer would his models. In *The History of Narrative Film*, David A. Cook defends Visconti's vision: "Realism . . . is a style, not an ideology, and it is an error to equate it with ugliness or desolation." Interestingly, Visconti here employed a strong depth of field reminiscent of Welles' *Citizen Kane* (1941).

**Rossellini's *Stromboli*, 1949.** Considered to be one of Rossellini's weakest films, it was the first of six collaborations between Rossellini and his wife Ingrid Bergman. The film's depiction of an outsider (Bergman) intruding into a tiny community is somewhat ironic if one views *Stromboli* as a case of art imitating life. (The casting of Hollywood star Bergman in a Neorealist film is something of an anomaly. Professional actors, let alone Hollywood stars, were forbidden by the Neorealist standards Zavattini had articulated.)

**De Sica's *Umberto D*, 1952.** *Umberto D* is considered the last of the true Neorealism films. Its subject is the lonely life of a weary and impoverished retired man struggling to maintain his dignity. In the end, the old man contemplates taking his own life. The film, which was written by Zavattini, infuriated Italian officials who believed it damaging to the country's image.

Because of its revolutionary leanings, the Neorealist movement was extremely unpopular among Italian government officials, who wanted to put an end to the movement. In 1949, the Italian film industry found itself in a state of financial crisis. Studies revealed that approximately 65 percent of films shown in Italy were Hollywood productions. Between 1945 and 1950, Italy had imported more than 1,500 American films while the United States had imported only 178 Italian films. An agreement was reached between Italy and the Motion Picture Export Organization which dramatically reduced the number of films imported from the U.S. while increasing the number of Italian films to be exported. It was after this agreement that the Italian government

> ### *Cinematic Firsts*
>
> The first fictional Italian film was *La presa di Roma, 20 settembre 1870* (*The Capture of Rome, September 20, 1870*), which was released in 1905.

passed the Andreotti Law, which gave the government the right to ban exportation of any Italian film it believed might depict the country in a negative light. As one might conclude, this meant that very few Neorealist films would be exported.

"Neorealist filmmakers depended upon foreign markets to help recoup their production costs," explains Millicent Marcus, author of *Italian Film in the Light of Neorealism*:

Andreotti's animus against practitioners of Neorealism, especially in their flaunting of Italy's dirty laundry before the eyes of the outside world, is well expressed in the famous letter he wrote to De Sica in 1952 with regard to *Umberto D*. "We ask the man of culture," wrote Andreotti, "to feel his social responsibility, which should not be limited to a description of the abuses and miseries of a system and a generation . . . If it is true that evil can be fought by harshly spotlighting its most miserable aspects, it is also true that De Sica has rendered bad service to his country if people throughout the world were to start thinking that Italy in the middle of the twentieth century is the same as in *Umberto D*."

When the government refused to export these films, the movement started to die. As many film scholars have noted, the movement appeared to be waning prior to the Andreotti Law, and likely would have wound down on its own without it.

The Neorealist cycle must be seen as a turning point in world cinema because it provided the blueprint for the character-driven avant-garde film. Unlike the films which preceded it, the Neorealist film gave importance to the day-to-day details of human life. These films, unlike their predecessors, focused on their characters first and foremost rather than plot. These works have made an indelible mark on the cinema, making way for Federico Fellini, Michelangelo Antonioni, cinema vertité, the French New Wave, the New Hollywood, and the Dogme 95 movement. The legacy of Neorealist filmmaking is films like *Five Easy Pieces* (1970) and *Lost in Translation* (2003), which dare to examine the simple details of everyday life.

Many methods by which the Neorealists sought liberation from cinema artifice would later be adopted by filmmakers of the French New Wave, some maverick American filmmakers (such as Nicholas Ray), the Brazilian Cinema Novo of the 1960s, and the Dogme 95 collective.

# Chapter 17

# André Bazin: Legitimizing Film Scholarship

Although he never made a single film, film scholar and essayist André Bazin is one of the most important figures in the history of cinema.

FRENCH FILM CRITIC André Bazin has arguably done more to make the cinema respected as an artform on par with literature or painting than anyone in history. It would be difficult to overestimate his importance regarding the perception of film. Before his intellectual writings on cinema appeared, filmic writing consisted of little more than industry-subsidized promotion and gossip-laden articles on the offscreen exploits of popular stars.

Bazin was born in Angers on April 18, 1918. He displayed signs of an extraordinary intelligence at a young age, teaching himself to read at age five. Throughout his school years, Bazin had an insatiable hunger for knowledge, and established himself as a gifted student with a passion for science and mathematics. With aspirations of becoming an educator, Bazin sought a well-rounded curriculum in college. (He attended college courses at La Rochelle, Versailles, and at the Ecole Normale Supérieure at St. Cloud.) He studied diligently and was a voracious reader. Nevertheless, because of his stammer, Bazin was unsuccessful in securing a teaching position.

After a brief stint in the army, Bazin became a member of the Maison des Lettres, which had been founded to educate students whose studies had been disrupted by World War II. In December 1941, Bazin and Jean-Pierre Chartier cofounded a cine-club, where they screened films. This is significant because cinema was held in very low esteem in France during this time. Motion pictures were generally considered a novelty to which no one of sophistication paid any attention. Nevertheless, Bazin and Chartier pressed on, screening hundreds of films and discussing them afterward. As France was under Nazi occupation at this time, numerous films had been banned. (The Nazis were especially eager to destroy prints of Charles Chaplin's films because he had just mocked Adolf Hitler in *The Great Dictator* [1940].)

Bazin and Chartier, through an elaborate network, managed to locate 16mm prints of various banned films and defiantly screened them, knowing full well that they were risking their lives to do so. Both men believed it important to show these works, and it was through his commitment to his cine-club that Bazin's lasting love for cinema came to flourish. Bazin the logician studied film as meticulously as he might a piece of classical art. Through these studies he developed a knowledge of the cinema and its conventions. As cine-club attendance gradually increased each week, spectators were privileged to hear Bazin introduce these screenings with insights both historical and artistic. Bazin and Chartier screened a diverse array of films from every genre. Although some spectators disapproved of his decision to screen some German films, Bazin stood his ground; he refused to ignore any aspect of the cinema for political reasons.

Bazin soon began to write about film in such publications as *L'Esprit* and *Le Parisien libéré*, carefully developing his own theories. Bazin enjoyed observing and theorizing in the still-evolving world of motion pictures—a world where new rules were created everyday and the possibilities of the art form seemed without limit. His writings and observations on film were more substantial than anything that had preceded them. Bazin wrote about film from a detached point of view more rooted in logic than in passion. His work and beliefs were heavily influenced by the writings of Jean-Paul Sartre, Charles Peguy, and Henri Bergson. In his writings Bazin sought to reconcile films with philosophy, science, religion, and politics. In his seminal study, *André Bazin*, film historian Dudley Andrew explains:

> Bazin wanted to teach and build, in the tradition of Roger Leenhardt, "a little school of the spectator." He wanted the spectator to become aware of lighting, camera, set design, editing, music, script, acting, and direction. But, even Leenhardt hadn't gone far enough for Bazin. The critic must do more than make people aware of the technical processes on which any aesthetics of film is based. He must point out as well the psychological, sociological, and economic factors which have given us the cinema we know and not some different cinema.

Cinema was gradually becoming accepted as an art, and Bazin was becoming synonymous with cinema. Further adding to his stature, Bazin was appointed director of cultural services at the newly established Paris film school L'Institut des Hautes Etudes Cinématographiques. Through this appointment he began to lecture as well as write on cinema, and table discussions at the cine-club.

In 1945, Bazin wrote his first great essay, "The Ontology of the Photographic Image" (for *Problèmes de la Peinture*) and "The Myth of Total Cinema" (*Critique*). Bazin often wrote about the perception of reality in motion pictures and how such perceptions are achieved. He questioned the role of the filmmaker and the possibility of a "pure" cinema. Bazin wrote at length about his disdain for montage because it so greatly condensed the passage of time. A subject that fascinated Bazin was the concept and process of literary adaptation. His colleague and disciple Eric Rohmer would later observe that Bazin's body of work "fits perfectly into [a] pattern of mathematical demonstration. Without any doubt, the whole of Bazin's work is based on one central idea, an affirmation of the objectivity of the cinema in the same way as all geometry is centered on the properties of a straight line."

While many point to Bazin as being the progenitor of the "auteur theory" later championed by *Cahiers du Cinéma*, this is an erroneous assumption. The auteur theory asserted that a film's director was the singular driving artistic force behind a film and, hence, its author. Bazin never agreed with this theory, which originated, in part, with André Malraux. Bazin believed that numerous factors decided the outcome of a motion picture rather than one figure; he saw the director, the cameraman, the actors, the script, the lighting, the circumstances of the produc-

### Did You Know?

André Bazin was a proponent of *mise-en-scène*, which contends that a psychological unity exists from one frame to the next. It was for this reason that Bazin was opposed to Eisenstein's montage, which he believed destroys the unity between frames.

tion, and its timing as all being of equal importance. (A thorough man, Bazin can, however, be credited with presenting Malraux's belief to his students even if he did not subscribe to it.)

As the cinema continued to gain respectability in the late 1940s, Bazin established (or, in some cases, helped to establish) many more cine-clubs throughout Europe. During this period Bazin wrote for the short-lived publication *La Revue du Cinéma*. In 1949, Bazin encountered a "wild child" from the Latin Quarter named François Truffaut. In this troubled sixteen-year-old, Bazin recognized a love and knowledge of cinema that equalled his own. Truffaut, like Bazin, had already established his own cine-club. Despite the respect he held for Bazin, the young Truffaut did not hesitate to debate any aspect of cinema on which he disagreed with him. Through Truffaut Bazin met a number of other Latin Quarter *cinéastes*, including Jacques Rivette, Jean-Luc Godard, and Eric Rohmer. That year Bazin also established the "Festival of Accursed Films" at which he screened motion pictures he believed to be deserving of a second look.

The following year Bazin successfully battled tuberculosis. He also established a new publication, *Cahiers du Cinéma*, with Jacques Doinol-Valcroz (with financing from a theater chain owner named Leonid Keigel). Bazin and Doinol-Valcroz attempted to fashion this new publication in the likeness of *La Revue du Cinéma*, for which they'd both written. At *Cahiers du Cinéma*, which would be regarded as the most distinguished and influential publication

---

### Cinematic Firsts

The first professional film critic to write for an American newspaper was the *New York Dramatic Mirror*'s Frank Woods in 1909.

---

in the history of cinema, Bazin served as father figure for a staff of talented young writers. This staff included Godard, Rivette, Rohmer, Claude Chabrol, and Truffaut, who would later, as filmmakers, stand at the forefront of the *Nouvelle Vague*, or New Wave. The first issue of *Cahiers du Cinéma*, which featured a yellow cover similar to those of *La Revue du Cinéma*, featured one of Bazin's most popular essays, "The Evolution of the Language of Cinema." Bazin also penned thoughtful, articulate book-length studies on the works of Chaplin, Welles, and Jean Renoir. (He never completed the book on Renoir. It was, however, completed after his death by Truffaut, who called it "the best film book written by the best critic on the best director.") By the mid-1950s Bazin was writing regularly for a number of publications, including *Le Parisien libéré*, *L'Esprit*, *L'Observateur*, *Radio-Cinéma-Télévision*, *Education Documentaire*, and *Cahiers du Cinéma*.

In 1955, Bazin wrote one of his most famous essays, "The Festival at Cannes Considered as a Religious Order." Bazin biographer Dudley Andrew observes:

> He preferred Venice to Cannes. It was, for him, more seriously interested in film art. Cannes had already become a promotional stage for producers and agents selling films and stars. Perhaps, being in the thick of things in Paris all year long, he was also more sensitive to the in-fighting over which French films would be represented, who would be on the jury, and so forth. At Venice he was honored as the man who had brought Italian cinema to high critical attention.

Ironically, it was at the 1954 Cannes Film Festival that Bazin received the worst possible news—that he was dying of leukemia. In the final years of his life, Bazin continued to write prolifically. (He wrote more than 2,000 essays in his lifetime, 116 pieces in ninety issues of *Cahiers du cinéma* alone.) He also wrote an outline for a documentary film on Romanesque churches that he'd planned to direct, entitled *Les Églises romanes de Saintonge*. Unfortunately, this project would never be completed. Bazin died on November 11, 1958, seven months after his fortieth birthday.

Claude Bellanger, editor of *Le Parisien libéré*, delivered this eulogy:

Who will ever account for the genius Bazin displayed at every moment? He possessed at one and the same time both passion and lucidity, the spirit of the quest and the spirit of analysis, both curiosity and certitude. He knew how to judge with absolute fairness and how to make himself understood without raising his voice, thanks to the inner truth he carried with him. His work, which has been interrupted so early, he accomplished as if it were a mission. And this is right, for today he seems to us like the missionary of a young art to which he consecrated his immense moral force and his limited physical stamina. His eyes come back to haunt us, luminous, tranquil, sincere, dreaming for an instant, then fired by the need to understand and to express. In these eyes one will never forget . . . He was a master.

Bazin's legacy survives today. Although a number of theorists had written on film before Bazin, most attempted to judge it by the standards of other artforms, such as poetry, literature, theatre, and art. Bazin recognized the need to create a distinct criterion by which to analyze and judge the cinema. In the mid-1940s Bazin predicted that film would one day be taught and studied at universities. He was correct. Interestingly, it is largely thanks to Bazin's writings that film began to be accepted as a legitimate field of study. Bazin brought a respectability and scholarship to the cinema that had not been present before.

In his essay "André Bazin on Film Technique: Two Seminal Essays," Bert Cardullo asserts:

The impact of André Bazin on film art, as theorist and critic, is widely considered to be greater than that of any single director, actor, or producer. He is credited with almost single-handedly establishing the study of film as an accepted intellectual pursuit, as well as with being the spiritual father of the French New Wave.

An unsigned *Sight and Sound* essay entitled "André Bazin: Divining the Real" echoes this sentiment:

It's no exaggeration to say that Bazin is the single thinker most responsible for bestowing on cinema the prestige both of an artform and of an object of knowledge.

Strangely enough, much of Bazin's legacy stands in opposition to his own views. Bazin once stated that a critic should not alter the path of art. Yet there can be no doubt that Bazin, directly or indirectly, achieved precisely that. Jean Renoir said, "After considering his writings I changed my own filming plans." Luis Bunuel remarked that Bazin discovered many "truths" within his work that even he had not seen. Hence, Bunuel began consulting with Bazin while planning and constructing his films.

Bazin, it has been said, did more to elevate film discourse than anyone else in the history of cinema. Jean Renoir once observed of him, "He it was who gave the patent of royalty to the cinema just as the poets of the past had crowned their Kings." It is ironic to note that Bazin, a man who early on gave up his plans to teach, became one of the most influential teachers of the twentieth century.

## Chapter 18

# HUAC and the Communist Witch Hunt

Director Elia Kazan, the man who named names.

FOLLOWING NAZI GERMANY'S 1941 attack on the Soviet Union, the United States and the Soviets became allies. Despite this alliance, after World War II a fear of all things Communist swept across America. This period would later become known as the McCarthy Era, after Wisconsin senator Joseph McCarthy, who insisted that Communists lurked in anonymity all around us. According to McCarthy and his cronies, these individuals sought to overthrow the government and put an end to the American way of life. Such paranoia led to the organization of the House Un-American Activities Committee (HUAC), led by J. Parnell Thomas, the purpose of which was to determine Communist affiliations of American citizens. During this dark time in American history, the United States government would, in essence, nullify its own constitution to criminalize political affiliation.

In 1947, the attention of HUAC fell upon Hollywood, which Thomas and his committee believed Communists had infiltrated with the intention of producing motion pictures filled with hidden subtext and propaganda. Even a film as harmless as *It's a Wonderful Life* (1946) was seen by some as a "Communist film." Mississippi representative John E. Rankin addressed his fellow congressmen by declaring, "Unless people in control of the industry are willing to clean house of Communists, Congress will have to do it for them." Vocal accu-

> ### Cinematic Firsts
>
> Hollywood's first blacklisted actor was comic Fatty Arbuckle, whose career was effectively ended in 1921 when he was accused of raping and murdering actress Virginia Rappe. Arbuckle was later found to be not guilty.

sations and condemnation of the film industry from paranoid conservatives spawned an atmosphere of uneasiness in Hollywood. Actor Kirk Douglas would later recall:

> The red scare had been growing for the last two years . . . Hollywood was conspicuous; we could do the most damage to the country by spreading propaganda, and they wanted to make an example out of us. Already, many people wondered why their telephones had stopped ringing, why there was no work, no parties, why they couldn't reach their agents—people like Edward G. Robinson, John Garfield, Larry Parks. You didn't have to be formally accused of anything—innuendo in the press could ruin you.

Behind closed doors, Thomas solicited the assistance of the FBI. On May 13, 1947, Richard B. Hood, head of the FBI's Los Angeles field office, turned over information to HUAC "with the understanding that under no circumstances will the source of this material be disclosed." The documents Hood provided the Committee listed the names of fifty-six "possible friendly witnesses" and eighty-nine "possible unfriendly witnesses."

In October 1947, HUAC subpoenaed the individuals named by the FBI to testify before them. These individuals were then questioned regarding their possible ties to Communist organizations whom, it was believed, sought to destroy the "American way of life." If these individuals refused to answer, they could be charged with contempt; if they answered that they had attended Communist meetings, they would be required to provide the names of others; if they answered that they had never been involved with the Communist Party, they would face charges of perjury.

Nineteen of those subpoenaed were deemed "unfriendly" because they refused to answer questions or spoke out against the unconstitutional nature of the proceedings. One of these witnesses was screenwriter Ring Lardner, Jr. Noted filmmaker Otto Preminger would later write:

> Ring Lardner, Jr., was one of the first to be summoned. Lardner was a gifted screenwriter who won an Academy Award in 1942 for the Katharine Hepburn–Spencer Tracy film *Woman of the Year*. He interrupted work with me on the script of *Forever Amber* to go to Washington. His testimony before the congressional committee is full of interruptions. He refused to discuss whether or not he had been a member of the Communist Party. As a descendant of one of the Minutemen at Lexington he didn't see how he could be labeled un-American. What he tried in vain to read into the record was a statement that the committee was attacking the freedom of American citizens.

The list of nineteen unfriendly witnesses was ultimately whittled down to ten artists who were known collectively as "the Hollywood Ten." (Bertolt Brecht had fled the country and the other eight unfriendly witnesses were not charged with contempt.) The "ten" individuals were Alvah Bessie, Herbert Biberman, Lester Cole, Edward

Dmytryk, Ring Lardner, Jr., John Howard Lawson, Albert Maltz, Samuel Ornitz, Adrian Scott, and Dalton Trumbo.

The American public—at least those who were paying attention—was blinded by the committee's accusations that these ten who would not cooperate were Communists and therefore posed a threat to America. Boycotts and protests were organized and a rash of anti-Hollywood editorials began to appear in newspapers across the country. This reaction worried the studio heads, who met in secrecy at New York City's Waldorf-Astoria on November 26, 1947. There, the moguls agreed to sacrifice the ten men to appease both the Committee and the public. They fashioned a statement for the Committee, which has since become known as the Waldorf Statement. It read:

> Members of the Association of Motion Picture Producers deplore the action of the ten Hollywood men who have been cited for contempt of the House of Representatives. We do not desire to pre-judge their legal rights, but their actions have been a disservice to their employers and have impaired their usefulness to the industry.
>
> We will forthwith discharge or suspend without compensation those in our employ and we will not re-employ any of the ten until such time as he is acquitted or has purged himself of contempt and declares under oath that he is not a Communist.

Film historian and critic William Triplett, among others, have suggested that the studios' willingness to assist the Committee might have been a ploy to break up the unions. (The primary targets of HUAC were all active members of the Screenwriters Guild, the Directors Guild, and the Screen Actors Guild.) With the drafting of the Waldorf Statement, the blacklist was imposed. The ten artists were terminated immediately and told that their actions violated the "morals clause" that appeared in every standard Hollywood contract of the time. Although the studios would insist that there was no blacklist, no one would publicly hire any of the ten men.

Paul Buhle, author of several books on the blacklist, including *Hide in Plain Sight: The Hollywood Blacklistees in Film and Television* and *Blacklisted: The Film Lover's Guide to the Hollywood Blacklist*, explains the Hollywood climate during this time:

Writers begin losing jobs and controversial films undergo a
sharp decline (as does film attendance) in 1947, although many
leftwing writers keep writing films until 1950. The anxiety about
producing anything that could be taken as critical of business or
U.S. global policies has the effect of demolishing the art film
project, connected with the independent productions, both considered hugely promising for a historic moment or two.

The HUAC circus then moved into a court of law, where Thomas
explained that these ten unfriendly witnesses had engaged in "Communist activities" (although he did not clarify) and insisted that arguments regarding "constitutional rights and the First Amendment"
should be disregarded. It was decided that there was sufficient evidence to proceed with a trial. The ten then requested a collective trial,
but their request was denied. The ten screen artists found their cases
caught in a judicial logjam, during which time some of them found
work writing under pseudonyms for drastically decreased wages.

In 1949, after two years of judicial red tape, the trials began. The
primary argument for the ten unfriendly witnesses was that their constitutional rights had been violated when they had been asked to
reveal their personal beliefs and associations, but the courts decided
that HUAC's fracturing of the witnesses' constitutional rights was fair.
At this point, the ten requested that their case be heard by the
Supreme Court. The Supreme Court refused. The ten were sentenced
to jail.

Before going to prison, the ten men rushed together a twenty-
minute film about their plight, entitled *The Hollywood Ten* (1949). In
their study *Inquisition in Hollywood* authors Larry Ceplair and Steven
Englund write:

> The film, like its makers, was blacklisted. The only distribution
> network which agreed to handle *The Hollywood Ten* was com-
> posed of the wives and friends of the jailed men. Sadie Ornitz,
> Sylvia Jarrico, Gale Sondergaard, and others carted the film from
> meeting hall to auditorium to living room. Even this circum-
> scribed distribution discomposed business and government
> circles. Although the powers did not fear that domestic com-
> mercial exhibitors would risk boycott and Red-baiting by allow-
> ing *The Hollywood Ten* to be shown on their premises, foreign

distribution was another question. *Variety* reported that "the Motion Picture Association of America, the United States State Department, and other groups concerned with U.S. public relations abroad, reportedly are agitated over efforts to give the film wide distribution overseas." Official and unofficial pressures emanating from the United States Government and American corporations hindered foreign, as well as domestic, play of the film.

Ironically, Dalton Trumbo ran into his old adversary Congressman Thomas during his incarceration at Danbury, Connecticut. Thomas was now an inmate, as well; the Congressman had been imprisoned for padding his office payroll.

In 1951, HUAC—now led by John S. Wood—returned to Hollywood for a second round of hearings. When subpoenas were issued, a number of those subpoenaed left the country for fear of following in the footsteps of the Hollywood Ten. This time HUAC was leaving no stone unturned; among those called to testify were Edward G. Robinson, Gale Sondergaard, and writer Dashiell Hammett, who was jailed for refusing to provide names. Waldo Salt, Larry Parks, and Richard Collins, who had been among the original nineteen unfriendly witnesses, were also called upon again. This time 110 unfriendly witnesses were called to testify. Fearing similar condemnation, fifty-eight admitted to having attended Communist meetings and supplied the Committee with names. (The number of names given by each witness ranged between six and 155.) Many witnesses simply gave the Committee names of people they already knew to have been linked to Communist groups. (Members of the Hollywood Ten were named again and again.) After begging the Committee not to force him to name names, actor Larry Parks broke down and gave up his comrades. Despite this concession Parks's career was effectively ended.

This time, a few "friendly" witnesses gave up names, as well. Actor Lloyd Bridges was allowed to offer his testimony in private. Actor Sterling Hayden gave up names to protect himself. The most famous of these stool pigeons is director Elia Kazan. Kazan supporters, such as actor Rip Torn, have suggested that the director had no choice. However, Kazan has admitted that his testifying was a conscious decision and something he felt needed to be done. Kazan told author Jeff Young:

I thought, nobody knows the truth about any of this. The Party was getting all kinds of money out of Hollywood and out of the theater. Communists were in a lot of organizations—unseen, unrecognized, unbeknownst to anybody. I thought, if I don't talk, nobody will know about it.

In the 1974 book *Kazan on Kazan*, however, the filmmaker confessed a darker reason for selling out his colleagues: revenge for his having been kicked out of the Communist Party. "I've never denied that there was a personal element in it, which is that I was very angry, humiliated and disturbed—furious, I guess—at the way they booted me out of the Party."

The 324 individuals named to the Committee were blacklisted immediately. In his book *Hollywood Babylon*, avant-garde director and author Kenneth Anger concludes: "The public was not amused. For it, politics and Hollywood just didn't mix. The Red Hunt did nothing to improve the quality of American films or American life."

Several blacklisted artists went to work in Europe. Others continued to find work with the use of pseudonyms. In 1956, a screenwriter named "Robert Rich" won the Best Screenplay Oscar for *The Brave One* (1955). However, Rich didn't attend the ceremony to pick up his statuette. It was later revealed that "Robert Rich" was actually Dalton Trumbo. (The Academy finally sent Trumbo his statuette in 1975.)

Otto Preminger led the charge for the dismissal of the blacklist in 1959. He would later write:

For years after it was discredited, McCarthyism remained a blight on the industry. In 1959, I hired Dalton Trumbo to write the screenplay for *Exodus*. One of the "Hollywood Ten," he was

### Did You Know?

Most film scholars agree that *On the Waterfront* (1954), directed by HUAC witness Elia Kazan, was his attempt to justify his actions. In the film, Marlon Brando's character testifies against underworld figures who are exploiting dockworkers.

making a meager living by working at low fees under assumed names. He and Michael Wilson, who collaborated on several scripts during their exile, received between $1,000 and $1,500 for an entire screenplay . . . United Artists financed and distributed *Exodus*. I made a luncheon date with its president and chairman, Arthur Krim and Robert Benjamin. I told them: "Trumbo has done a first-rate job on this script. You people are always saying that the blacklist is fiction, so I will give him the credit he deserves. I shall use his real name as author of the script."

Trumbo's being credited on the film effectively led to the end of the blacklist. However, the finest years of many of these artists' careers were taken away from them while our nation went mad with a naive fear of something it didn't fully understand.

Although we now know that most (if not all) of the so-called Hollywood Ten did attend Communist group meetings, does this make them any less American? Before invoking any preconceived notions of what being a member of a Communist group means, ponder this: future U.S. President Ronald Reagan later admitted having not only attended meetings with Dalton Trumbo, but also serving on this group's board of directors! Making this all the more interesting is Reagan's claim that it was his own fear of "neo-fascism" which led him to join this group in the first place. In a 1960 letter to *Playboy* mogul Hugh Hefner, Reagan wrote:

Following World War II my interest in liberalism and my fear of "neo-fascism" led to my serving on the board of directors of an organization later exposed as a "communist front"; namely the "Hollywood Independent Citizens Commission of the Arts, Sciences and Professions." Incidentally (Dalton) Trumbo was also on that board.

Today the blacklist is a thing of the past. Most of those who were blacklisted are now deceased. Nevertheless, the saga of HUAC, the Hollywood Ten, and the blacklist remains one of the most embarrassing incidents in the history of the United States. Its ramifications reach far beyond the film industry. The House Un-American Activities Committee's complete disregard for the Constitution weakened its powers and demonstrated, for all the world to see, our government's willingness to suspend its own laws when it sees fit. This period also caused studios to discontinue producing "message" and art films, thus stunting the artistic growth of the film industry.

This terrible period must be seen not simply as archaic history, but as an example from which we as a society must learn. Unfortunately, the film industry may not be as far removed from these events as we would like to believe. Witness the near blacklisting of liberal actors who vocally opposed the war in Iraq in 2003. (Petitions were circulated requesting the firing of actor Martin Sheen from the television series "The West Wing" and actress Janeane Garofolo actually lost a number of jobs because of her antiwar stance.) Can America learn from its mistakes or is it doomed to repeat them? Only time will tell.

# Chapter 19

# The Emergence of Television

An early advertisement for Sylvania brand television sets.

IT WOULD BE DIFFICULT to overstate the impact of television on Hollywood. The impending threat of this new medium emerged as early as the mid-1930s, but the outbreak of World War II delayed television's development. During this period Hollywood moguls considered buying their way into television, with the intention of controlling it as they had done previously with radio broadcasting. Warner Bros., Paramount, MGM, and 20th Century-Fox had all applied for television station licenses, an idea that was quickly shot down by the Federal Communications Commission (FCC) in 1945. As an antitrust investigation was already looming, the FCC advised studio owners against venturing into television. Making matters worse, motion picture theater attendance was already declining; a 1949 *Wall Street Journal* survey of twenty major markets found lower attendance.

Movie mogul Samuel Goldwyn predicted television's impending impact in "Hollywood in the Television Age" (*Hollywood Quarterly*, Winter 1949/1950):

> We are about to enter what can be the most difficult competition imaginable with a form of entertainment in which all the best features of radio, the theater, and motion pictures may be combined. Today there are fifty-six television stations on the air, with sixty-six additional stations in the process of construction. The chairman of the Federal Communications Commission points out that by 1951 there may be 400 stations in operation. There are now 950,000 receiving sets installed, sets are being produced at the rate of 160,000 per month, and next year that rate will be doubled. Soon, there will be a potential audience of 50 million people or more. Here, we have the development that will change the entire entertainment business. Fifty million Americans will be able to sit at home and take their choice of visiting the ball park, the prize-fight matches, the wrestling bouts, the legitimate theater, and the motion pictures without stirring from their own living rooms. It is going to require something truly superior to cause them not only to leave their homes to be entertained, but to pay for that entertainment.

Some weren't so sure. One mogul remarked that viewers would "soon get tired of staring at a plywood box every night." This prediction, of course, turned out to be dead wrong. By the mid-1950s, television had effectively integrated itself into American life. This had a swift impact on the film industry. Whereas average weekly motion picture attendance in 1946 had been charted at 82,000,000, by 1955 it sank to 46,000,000. A 1953 survey of television owners found that its subjects had gone to the movies an average of 2.8 times per week prior to purchasing a television, but now went only 0.7 times per week.

> ### *Cinematic Firsts*
> The first feature film to be shown on television was Burton L. King's *The Police Patrol* (1925), aired in April 1931.

In their book, *The Complete Idiot's Guide to Movies, Flicks, and Film*, Mark Winokur and Bruce Holsinger measure the effect of television and describe the resulting innovations which have since occurred:

> Per day, for every American who goes to the cinema to watch a film on-screen, something in the neighborhood of fifty Americans rent a movie from Blockbuster, purchase a pay-per-view showing, or watch a movie broadcast on network or cable television. What this means is that only 2 percent of Americans watching a movie today, as you read this, will do so in a commercial theater designed for that purpose. In 1950 that figure was almost 100 percent.

None of this was lost upon the motion picture studios, who immediately responded by cutting costs and raising rental fees. This in turn caused distributors to raise prices, which compelled exhibitors to increase ticket prices. Newsreels quickly became a thing of the past because television news programs could relay stories in a more timely fashion. The studios began to make more spectacular films, with which television programs could not compete, but the cost of producing such films was high, and Hollywood's production levels dropped. (By 1951 Hollywood was producing roughly 25 percent fewer films than it had before World War II.) As a result, the larger studios ceased production of "B" movies, and because of the competition of daytime television drama, produced fewer melodramas made for the female audience.

The emergence of television led to technological improvements in motion pictures; Hollywood wisely decided to focus on areas of production in which television could not compete. Some of these innovations would be more successful than others, among them:

**Converting to color.** While numerous color processes had long been available, the vast majority of Hollywood films were still being produced in black-and-white prior to television's emergence. Because television transmission was for some years strictly monochrome, Hollywood productions were filmed in color much more often. (In 1947, only 12 percent of American films were produced in color. By 1954, more than half of all American films were in color.) CBS broadcast the first color program on June 21, 1951, but as only twenty-five receivers in the entire U.S. could accommodate color, more than 12 million viewers found themselves staring at a blank screen.

**Widescreen.** Hoping to remind television owners of the advantages of viewing films theatrically, Hollywood studios began experimenting with processes which gave images greater width and depth. Perhaps the most famous of these processes was Cinema-Scope, which had been invented in the late twenties. With the much bally-hooed Cinerama, images were shown at six times their normal size. This, however, ultimately became unwieldy because of the expenses required to install Cinerama projection equipment and three-panel screens. Other widescreen processes included Techniscope, Technirama, VistaVision, and Ultra Panavision.

**Gimmicks.** A number of fads had their moment during the 1950s, as producers hoped to lure people away from their televisions. One of the most memorable was 3-D, a process that made images look as though they were popping out of the screen, a particularly effective gimmick for horror films. However, 3-D proved to be a short-lived phenomenon thanks in part to the headaches that frequently arose as a result of the cardboard glasses worn by audience members in order to see the effect. Another short-lived gimmick was "Smell-O-Vision," which was designed to provide viewers with the scents referred to on-screen.

Nearly twenty years earlier, actress/producer Mary Pickford had encouraged the film industry to merge with television. This, she believed, would stop television from crushing the motion picture industry. "Opposition to progress is forever futile," Pickford wrote in

a 1934 essay. "And he who maketh use of his enemy is indeed wise."
It was in this spirit that Hollywood came to embrace television. The
studios derived three methods from which to earn revenue through
television: the production
of syndicated and nonsyn-
dicated programming for
television; experimenting
with "theater television,"
in which television pro-
grams could be projected
in a motion picture theater;
and the development of
pay-television systems that
would deliver brand-new motion pictures. The FCC intervened and
put a stop to development of pay television. By the mid-1950s the studios began licensing for broadcast blocks of older films from which
they could no longer profit theatrically. (The bulk of these were produced by RKO and MGM.) This practice led comic Bob Hope to quip,
"Television? That's where old movies go when they die." The 1960s
saw studios selling newer, high-profile films to the networks. When, in
1966, *The Bridge on the River Kwai* (1957) was sold to television for
$2 million, the film drew an estimated 70 million viewers, a success
that led to higher fees for hit films sold to television. In 1971, financial interest and syndication laws were passed requiring networks to
reduce their in-house productions. As a result, the studios became
more involved with the production and syndication of network television programs.

Although Hollywood never fully recaptured the dedicated audience it enjoyed before the advent of television, it did manage to adapt
to the medium and survive.

> ### *Did You Know?*
> The Cinerama process that
> debuted in 1952 was essentially
> the same widescreen process
> Abel Gance had used in 1927
> for *Napoleon*.

# Chapter 20

# American International Pictures: A Blueprint for Success

PHOTOFEST

By producing drive-in fare that targeted teenagers, American International Pictures founders Samuel Z. Arkoff and James H. Nicholson revolutionized the film industry and provided a blueprint for other independents.

SAMUEL Z. ARKOFF, a lawyer from Iowa hoping to work in the film industry, got his first taste of the business when he and his old friend Hank McCune served as producers on McCune's NBC television series in 1950. A few years later Arkoff was hired by schlock producers Alex

Gordon and Edward D. Wood, Jr., who believed they had been wronged by a production/distribution company known as RealArt Productions. After their screenplay *The Atomic Monster* was rejected by RealArt, Gordon and Wood had understandably become angry when RealArt later released a different picture with that title. Arkoff knew the two producers didn't have a case, but he accepted the job anyway with the ulterior motive of trying to parlay this into a job in the film industry. RealArt chief Jack Broder had no memory of his meeting with the two producers, but Arkoff nonetheless managed to get a $500 settlement for his clients. It was then that Arkoff met James H. Nicholson, who was working as a sales manager for RealArt. The two men found that they shared the same goals, and they pooled their resources to establish American Releasing Company in 1954. (The company would be rechristened American International Pictures two years later.) At that time no one—not even Nicholson and Arkoff—could have imagined the impact their company would have upon the American film industry.

At first, Arkoff and Nicholson were laughed at. The two men had very little experience in the industry and independent studios rarely stayed afloat for long. However, Arkoff and Nicholson proved to be the exception to the rule. By hiring a team of talented young producers and directors, which included Roger Corman, Herman Cohen, Bert I. Gordon, and the aforementioned Alex Gordon, AIP became the first studio to recognize the tremendous untapped teen market. AIP films made a handsome profit. "The older people and parents were staying home and watching TV," Arkoff would later recall. "Who wanted to go to the theater? The teenagers! These kids wanted to get out of the house, and their parents

> ### *Did You Know?*
> Former American International Pictures model builder James Cameron directed the hit film *Titanic* (1998), which nabbed a record fourteen Oscar nominations, an honor *Titanic* shares with *All About Eve* (1950).

were delighted to get them out of the house . . . and to pay for them to get them out of the house!" This realization also led to the modern-day summer releasing season. "Summer was not the big time then,"

Arkoff would later say. "It was considered the off-season. But we understood that was our biggest season of the year. We were making drive-in pictures for kids [who] had cars."

Arkoff claimed that he and Nicholson made movies with one key rule firmly in mind at all times: "Thou shalt not put too much money into any one picture. And with the money you do spend, put it on the screen; don't waste it on the egos of actors or on nonsense that might appeal to some highbrow critics." Arkoff expounds upon this Golden Rule in Mark Thomas McGee's *Fast and Furious: The Story of American International Pictures:*

> We were in a business. It was a business we liked and enjoyed. But at the same time we had to get a return on our investment. Unless we did, we were going to go bankrupt. Unlike the Michelangelos, we had no Medicis or Popes or government subsidies or anything else. So it's always been a first rule that when you're in a business, like any other businessman, you must get your money back, make a profit, and continue on. Always more important to continue on than it was to go out on a limb and make some arty-farty picture which might very well never get its money back, do you no good, and end your existence.

AIP was well known for the economical projects it churned out. Sometimes pages were ripped from scripts to keep productions from going overschedule. To keep costs down, sets and costumes often were used for a number of different films, sequences from older AIP films were reedited into new productions. One of the most famous stories to illustrate AIP production methods involves *The Beast with 1,000,000 Eyes* (1956). Because producer Roger Corman had gone over budget with his previous film, he was given a paltry $29,000 with which to complete the film. Because of his limited budget Corman decided to eliminate the monster from the film entirely—this in a film entitled *The Beast with 1,000,000 Eyes*!

In typical AIP fashion, Arkoff and Nicholson saved the day by creating a monster themselves. This was accomplished by poking forty holes (representing the beast's "million" eyes) into the sides of a teakettle. Blurry shots of the teakettle emitting steam from its forty holes were shot and edited into the film, thus providing the title role of the "beast." (Some sources have questioned whether this anecdote is true, but it originated with Arkoff himself.)

Another famous tale of AIP penny-pinching is the casting of the same actors to play both the cowboys and the Indians in a Western film. In another instance, Corman filmed the hit film *Little Shop of Horrors* (1960) in less than three days! "I filmed it in two days and a night," Corman recalls proudly. "I did it almost as a joke, simply to see if I could do it. When I finished, [screenwriter] Bob Towne, who is a good friend of mine, said, 'You should remember, Roger, making films is not like a track meet. It's not how fast you go.' And I said, 'You're right, Bob. I'll never make a two-day picture again.'"

"I've never known a movie producer at any level who didn't try to cut costs to the bone," observes Joe Bob Briggs, author of *Joe Bob Goes to the Drive-In* and *Profoundly Disturbing: Shocking Movies That Changed History.* "Arkoff and Nicholson were laboring in the B movie world, where they were sometimes making second features that were licensed for a flat rate, so it's not surprising they pinched pennies. You can't argue with their success."

Between 1954 and 1960 AIP enjoyed an impressive run, during which the studio did not produce a single film that lost money. Although they were essentially the same, AIP produced pictures that were considered "A" films as well as "B" films. By doing this, they could issue double features, which had traditionally consisted of a big studio "A" film followed by a lesser "B" film. By producing both films, AIP earned all the rental fees rather than just those of the bottom-billed picture. The typical AIP film cost approximately $300,000 to produce and was shot in a week to ten days. These films, known as "exploitation" films, were geared toward the latest teen trends. The success of AIP spawned countless imitators, but few had AIP's uncanny ability to recognize the end of one trend and sniff out the beginning of another. These trends included, among others: biker films, Westerns, drug culture, juvenile delinquency films, monster movies, women-in-prison movies, Edgar Allen Poe adaptations, gangster pictures, beach party movies, blaxploitation, espionage movies, kung fu, redneck movies, and science fiction.

In *Film History: An Introduction* Kristin Thompson and David Bordwell explain the methods employed by AIP and the other independents who emerged in their wake:

Obliged to work on shoestring budgets, AIP and other exploitation companies pioneered efficient marketing techniques. AIP would often conceive a film's title, poster design, and advertising campaign, test it on audiences and exhibitors, and only then begin writing a script. Whereas the major distributors adhered to the system of releasing films selectively for their first run, independent companies often practiced "saturation booking" (that is, opening a film simultaneously in many theaters). The independents advertised on television, released films in the summer (previously thought to be a dead season), and turned drive-ins into first-run venues. All these innovations were eventually taken up by the majors.

One of AIP's most important strengths was their ability to draw interest in their products with sensational advertising, taglines, and titles. Some of the most outrageous titles from the AIP catalogue include *Viking Women and the Sea Serpent* (1957), *Attack of the Puppet People* (1958), *War of the Colossal Beast* (1958), *Teenage Caveman* (1958), *Attack of the Giant Leeches* (1959), *The Ghost of Dragstrip Hollow* (1959), *The Ghost in the Invisible Bikini* (1966), and *1,000 Convicts and a Woman!* (1971). AIP was often able to lure viewers away from mainstream releases and into theaters to see movies they knew absolutely nothing about based on nothing more than their curiosity-inspiring titles. Many of AIP's titles were so sensational and bizarre that one could often find commentary on them in film reviews. (More often than not the titles were more interesting than the films themselves.) In his review for *I Was a Teenage Werewolf* (1957), *Los Angeles Examiner* critic S.A. Desick once wrote:

To take first things first, the title is a magnificent piece of composition. It has a haunting quality about it, and I ought to caution you that if you let it pierce your consciousness it will echo in your brain in a constant refrain—*I Was a Teenage Werewolf, I Was a Teenage Werewolf*. The title, in other words, is by way of being a little monster itself.

Despite the studio's many successes, internal conflicts soon erupted. A number of filmmakers and producers broke from AIP because they felt they were being cheated out of money. Roger Corman, the studio's most respected producer/director, left to form his own company. When Nicholson's divorce left him without a significant portion of his share in the company, his role in the business began to erode. Arkoff and Nicholson were good friends, but Arkoff was first and foremost a businessman, and Nicholson resigned from AIP in 1971. (He inked a six-picture production deal with Fox, completing only one [*The Legend of Hell House,* 1973] before dying of a brain tumor in 1972.) Arkoff and AIP spent much of the seventies on the receiving end of lawsuits, one of which involved the charge that AIP's 1974 film *Abby*, was a ripoff of Warner Bros.' *The Exorcist* (1973).

> ### *Cinematic Firsts*
>
> The first film to be released by James Nicholson and Samuel Arkoff was *The Fast and the Furious* (1954), directed by John Ireland and Edward Sampson and starring Ireland, Dorothy Malone, and Bruce Carlisle.

The success of American International Pictures led to a rise in independent producers that challenged the major studios and influenced them to change their own distribution methods and production standards. The strategy of Arkoff and Nicholson served as a blueprint for other independent filmmakers. AIP is also significant because of its role in the black film explosion of the 1970s (see Chapter 24) and because it was home to many talents who started their careers there, including Martin Scorsese, David Cronenberg, Bruce Dern, Peter Bogdanovich, Dennis Hopper, Woody Allen, Francis Ford Coppola, John Milius, Jack Nicholson, Charles Bronson, Jonathan Demme, Robert De Niro, Nick Nolte, and Monte Hellman, among others.

## Chapter 21

# La Nouvelle Vague:
# The French New Wave

Young Antoine Doinel (Jean-Pierre Leaud) feels trapped in François Truffaut's 1959 masterpiece *Les quatre cents coups* (*The 400 Blows*).

IN 1954, *Cahiers du Cinéma* critic François Truffaut published a scathing indictment of contemporary French cinema entitled "Une certaine tendence du cinéma français" ("A Certain Tendency of the French Cinema"). In this essay, Truffaut lashed out at the French film industry and its so-called "tradition of quality," which he saw as justifying the production of bloated, overproduced historical costume dramas and literary adaptations. For some time Truffaut and his *Cahiers du Cinéma* colleagues had been calling for a new cinema. However, they had never gone about it so directly. In Truffaut's essay, he pinpointed individual filmmakers and proceeded to dismantle their films one by one. This essay would become a manifesto of sorts for a movement which would be dubbed *la Nouvelle Vague* (the New Wave). The *Cahiers* writers who would later become the filmmakers of the New Wave championed the work of American auteurs such as John Ford, Howard Hawks, Nicholas Ray, and Budd Boetticher, whom they believed made personal films within the constrictions of the studio system.

Much of the credit for the movement belongs to filmmaker Roger Vadim. The tremendous success of Vadim's 1956 *Et Dieu crea la femme* (*And God Created Woman*) promoted an atmosphere in which young, untested directors were given opportunities behind the camera. These filmmakers were able to craft inexpensive films by shooting primarily on location with portable equipment, using unknown actors, and employing miniscule crews. Some aspiring filmmakers, unable to secure financing for their films, took destiny into their own hands. The most important of these was Claude Chabrol, who used his wife's inheritance to finance his 1958 debut *Le Beau Serge* (*Handsome Serge*). The success of Chabrol's next film, *Les Cousins* (*The Cousins*, 1958), allowed him to establish his own production company and give other young filmmakers an opportunity to work on feature films. (Truffaut and Jean-Luc Godard had been making short films as early as 1954.)

There has been some debate as to when the New Wave actually began. While some films possessing the aesthetics of a New Wave film were released in 1958, the term *nouvelle vague* didn't gain currency until 1959. It was in this banner year that Truffaut's debut feature *Les quatre cents coups* (*The 400 Blows*) was released to great acclaim. The presence of New Wave films at the 1959 Cannes festival announced a new direction for cinema. In the Summer 1960 issue of *Film Culture*, Jonas Mekas writes:

> Overnight the Cannes film festival became a camp of insurgents. Not only did they take over the prizes and the publicity, they also gathered together—some twenty of them—and attempted to arrive at a manifesto. However, there happened

to be present as many different personalities, styles, and directions as there were heads, and no common agreement was reached. They stressed insistently that they were not a movement but, using Truffaut's words, an eruption of new filmmakers whose first and fundamental characteristic, and the only one on which they all agreed, was to have complete control over their own productions. In Venice, two months later, with Rossellini himself presiding, there was another attempt made to get out a common statement—but again it failed. In the true French spirit, they insisted on their own independent individualities.

In his book *Cinema Eye, Cinema Ear*, which was written during the first flush of the New Wave, John Russell Taylor writes:

> Like most such labels, "New Wave" was most useful when it meant nothing very specific; when it meant simply a conglomeration of new directors with for the most part no particular affiliations with one another, and only related by the incidental fact that conditions in the French film industry at the time permitted, indeed encouraged, them all to break into commercial cinema during the same relatively short period. Some of them—in most respects, certainly, the most interesting of them—were film critics turned creator; virtually all the founders and regular early contributors to the monthly review *Cahiers du Cinéma* have directed at least one feature film, and three of them, François Truffaut, Jean-Luc Godard, and Claude Chabrol, have become dominating figures in the new French cinema. But others have come from documentary, like Alain Resnais, Agnès Varda, and Georges Franju, yet others, like Chris Marker, Jean Rouch, and the proponents of "cinema verité," have stayed with documentary, and others again have come up during the "New Wave" period by the most traditional route in the French cinema, graduation to full directorship after a period as "apprentices" learning the craft by assisting already established directors.

Despite the initial difficulties in pinpointing similar aesthetic qualities of the New Wave films, it is apparent today that these works share a number of characteristics. Like the filmmakers of the second Italian

Renaissance, the New Wave filmmakers frequently constructed plots around chance occurrences. Their films were filled with non sequiturs and self-referential jokes regarding the cinema that had preceded the New Wave. These films often recalled the work of the Italian Neorealists, as they were designed to appear choppy and casual, in a response to the polished product of Hollywood and the French tradition of quality. New Wave filmmakers frequently used handheld cameras, and their films featured jerky editing. A great number of these films were shot with natural lighting because of budgetary considerations, and many utilized open-ended narratives and were based in contemporary times. "[T]he *Nouvelle Vague* was the first group of directors to refer systematically to prior film traditions," write Kristin Thompson and David Bordwell in *Film History: An Introduction*. "For these former critics, film history was a living presence."

In December 1962 *Cahiers du Cinéma* dedicated an entire issue to the New Wave. This sixty-six-page issue set an interesting trend in defining the filmmakers involved with the movement (or nonmovement, if you will); despite the magazine's heralding the 162 "new" filmmakers making up the New Wave, the issue focuses only on the work of Truffaut, Godard, and Chabrol. Likewise, in the years since, writers often acknowledge that a large number of filmmakers comprised the New Wave, but go on to define the movement by singling out the former *Cahiers* critics-turned-filmmakers. This approach may at first seem to provide a disservice to the many other unmentioned filmmakers, but it limits the discussion to a mere handful of films, making it somewhat easier to pinpoint aesthetic characteristics of a New Wave film. Again, this method of evaluation may seem incomplete, but for the most part the films of the *Cahiers* writers were the ones to exert the greatest impact on the international film industry. In this light the New Wave can be seen more as a collection of filmmakers than of films.

Five of the most important filmmakers of the New Wave were:

**François Truffaut.** Under the wing of film critic and theorist André Bazin, this passionate cinéaste wrote many famous and highly praised essays for *Cahiers du Cinéma*. While writing for *Cahiers*, Truffaut called for a cinematic revolution which broke away from the slick, highly-polished films of the time. Seeking to prove that this new form of cinema could in fact exist, Truffaut began making films in 1954 with the 16mm short *Une Visite*. Because of the controversy that surrounded his critical writings, Truffaut was barred from the 1958 Cannes Film Festival. The following year, however, he was greeted at the festival with open arms; there he won the award for Best Director for his debut feature *Les quatre cents coups* (*The Four Hundred Blows*). Today this film remains one of the most popular works of the New Wave, and one of the most influential films ever produced. Truffaut's other significant directorial efforts include *Tirez sur le pianiste* (*Shoot the Piano Player*, 1960), *Jules et Jim*, *La Mariée état en noir* (*The Bride Wore Black*, 1968), *Baisers volés* (*Stolen Kisses*, 1968), and *La Nuit américaine* (*Day for Night*, 1973).

> ### *Did You Know?*
>
> Among the materials burned in François Truffaut's film *Fahrenheit 451* (1966) is a copy of *Cahiers du Cinéma,* for which several of the New Wave directors wrote (including Truffaut). The film pictured on the cover of the issue in flames is Jean-Luc Godard's *À bout de souffle* (*Breathless,* 1960).

**Jean-Luc Godard.** Godard made his feature debut in 1959 with *À bout de souffle* (*Breathless*), which was cowritten by Truffaut. This film and Truffaut's *Les quatre cents coups* are generally considered the works that first signaled the New Wave's arrival to cinéastes outside France. Like Truffaut's *Tirez sur le pianiste*, *À bout de souffle* is an homage to the Hollywood gangster film, and contains many obscure film references. Godard utilizes long takes to great effect, and he uses a great many jump cuts. Much of the film was improvised, lending the production a feeling of spontaneity. Although Godard would make nearly twenty films in less than a decade, *À bout de souffle* is his most significant contribution to the New Wave.

**Claude Chabrol.** Chabrol demonstrated that films could be financed and constructed outside the normal film industry channels. His 1958 debut *Le Beau Serge* is considered by many to be the first of the New Wave films, and his second, *Les Cousins*, proved to be a substantial hit. Chabrol continued working, producing a succession of thrillers that paid homage to his cinematic hero, Alfred Hitchcock. However, because his body of work as a whole is extremely inconsistent in quality and vision, his other works from the New Wave era tend to be overlooked. The prolific Chabrol shot eight features between 1958 and 1962, but of these only the first two were successful commercially or critically.

**Eric Rohmer.** Rohmer assumed the duties of chief editor at *Cahiers du Cinéma* after the 1958 death of André Bazin. After making his directorial feature debut with *Le Signe du lion* (*The Sign of the Lion*) (1959), he crafted what he called his Six Moral Tales: *La Boulangère de Monceau* (*The Baker of Monceau*) (1963), *La Carriére de Suzanne* (*Suzanne's Profession*) (1963), *La Collectionneuse* (*The Collector*) (1967), *Ma nuit chez Maud* (*My Night at Maud's*) (1968), *Le Genou de Claire* (*Claire's Knee*) (1970), and *L'Amour l'après-midi* (*Chloe in the Afternoon*) (1972). As Douglas Gomery points out in *Movie History: A Survey*, all six films share essentially the same plot: "A young man on the verge of committing himself to one woman meets by chance another whose charms cause him to question his initial choice. His entire way of thinking, his very moral center, seems to unravel." Rohmer's films are stylistically different from many of those categorized as New Wave; in fact, his style invites comparisons to that of Jean Renoir. This difference in sensibility is perhaps attributable to the age difference between Rohmer and his colleagues; he was approximately a decade older than the other *Cahiers* writers, and only two years younger than André Bazin. Truffaut and company would later argue that *Cahiers*—in Rohmer's charge—concentrated too much on American productions while ignoring those of the New Wave, a charge that ultimately led to Rohmer's dismissal from the publication.

**Jacques Rivette.** Rivette began his career as a writer for *Gazette du Cinéma* (where Eric Rohmer was his editor). Rivette lashed out against the older generation of critics—Bazin among them—whom he believed were now ignoring the *mise-en-scène* (stage setting) criticism. Rivette joined the staff of *Cahiers du Cinéma* in 1953. He later worked as an assistant director to Jean Renoir. In 1957, after making a few short films, Rivette decided he would direct a feature, and like Chabrol, he chose to finance his own production, borrowing his first $150 from *Cahiers du Cinéma*. Thus he began filming *Paris nous appartient* (*Paris Belongs to Us*) in 1958, much of it improvised and shot silent, the actors' voices were dubbed in later. Still working on the film in 1960, Rivette was forced to borrow money from Truffaut and Chabrol to complete it. The final budget has been estimated at somewhere between $100,000 and $140,000. Rivette's meticulous attention to detail is the stuff of legend; editing took more than a year and Rivette recut the film almost daily. As Richard Neupert points out in *A History of the French New Wave Cinema*, Rivette was not "considered as a major figure of the New Wave" until a censorship battle erupted over his film *La Religieuse* (*The Nun*) in 1966. Rivette's work favors the art-house crowd; one of his films, *L'Amour fou* (*Crazy Love*, 1969) runs four hours and another, *Out 1* (1971), runs twelve.

Upon first glance one might think that *Cahiers du Cinéma* used its influence to champion its own writers turned directors. However, according to Richard Neupert that was not necessarily the case:

My assumption was that *Cahiers du Cinéma* had played such a strong public relations role in championing the first films by its own members that it had permanently warped public perception of the New Wave. And to a certain degree that is true. . . . Tests of popular and even competing journals reveal that Chabrol, Truffaut, and Godard were indeed the key figures, for better or worse, for most contemporary observers of the New Wave. Their critical audacity, avowed debt to auteurs from both distant and recent film history, their marketing savvy, technical innovation, and narrative experimentation, all seemed to set these three apart from their peers in 1960. Contemporary observers found these fellows to possess all the important youthful traits expected of New Wave filmmakers, while many other directors shared only only several of those most pertinent qualities.

The end of the New Wave is difficult to pinpoint. Some studies cite 1964, others 1967. Later works of these filmmakers produced in the seventies and eighties are sometimes considered part of the New Wave. By general consensus, however, the period dates roughly from 1959 through 1964.

The writings and films of those involved with the New Wave—particularly the *Cahiers* crowd—had an immediate impact on cinema around the world. The questioning of narrative conventions in New Wave films rejuvenated cinema in the United States and Britain, and led to smaller movements throughout Europe bent on innovation. The French New Wave continues to influence filmmakers today, and its influence can be felt in the works of filmmakers as varied as Lars von Trier, John Cassavetes, and Quentin Tarantino.

### Cinematic Firsts

The first film to employ a total of eleven cinematographers was *Close Encounters of the Third Kind* (1977), which featured New Wave director François Truffaut on-screen as a member of the cast.

## Chapter 22

# Relaxing Restrictions:
# The MPAA Ratings System

Mike Nichols' *Who's Afraid of Virginia Woolf?* (1966) was one of the films that convinced Jack Valenti to adopt the voluntary ratings system.

THE MOTION PICTURE ASSOCIATION OF AMERICA hired Jack Valenti as their new president in May 1966. Prior to this, Valenti had served as special assistant to United States President Lyndon B. Johnson. The late sixties was a time when the country was in a state of political and cultural upheaval, and with this breakdown of traditional values, literature, film, art, and music began to challenge existing boundaries of what was considered socially acceptable. Such challenges stood in clear opposition to the Hays Code, which had failed to grow or adapt since its establishment in 1934. Controversial pictures like *Lolita* (1962) and *Hud* (1963) had already pushed the envelope, and Warner Bros. was preparing an adaptation of Edward Albee's award-winning play *Who's Afraid of Virginia Woolf?* (1966).

This was nothing new. A showdown had long been expected, as MPAA had issued a string of requests and veiled threats to Warner Bros. regarding the project as early as March 1963. However, studio chief Jack Warner and director Mike Nichols refused to cooperate, arguing that *Who's Afraid of Virginia Woolf?* would be shorn of its impact if its shocking dialogue was toned down. (Valenti's predecessor Geoffrey Shurlock had conceded that the film would be significantly diluted if the "profanity and . . . blunt dialogue" were removed.) Warner Bros. decided to film the $7.3 million adaptation with the questionable scenes and dialogue fully intact. As a result, the film was denied the Production Code Administration's seal of approval, a decision Warner Bros. then appealed.

> ### Did You Know?
>
> Mike Nichols' *Who's Afraid of Virginia Woolf?* enjoyed an exceptional honor at the 1966 Academy Awards: every member of its cast (there were four) was nominated for an Oscar.

Citing the film's quality, Valenti convinced the MPAA to allow the film to be released as a one-time exemption as long as it bore the label "S.M.A." (Suggested for Mature Audiences) and children were not allowed entrance into theaters, an action that can be seen today as a precursor to the MPAA ratings system. Hoping to avoid any misunderstanding, MPAA's Board of Directors explained the film's exemption:

This exemption means exactly that—approval of material in a specific, important film, which would not be approved for a film of lesser quality, or a film determined to exploit language for language's sake. This exemption does not mean that the floodgates are open for language or other material. Exemption means precisely the opposite. We desire to allow excellence to be displayed and we insist that films, under whatever guise, which go beyond rational measures of community standards will *not* bear a Seal of Approval.

Only a few months later, the MPAA issued its second exemption to *Alfie* (1966). Sensing that the traditional rules were no longer sufficient to address films such as these, Valenti resolved to revise the Code. In his essay "How It All Began," Valenti recalled:

It was plain that the old system of self-regulation, begun with the formation of the MPAA in 1922, had broken down. What few threads there were holding together the structure created by Will Hays, one of my two predecessors, had now snapped. From the very first day of my own succession to the MPAA president's office, I had sniffed the Production Code constructed by the Hays Office. There was about this stern, forbidding catalogue of "Do's and Don'ts" the odious smell of censorship. I decided to junk it at the first opportune moment.

In late 1966 Valenti unveiled his newly revised version of the Production Code. Edward J. Leff and Jerold L. Simmons describe it in *The Dame in the Kimono*:

The old principles had ruled that "no picture shall be produced which will lower the moral standards of those who see it." The new one recommended that movies "keep in closer harmony with the mores, the culture, the moral sense and the expectation of our society." Valenti had had enough of the "excessive exposure" wars. He and Jack Warner had argued over "screw you" and "Hump the Hostess" for three hours, and it "seemed wrong that grown men should be sitting around discussing such matters. More, I was uncomfortable with the thought that this was just the beginning of an unsettling new era in film, in which we would lurch from crisis to crisis, without any suitable solutions in sight." The new Code replaced rules on murder, drug addiction, and nudity with more general rules that preached caution on scenes of violence, exposure, criminal behavior, and sexual intimacy.

Despite changes, it seemed apparent to everyone that some sort of ratings system would be implemented in the not-too-distant future by either the government or the MPAA. A number of highly vocal organizations were in favor of an MPAA-implemented system, among them the Catholic Legion of Decency, the Protestant Broadcasting and Film Commission of the National Council of Churches, the National Congress of Parents and Teachers, the American Library Association, the American Jewish Committee, and the General Federation of Women's Clubs. Msgr. Thomas F. Little of the National Legion of Decency observed that "such classification would serve several purposes. (1) It would be an information service for the parents. (2) It could be a guarantee that morally wholesome adult films would be produced for the public. (3) It would forestall undesirable action by the states." A number of distinguished film directors, including Elia Kazan, Otto Preminger, William Wyler, and Billy Wilder, expressed their support of such a system.

However, the suggestion of self-regulation found its share of opposition. Those who opposed classification argued that such labeling was blatant censorship. These parties also believed that a self-imposed classification system could result in governmental classification. Noted filmmaker Stanley Kramer spoke out against such a system, admitting, "I am not sure that even my censorship would be objective." Both the exhibitors and the studios were strongly against classification as they feared such labeling could hurt business.

Despite much debate, the motion picture industry was evolving, and films were being produced that depicted all manner of sexual misconduct, acts of violence, and contained lurid language which had not been shown previously. In 1967 the first two films were released in which the word "fuck" was uttered (*I'll Never Forget What's His Name* and *Ulysses*). In his book *See No Evil* MPAA board member Jack Vizzard explored the factors in the industry which had led to the lack of "quality control":

Mainly, there was a process of depersonalization going on in the film companies. The trend toward conglomerates that was so pronounced in the economy as a whole was touching the studios in a special manner. Paramount was taken over by Gulf and Western Industries. United Artists had been absorbed into the huge Transamerica Corporation. Universal-International, already a subsidiary of MCA, was to receive flirtations from Westinghouse Electric, and when this was frowned on by the Justice Department, by Firestone Tire & Rubber. An important position was taken in M-G-M by people from Schenley Industries. Avco, the aviation conglomerate, was about to take over Embassy Films. And so it went. The result of this process was a diffusion of interest at the top. Harry Warner, in the old days, used to use the homely Russian adage that a "fish stinks from its head." With the diminishing of clear and sharp leadership at the head of the industry, authority was seized by individual picture makers at the actual shop level. Directors became tyrannous in their demands and in their assertions of rights. They pushed for liberties that were sometimes out of proportion to their talents, so that men of secondary ability were forced to substitute shock for skill, and to pawn off boldness for inventiveness. And since anything innovative was in the vogue, the public was giving the appearance of standing behind these men, making them seem like pioneers in the opening of brave new worlds.

In 1968, a self-imposed MPAA classification system was put into effect as the result of two Supreme Court decisions. The first, *Ginsberg v. New York*, dealt with a New York mother's objections to her sixteen-year-old son being sold pornographic material (i.e., a "girlie magazine"). The second, *Interstate Circuit v. Dallas*, found in favor of a Dallas exhibitor who objected that municipal censors had banned children from attending the Brigitte Bardot vehicle *Viva Maria* (1965). Interestingly, the Supreme Court ruled on both cases on the same day. With *Ginsberg v. New York*, the Supreme Court decided that the government could protect minors from materials depicting nudity and graphic sexual conduct. In the case of *Interstate Circuit v. Dallas* the court declared the municipal censorship unenforceable because it was too vague.

Spurred on by these two decisions, which when viewed in tandem suggested that legislature could close the box office to children, Valenti pushed hard for a classification system. "I knew that the mix of new social currents, the irresistible force of creators determined to make 'their' films, and the possible intrusion of government into the movie arena demanded my immediate action," Valenti would later recall. He began to meet with governing members of the National

Association of Theater Owners (NATO) and the International Film Importers & Distributors of America (IFIDA). These discussions lasted approximately five months, during which time Valenti also sought the opinions of religious organizations, directors, producers, studio chiefs, film critics, screenwriters, and labor unions.

Valenti announced the implementation of a new voluntary ratings system on November 1, 1968, under which producers would voluntarily submit their films for rating. The films would then be viewed by a ratings board comprised of seven people, who would assign ratings based on four criteria: theme, language, violence, and nudity and/or sexual content. The producers would be allowed to appeal this rating or to recut their films in order to receive a milder rating. Initially, there were four ratings:

- **G**   Material is acceptable to general audiences.
- **M**   Material is for mature audiences.
- **R**   Material is to be restricted to children under the age of sixteen unless they are accompanied by an adult.
- **X**   Children under the age of seventeen not admitted.

Under this system, all the ratings symbols were trademarked except X. This allowed filmmakers who didn't want to submit their films to self-apply the X rating. Valenti's initial plan had been to use only three labels (G, M, and R); NATO suggested adding the X rating.

The ratings system would later be modified. The first change came in 1969, the result of confusion as to the nature of the M rating—many parents believed that M implied that a film contained more adult content than those

> ### *Cinematic Firsts*
>
> The first film slapped with an X rating by the MPAA was Brian De Palma's *Greetings* (1968), starring Robert De Niro.

labeled R. M was replaced by the GP rating (Parental guidance suggested). The following year GP became PG, and the age limit was increased to seventeen.

The system was changed again in 1984 when two Steven Spielberg films, *Gremlins* and *Indiana Jones and the Temple of Doom*—both heavy on violence but devoid of sex—were released. These films were thought to be too wild for the PG rating, but not rough enough to be rated R. With this distinction in mind, the MPAA introduced the PG-13 rating on July 1, 1984. This meant that children under the age of seventeen could still be admitted, but that parents were strongly cautioned to consider the possible impact of the film on their children. (The first film to receive a PG-13 rating was John Milius's *Red Dawn* (1984).) In 1990, the X rating was changed to NC-17: no children under the age of seventeen could be admitted to films so rated, with or without adult supervision. The reason for this, Valenti said, was because the X rating had taken on a "surly meaning in the minds of many people." Because films that were not pornographic in nature had been slapped with the X rating, he hoped that the more neutral NC-17 would mitigate the pornographic connotations associated with the X rating.

In the years since the ratings system was implemented, there has been an unending debate as to its effectiveness. One heavily argued objection to ratings is the effect they have on a film's box-office earnings. Valenti and other MPAA members have argued that ratings have no impact upon a film's financial outcome, but despite their insistence to the contrary, the MPAA ratings can significantly impact a film's financial outcome. Adults have proven less likely to attend a non-children's movie with a G rating. Several films, such as *Sneakers* (1992), have had *more* provocative material intentionally added to them to secure a PG rating. R and NC-17 movies clearly impact a film's audience as a huge moviegoing demographic group is excluded. Because MTV star Tom Green's fan base is comprised primarily of teenagers, the R rating assigned his film *Freddy Got Fingered* (2001) effectively prevented most of his target audience from seeing it. Had it been released with either a PG or PG-13 rating, chances are it would have made more money in its opening weekend. Also affecting some films' earning power is the decision by many theaters to not show either NC-17 or X rated films, which all but obviates any hope of a box-office success.

One of the biggest objections to the ratings system is that films are judged on a case-by-case basis, which often leads to discrepancies in the way films are rated. "There are no guidelines that are strictly adhered to," observes director Jeff Burr, who battled the MPAA ratings board over his film *Leatherface: Texas Chainsaw Massacre III* (1990). (To receive an R rating the film was ultimately cut and recut to the point of incoherence.) "There are different rules for studios than there are for independents. There are different rules for major directors within studios than there are for normal directors. There is no rhyme or reason to it. It's not like if you say 'fuck' twice, you get an R rating, and if you say it once, you get a PG-13, or if you show five bullet hits on one character, that's R violence, and if you show two bullet hits on a character, then it's PG-13 violence. There are no guidelines. . . . It's all about how the thing feels. You can make a film with no gore, where the mood is incredibly repellent, and you'll get an R, where it should be a PG-13; they penalize you for doing your job well. And they're slaves to the studio system because that's who supplies the money for the MPAA. So naturally they're going to be a lot harder on independent movies, which was more of a problem in the eighties because there were more independent movies being made."

Although the MPAA denies the charges that it treats some film-makers differently, there is sufficient evidence to support such a claim. Director Steven Spielberg, often regarded as Hollywood's favorite son, is treated conspicuously differently than other filmmakers when his films are submitted for rating. In the case of *Saving Private Ryan* (1998), by far the goriest and most violent film to ever receive an R rating, a film depicting considerably more violence than, say, the aforementioned *Leatherface*, is accorded what some take to be special treatment by the ratings board.

"It's annoying because you feel like you're being screwed over all the time," filmmaker Rusty Cundieff observes of the ratings system. "Look at *Saving Private Ryan* . . . I think that's the most intense shit I've ever seen! Compare that to *Tales from the Hood* (1995) where they made us take out an officer hitting someone in the head with a baton because they were going to damage someone. You just kind of go, 'Um, okay. I can see where one more baton hit is going to be the difference between peace and civil disobedience.'"

Sometimes battles with the ratings board have been almost absurd in nature. Bill Unger, executive producer of *True Romance* (1993), recalls one such conflict with Valenti over the use of the word "pussy". "We had this murderous battle with the ratings board in which the man who had headed the board for years took offense to the number of times the word *pussy* was used. As I recall, we literally had memos going back and forth amongst grown men that we were laughing at, but almost crying about too, that in the first cut the word *pussy* is used twelve times, and it is now limited to seven times. So then we would get back a memo that this wasn't enough. So we would be looking at each other and kind of asking with a sense of absurdity how many times you could use the word *pussy* and not offend this man."

It can be argued that the MPAA ratings system is in need of more clearly defined guidelines, consistent for every film submitted. Nevertheless, it's a system clearly superior to the Hays Code if only because it shows more respect to the artists responsible for the films. Both Valenti's revision of the Code and his institution of the ratings system represent a turning point in how we view films in a more relaxed, less overtly censorious atmosphere. Much of the violent and sexual content of films released since 1968 would not have been permitted under the Hays Code, and by regulating themselves, the motion picture industry successfully forestalled any government regulation of movies.

# Chapter 23

# The New Hollywood: America's New Wave

Jacy (Cybill Shepherd) flirts with Sonny (Timothy Bottoms) in a scene from Peter Bogdanovich's *The Last Picture Show* (1971).

THE EARLY 1970S saw the birth of a new kind of film. Younger film-makers fresh out of film school, along with others who had started out in television, invaded Hollywood en masse. Unlike most filmmakers before them, these new directors had been able to study the films of the directors who had preceded them and, well versed in Hollywood's conventions, sometimes broke away from them in the name of art.

The new breed was also heavily influenced by the works of Italians like Federico Fellini and by the French New Wave. Thanks to influential writers such as Bazin and Truffaut, film was for the first time seen as an acceptable subject for study in the United States. Once exposed to the auteur theory, which concluded that the director was the creative force behind a film, these young Americans, like those of the French New Wave before them, saw themselves as auteurs. They sought to make films very different from the normal Hollywood fare. When given the opportunity, many of these filmmakers would discard plot in favor of character development and improvisation. As a result, their films were generally more personal than those produced by older, more established directors in the American film industry.

In the mid-1960s, screenwriters Robert Benton and David Newman completed their script for *Bonnie and Clyde* (1967). Because the screenplay was influenced by the French New Wave, they sent *Bonnie and Clyde* to Truffaut hoping he might want to produce or direct it. Truffaut immediately fell in love with the script, but already had a number of projects in the works, so he passed it along to Jean-Luc Godard, who flirted with the project for some time. When, in 1966, Truffaut had dinner with actress Leslie Caron and her then-lover, Warren Beatty, Beatty announced that he was seeking a project to produce, Truffaut gave him a copy of *Bonnie and Clyde*. "It needs to be made by an American," Truffaut said. Beatty read the script, loved it, optioned it, and then convinced veteran filmmaker Arthur Penn to direct. Penn helmed the film with some flair, but it was producer/star Beatty who shepherded it through the system and molded it as he saw fit. When the film was released, with Beatty and Faye Dunaway in the lead roles, it received a critical pounding. This wasn't the type of film American critics were accustomed to, but most of them changed their minds by the end of the year, and many who had condemned the film ended up listing it as one of the best films of 1967. (*Time* magazine went so far as to run a retraction of its initial review.) *Bonnie and Clyde* caused quite a stir with its anti-authoritarian stance, underlying homosexual tensions, and the two antiheroes at its center. The film's climax set a new high-water mark for violence—which would be surpassed only two years later by Sam Peckinpah's *The Wild Bunch* (1969).

*Bonnie and Clyde* reinforced the young American auteurs' belief that Hollywood films could be produced in a different way. With the

MPAA's new ratings system, filmmakers felt freer to investigate aspects of life that had never before been considered acceptable, and to do so in ways that had never before been permitted. If *Bonnie and Clyde* had unlocked the door for unrestrained creativity, the MPAA's new ratings system kicked it wide open.

*Bonnie and Clyde* can be seen as a catalyst for the New Hollywood, much like Visconti's *Ossessione* (1943) was for Italian Neorealism. The era of the "New Hollywood" lasted roughly from Dennis Hopper's *Easy Rider* (1969) to Martin Scorsese's *Raging Bull* (1980). Although the number of highly personal works clustered in the first half of the 1970s—before the release of *Jaws* (1975)—a number of significant works also emerged in the latter half of the decade. The decline of the New Hollywood parallels the rise of the modern blockbuster which, ironically, was intensified by the works of two young turks, Steven Spielberg and George Lucas—who formerly had been a part of Hollywood's New Wave.

Dennis Hopper's *Easy Rider* is recognized as the New Hollywood's first salvo, an experimental film—Hopper's first as director—intended to "show the violence underlying everything in America." The film, in which Hopper, Peter Fonda, and Jack Nicholson play castabouts attempting to make their way across the country on motorcycles, was a mammoth hit, and its success would tempt Hollywood to embrace new ideas and untested filmmakers. Director Peter Bogdanovich explains the impact of the film in George Hickenlooper's *Reel Conversations*:

> Certainly *Easy Rider* was one of the first of Hollywood's more radical films to find success, which I think had a very positive effect on mainstream movie making. And, of course, *Easy Rider* was the first movie made outside the studios to gross enormous sums of money. It became a real blockbuster, and that impressed everyone, even the most conservative executives at the time. It cost something like seven or eight hundred thousand dollars and made millions. In 1969, that same year, I was under contract at Paramount where they had spent almost a hundred million dollars on five or six movies, and I remember everybody standing around wondering what had happened. So then toward the end of the sixties, everybody started saying this was the way to make pictures. Go out on location with a million dollars, take a script that was a little different to a new

director and do it. At the time I remember making a joke that
the easiest way to make a picture was to not have made one.

In her book *Dennis Hopper: A Madness to His Method*, Elena Rodriguez
adds:

> Dennis was suddenly being called a genius by a whole new
> generation of movie directors who were coming onto the
> scene at the end of the sixties. *Easy Rider* was more than a
> countercultural phenomenon, so much so that it altered the
> economics of Hollywood production for some time afterward.
> It was made for less than $400,000 and grossed more than
> $50 million. It pulled in the youth audience that the big stu-
> dios had not been able to attract. Hopper also had brought
> the film in on schedule and under budget. Coming on the
> heels of several $20 million, big-budget flops, the phenome-
> non shifted the studios' attention to small, interesting, risky
> productions. The brief brave new world of the "New Holly-
> wood" was born. . . .

### Did You Know?

*Easy Rider* (1969) was the second film on which Dennis Hopper, Jack Nicholson, and Peter Fonda collaborated. The first was Roger Corman's *The Trip* (1967), in which Hopper and Fonda appeared as actors and for which Nicholson wrote the screenplay. Hopper also served as a second unit director.

As Peter Biskind observes in *Easy Riders, Raging Bulls*, the success of Italian director Michelangelo Antonioni's English-language film *Blowup* (1966) also deserves some credit for this new wave of American filmmaking. Holly-wood execs were dumb-founded by this film, which they believed to be "about nothing." Because of their confusion regarding *Blowup* and, later, *Easy Rider*, these executives began greenlight-ing pictures to which they normally would not have given even the slightest consideration.

While a startling number of landmark films were produced during this era, it is most generally the filmmakers behind them who are remembered. (This is, perhaps, fitting considering that the New Hollywood respected the director as auteur.) These filmmakers came to directing from a variety of backgrounds, and each possessed his own individual aesthetic sense. The following (listed in alphabetical order) are a few of the noted filmmakers who emerged and/or flourished during this era:

**Woody Allen.** Allen was hired as a screenwriter on *What's New, Pussycat?* (1965) after Warren Beatty observed his nightclub comedy act. As the story goes, Allen wanted more money than producer Charles Feldman was willing to offer, but said he would work for less if Feldman would cast him as an actor. Feldman agreed, and the rest is history. Allen purchased the rights to a 1964 Japanese spy thriller called *Kagi no kag* and overdubbed the film with silly one-liners and a nonsensical plot revolving around an egg salad recipe; the result was *What's Up, Tiger Lily?* (1966). He soon made his "proper" directorial debut with *Take the Money and Run* (1969), which led to a string of successful comedies, including *Bananas* (1971), *Everything You Ever Wanted to Know About Sex (But Were Afraid to Ask)* (1972), *Sleeper* (1973), and *Love and Death* (1975). In these films Allen adopted the persona of a neurotic schnook, which he played to perfection in *Annie Hall* (1977). *Annie Hall* became a monumental hit and earned Allen Oscars for writing and directing. *Interiors* (1978), a chamber drama highly influenced by the works of Ingmar Bergman, got a bit too heavy-handed for most audiences, but with *Manhattan* (1979) Allen scored another critical and commercial success as well as an Oscar nomination for Best Screenplay. His next film was the largely autobiographical *Stardust Memories* (1980). In the decades since, Allen has continued to play the same melancholy neurotic he perfected in *Annie Hall*.

**Robert Altman.** Although directing his first feature, *The Delinquents*, in 1957, Altman spent most of the sixties working in television. He returned to feature filmmaking largely unnoticed with *Countdown* (1968) and *That Cold Day in the Park* (1969), but *M*A*S*H* (1970), a black comedy about wartime medics, was a departure from the usual studio products. The irreverent film was truly a product of its times; with its strong anti-authoritarian stance, its racial and sexual stereotyping, and its cavalier regard to its own sexist nature, *M*A*S*H* could not be made today. A giant success, it established Altman as a unique filmmaker, and Altman received an Oscar nomination for Best Director. He then directed the revisionist oater *McCabe and Mrs. Miller* (1971), followed by *Images* (1972), *The Long Goodbye* (1973), *California Split*, and *Thieves Like Us* (both 1974). While these films failed to make an impact at the box office, they are, in hindsight, as potent and imaginative as anything on the prolific filmmaker's filmography. For his next project, the visionary *Nashville* (1975), featuring interconnecting storylines about the Nashville music scene, Altman received Oscar nominations as both producer and director. By the end of the decade, Altman fell victim to the excesses of the 1980s with the ill-fated *Popeye* (1980). Altman's output has since been constant, but uneven, and although the era of the New Hollywood is long gone, Altman continues to take risks and thumb his nose at conventional filmmaking. Of his relationship with the mainstream Altman once quipped, "We're not against each other. They sell shoes, and I make gloves."

> ## Cinematic Firsts
>
> The first major release in which all the music on the soundtrack is performed by the actors live in front of the camera was Robert Altman's *Nashville* (1975).

**Hal Ashby.** Ashby worked at Universal as an editor before making the leap to directing. He received an Oscar nomination for editing on *The Russians Are Coming! The Russians Are Coming!* (1966) and won the statuette for *In the Heat of the Night* (1967). Ashby made his directorial debut with *The Landlord* (1970), which he took over after Norman Jewison resigned. Heralded as a bright new talent with the release of *Harold and Maude* (1971), he followed this with *The Last Detail* (1973), which was critically and commercially well-received. Ashby reteamed with *Last Detail* scribe Robert Towne on *Shampoo* (1975), starring Warren Beatty. Although Ashby's stunning film about the life of folk singer Woody Guthrie, *Bound for Glory* (1976), failed to find an audience, he received an Oscar nomination for Best Director for *Coming Home* (1977). His 1979 Peter Sellers comedy *Being There* was Ashby's last film during the New Hollywood era, and his last to meet with any success before his death in 1988.

**Peter Bogdanovich.** As a youth, Bogdanovich wanted to be an actor. He studied under noted acting coach Stella Adler in the 1950s, and appeared in minor roles on a handful of television series. Bogdanovich was also a cinéaste and a film scholar who immersed himself in cinema, and began writing essays on cinema for such major publications as *Esquire*. Through these assignments he met and became an apprentice of sorts to filmmakers John Ford, Howard Hawks, and Orson Welles. In the mid-1960s Bogdanovich was hired to work as a jack-of-all-trades at American International Pictures, where he directed his first film, *Targets* (1967). In 1971, his first major league feature, *The Last Picture Show*, became a critical and commercial success and landed Bogdanovich an Oscar nomination. The director soon began making tabloid headlines when he left his wife Polly Platt for starlet Cybill Shepherd. He then directed the screwball comedy *What's Up Doc?* (1972), scripted by Buck Henry, and *Paper Moon* (1973), which earned Tatum O'Neal an Oscar. All four of these films made knowing reference to classic films of the past. Although Bogdanovich continued working throughout the decade, most of his output attracted meager attention and showed little of the magic of his earlier films. Although his recent work has been uneven, in the decades following the New Hollywood era Bogdanovich has enjoyed a number of successes, including *Mask* (1985) and *The Cat's Meow* (2001).

**John Cassavetes.** As Leonard Maltin writes, Cassavetes's "experimental, inexpensive features were American counterparts to the films that were the product of France's New Wave." Cassavetes began his career in the fifties as an actor, appearing in such urban films as *Taxi* (1953) and *Edge of the City* (1957). In 1960, Cassavetes directed his first film, *Shadows*, which many believe catalyzed the American independent cinema. Cassavetes, who utilized an improvisational approach to filmmaking, is today considered a pioneer in American cinema verité. Cassavetes worked as an actor in mainstream features such as *The Dirty Dozen* (1967) and *Rosemary's Baby* (1968) to make money with which he could finance his own productions. "I'm sort of my own Mafia," Cassavetes once joked. "You know, breaking my own knees." Although he began directing a full decade before the birth of the New Hollywood, Cassavetes's work was strongest during this period. Between 1969 and 1980 Cassavetes directed the grim, gritty, critically acclaimed films *Husbands* (1970), *Minnie and Moskowitz* (1971), *A Woman Under the Influence* (1974), *The Killing of a Chinese Bookie* (1976), and *Gloria* (1980). Cassavetes also received three Oscar nominations: Best Supporting Actor for *The Dirty Dozen*, Best Original Screenplay for *Faces* (1968), and Best Director for *A Woman Under the Influence*.

**Francis Ford Coppola.** With a composer for a father and an actress for a mother, Francis Coppola's career in the entertainment business was probably inevitable. Like a number of his New Hollywood alums, Coppola went to work at AIP. There he worked in several capacities before directing *Dementia 13* (1963). (In a rare feat, Coppola actually made his commercial debut before he graduated from USC film school.) Warner Bros. hired Coppola to direct the musical *Finian's Rainbow* (1968), which bombed. He served as a screenwriter on numerous projects, including *Is Paris Burning?* (1966) and *Patton* (1970), for which he received an Oscar. In 1969, Coppola directed *The Rain People* and also established his own production company, American Zoetrope, through which he produced George Lucas's *THX 1138* (1971) and *American Graffiti* (1973). But it was with *The Godfather* (1973) that Coppola came into his own as a filmmaker, earning him critical acclaim and a huge box-office success. For his next, *The Conversation* (1974), which was very much influenced by the French New Wave, he received the prestigious Palme d'Or at the Cannes film festival. For *The Godfather Part II* (1974), which many consider the finest sequel ever produced, Coppola received Oscars for his work as producer, screenwriter, and director. *Apocalypse Now* (1979), which took him three years to complete, was another critical and commercial success, and yet again Coppola received Oscar nominations for his work as producer, screenwriter, and director. Coppola's career has been largely a series of missteps in the decades following *Apocalypse Now* (most notably the ill-advised *Godfather Part III*, 1990).

**Brian De Palma.** In the early 1960s De Palma helmed a number of interesting shorts, one of which, *The Wedding Party* (1963), was given theatrical release in 1969 after actors Robert De Niro and Jill Clayburgh had established themselves. His 1968 feature *Greetings* reteamed him with De Niro, and the two collaborated again on *Hi, Mom!* (1970). De Palma scored a minor hit with *Sisters* (1973), in which he revealed an obvious fascination for the work of Alfred Hitchcock. After the musical horror film *Phantom of the Paradise* (1974), he continued his public obsession with Hitchcock and De Palma became recognized for his voyeuristic camera and Hitchcockian homages. *Obsession* (1976) is startlingly similar to Hitch's *Vertigo* (1958) and *Dressed to Kill* (1980) bears a striking resemblance to Hitchcock's *Psycho* (1960). De Palma also adapted Stephen King and John Farris novels about telekinetic children: *Carrie* (1976) and *The Fury* (1978). De Palma has since continued a successful career in which he has copied Hitchcock more often than not. Despite this, De Palma's work is at its peak when he avoids Hitchcockian tropes in *Scarface* (1983), *The Untouchables* (1987), and *Casualties of War* (1989).

**William Friedkin.** Friedkin began his career working for a local television station in Chicago, after which he moved into network television, where he directed episodes for a number of series. He made his directorial debut with *Good Times* (1967), which starred Sonny & Cher. Attracting critical attention with *The Night They Raided Minsky's* and *The Birthday Party* (both 1968), followed by *The Boys in the Band* (1970), he directed the hit *The French Connection* (1971), starring Gene Hackman, followed by the equally impressive *The Exorcist* (1973). With the success of the last two films, it appeared that Friedkin was on the verge of becoming one of the most successful directors in history. His fortunes turned when the ambitious *Sorcerer* (1977) was a huge bomb, and the thriller *Cruising* (1980) an even bigger one. Friedkin has continued working in the decades which have followed, but results have been mixed to say the least.

**Dennis Hopper.** Method actor Hopper began his career with minor roles in *Johnny Guitar* (1954) and *Rebel Without a Cause* (1955). While working on the latter, Hopper became close friends with James Dean, with whom he also appears in *Giant* (1956). In 1969, Hopper directed *Easy Rider*, which kicked off the era that has become known as the New Hollywood. Hoping to make a similar splash with an even more daring project, Hopper directed *The Last Movie* (1971), a bold experimental film that was largely hit-or-miss, unsuccessful critically and commercially. Mostly improvised (its credits do not appear on-screen until approximately thirty minutes into the film), *The Last Movie*'s successes can be attributed to Hopper's far-reaching ambitions, and its failures can be chalked up to his acknowledged drug abuse during shooting. In many ways, this was Hopper's "last movie" as a director. After a nine year hiatus from filmmaking, Hopper began directing again in 1980, but his subsequent films as a director have been largely forgettable.

**George Lucas.** As a young man George Lucas dreamed of making "abstract films that are emotional." After making a number of short films, Lucas won an internship under Francis Ford Coppola on the film *The Rain People*. Coppola and Lucas became friends immediately, and Coppola allowed Lucas to shoot a documentary about the making of his film (*Filmmaker*, 1968). Coppola secured financing for Lucas's feature debut, *THX-1138* (1971) but the sci-fi film tanked. Coppola convinced Lucas to come up with a more mainstream project, and the result was the largely autobiographical *American Graffiti* (1973). The film scored at the box office, garnering Lucas Oscar nominations for his work as both screenwriter and director. His next film was much more ambitious, and took him several years to write. *Star Wars* (1977) soon became the biggest moneymaker in history, and made Lucas an extremely wealthy man. Despite such unparalleled success, *Star Wars* lacked the well-rounded acting and strong character development of *American Graffiti*. Nevertheless, Lucas snagged Oscar nominations for writing and directing the sci-fi extravaganza. In the decades following the New Hollywood era, Lucas has overseen the *Star Wars* film series and has produced a number of other successful films.

**Mike Nichols.** As an actor Nichols studyied under Lee Strasberg, and later helped form the improvisational comedy troupe known as Second City. Nichols then turned to Broadway, first as an actor and later as director, and on film he made a substantial splash with his directorial debut, *Who's Afraid of Virginia Woolf?* (1966). This gritty film starring Richard Burton and Elizabeth Taylor snagged Nichols an Oscar nomination for Best Director and played a vital role in the advent of the MPAA's voluntary ratings system. None of this, however, could prepare Nichols for the success his next film would enjoy. *The Graduate* (1967) was a monstrous hit, and won Nichols an Oscar. His next projects were the highly ambitious but underachieving adaptation of Joseph Heller's novel *Catch-22* (1970) and the frank, unblinking *Carnal Knowledge* (1971). Unfortunately, neither *The Day of the Dolphin* (1973) and *The Fortune* (1975) fulfilled the promise of his earlier work, and Nichols took a lengthy hiatus from film. He returned to film in 1983 with *Silkwood*.

**Bob Rafelson.** Rafelson, Bert Schneider, and Steve Blauner founded a production company known as BBS in the mid-1960s, and were instrumental in assembling the music group the Monkees for the television series of the same name. Rafelson directed several episodes of the series before making his feature debut with the Monkees film, *Head* (1968), which Rafelson cowrote with actor Jack Nicholson. A hallucinatory exercise in surrealism, *Head* established Rafelson as a genuine talent with a unique voice. However, it was his second film that garnered him the critical accolades befitting a veteran director. *Five Easy Pieces* (1970) features Jack Nicholson in a virtuoso performance as a concert pianist struggling to find himself and received Oscar nominations for Best Screenplay and Best Director. This film, along with *Easy Rider* and *The Last Picture Show*, serves as perhaps the finest example of the New Hollywood's approach toward conventions and its debt to both the Italian Neorealist and French New Wave movements. Rafelson's next film, also with Nicholson, *The King of Marvin Gardens* (1972), served up a grim depiction of the American dream and the nightmare it can quickly become. Rafelson then suffered a number of setbacks, among them the lackluster *Stay Hungry*

(1976) and his being fired from *Brubaker* (1980) as a result of an artistic disagreement with star Robert Redford. Rafelson would make a comeback with his bleak remake of *The Postman Always Rings Twice* (1981), teaming up again with Jack Nicholson.

**Martin Scorsese.** Scorsese considered becoming a priest before he went into filmmaking. Upon graduating from New York University Scorsese directed a number of short films and made his feature directorial debut with *Who's That Knocking at My Door?* (1968), which featured Harvey Keitel. Scorsese was hired by AIP to direct *Boxcar Bertha* (1972), a loose sequel to Roger Corman's *Bloody Mama* (1970). Scorsese then began shopping around a script he called *Season of the Witch*. Corman offered to produce the film—which would ultimately become *Mean Streets* (1973)—if Scorsese would agree to make it as a blaxploitation film. Because the very personal film deals largely with Italian-American culture, Scorsese declined, found other financing, and made the film starring Keitel and Robert De Niro. The film's success brought acclaim to Scorsese and his stars. His next, *Alice Doesn't Live Here Anymore* (1974), was both a critical and commercial success. The film was championed internationally and received a nomination for the prestigious Palme d'Or at Cannes. He followed this up with the extraordinarily successful, if grim, *Taxi Driver* (1976), which reunited him with both Keitel and De Niro. He returned to Cannes with *Taxi Driver*, and this time won the Palme d'Or. The success of *Taxi Driver* gave Scorsese the leverage to make a big-budget musical, *New York, New York* (1977), starring De Niro and Liza Minnelli. It was a flop, but an interesting one, because it's possibly the darkest musical ever made. In 1980, Scorsese redeemed himself with the Jake LaMotta biopic *Raging Bull*, which many critics have called the finest film of the 1980s. That film also earned Scorsese his first Oscar nomination. In the following years, Scorsese has continued working with very few missteps.

**Steven Spielberg.** Spielberg broke into the film industry through television, notably directing a segment for the TV-movie *Night Gallery* (1969), which served as a pilot for the anthology series of the same name. Among his several telefilms, *Duel* (1971), the story of a man terrorized by an anonymous semi truck driver, was so acclaimed that it was eventually given a theatrical release. This led to his first true theatrical feature, *The Sugarland Express* (1974), an underappreciated film that received enthusiastic notices but failed to score at the box office. Spielberg's next was the wildly successful *Jaws* (1975), a superbly crafted film that started the modern blockbuster craze and made Spielberg a celebrity. For the sci-fi epic *Close Encounters of the Third Kind* (1977) he received his first Oscar nomination. Spielberg's final film during the New Hollywood era was the so-so World War II comedy *1941* (1979), but in the decades that followed, Spielberg has continued to produce extraordinary work.

Other American auteurs who rose to prominence during this period include John Milius, George Romero, Wes Craven, Paul Schrader, Michael Cimino, Terrence Malick, John Carpenter, and David Lynch. The free-wheeling atmosphere during the years of the New Hollywood allowed a number of foreign filmmakers to work in America, and several veteran helmers, such as Sam Peckinpah, produce some of their finest work.

In *Easy Riders, Raging Bulls*, Peter Biskind concludes:

[T]he '70s was truly a golden age, "the last great time," in the words of Peter Bart, who was vice president of production at Paramount until mid-decade, "for pictures that expanded the idea of what could be done with movies." It was the last time Hollywood produced a body of risky, high-quality work that was character-, rather than plot-driven, that defied traditional narrative conventions, that challenged the tyranny of technical correctness, that broke the taboos of language and behavior, that dared to end unhappily. These were often films without heroes, without romance, without—in the lexicon of sports, which has colonized Hollywood—anyone to "root for."

By 1981, trends had changed and financing had all but dried up for personal, artistic films. The New Hollywood was dead, and the films it produced—modern classics as most of them are—are now a relic of a bygone era.

# Chapter 24

# The Blaxploitation Cycle

It may not be one of the more famous entries in the cycle, but Ralph Bakshi's animated film *Coonskin* (1975) serves as an apt representative of the blaxploitation film.

Before discussing the blaxploitation cycle, we must first define just what blaxploitation is. Perhaps the best explanation yet comes from Mikel J. Koven's book *Blaxploitation Films*:

> The first thing to note, rather obviously perhaps, is that this genre, this period of filmmaking if you prefer, is a fusion of two different words—black and exploitation. Blaxploitation films are, by definition, "black exploitation" films. But the problem comes when we ask who is being exploited? We know that most forms of exploitation cinema, for example, splatter movies or pornography, exploit images of violence and/or sexuality; the *raison d'être* of the films is the presentation of sex or violence, not their discourse or analysis. Any semblance to plot or story is purely accidental. These filmmakers exploit our desire to watch violence and/or sex, and if producers could get away with it (and let's face it, some have) they would give us nothing more than scenes of what we've paid to see. Extending this to include blaxploitation films, these must be films that exploit our desire to see black people, specifically African-Americans, on-screen, doing presumably what one expects or wants to see African-Americans doing.

The term "blaxploitation" has always caused confusion. Is the term meant to be derogatory? Are these films degrading to their audience and the black characters they present? Roger Corman, who was one of the top producers of blaxploitation films, goes a step further in his explanation of the term:

> Blaxploitation is exactly the same as the word exploitation, which you could call "whitesploitation." It's the same type of picture, except that you have blacks instead of whites. There's no particular difference. If you look at them, you see that they followed the same basic genres as any other exploitation film. Crime stories, action stories, mystery, adventure, so forth. These are the same genres, but they appealed specifically to the black audience.

---

### *Cinematic Firsts*

Oscar Micheaux became the first black to produce a motion picture with *The Homesteader* (1919), and later became the first black to produce a talkie with *The Exile* (1931).

---

The roots of the blaxploitation film can be traced to 1965, the year director Sidney Pollack hired a young up-and-comer named Quincy Jones to score the Sidney Poitier-starrer *The Slender Thread*. Pollack asked Jones for a different type of score, and gave him room to experiment. What Jones delivered was a soulful score featuring brassy instrumentation. The success of this film made it acceptable to craft films with soulful soundtracks. Though these mainstream films are very different from what we now refer to as blaxploitation, they provided the cultural atmosphere which made the blaxploitation era possible.

The years 1968 and 1969 served as an important point of transition regarding blacks and their participation and depiction in motion pictures. Jules Dassin's *Up Tight* (1968) and Robert Alan Aurthur's *The Lost Man* (1969) did much to change the characterizations of black characters. (Both were remakes of "white" films: *Up Tight* of *The Informer*, 1935; *The Lost Man* reworked Carol Reed's *Odd Man Out*, 1947.) Far more significant, however, were *The Learning Tree* (1969) and *Cotton Comes to Harlem* (1970). Both were written and directed by black filmmakers—Gordon Parks and Ossie Davis respectively—and served to demonstrate to those in the business who persisted in doubting it that a black man was more than capable of directing a motion picture. (With *The Learning Tree*, Parks became the first black filmmaker to helm a motion picture released by a major U.S. studio.)

The following year saw the release of *Sweet Sweetback's Baad Asssss Song* (1971), which is generally cited as the first true blaxploitation film. How that revolutionary film came to be made is the incredible story of writer/director Melvin Van Peebles. After working as a painter and a writer, Van Peebles had decided he wanted to try film. He shot a few short films in San Francisco in the late sixties and then journeyed to Hollywood. After screening his films for studio execs, Van Peebles was offered a job—working as an elevator operator! When he informed them that he wanted to direct films, he was then offered a job as a dancer. Many academians believe this anecdote to be Van Peeble's own creation, but it nonetheless serves as an accurate illustration of the extent of black involvement in the film industry prior to the blaxploitation cycle. Subsequently Van Peebles moved to Holland, where he earned his Ph.D. in astronomy, after which he settled down in France where he became a journalist and wrote novels. There he learned that any French writer or director was eligible for a director's permit. This meant he or she was allowed access to costly filmmaking equipment at the French Film Center. Van Peebles applied for and received a permit, and shot his first film, *La Permission (The Story of a Three Day Pass)* (1968). After receiving accolades and awards for the film, Van Peebles returned to the United States. Hailed as a visionary French director despite his hailing from Chicago, Van Peebles landed a job directing *Watermelon Man* (1970) for Columbia. Following this, Van Peebles raised enough money to finance *Sweet Sweetback's Baad Asssss Song*.

The gritty, unflinching film, which told the story of a male prostitute, earned $14 million in the United States. More than three decades later, the film remains on the list of the all-time biggest independent moneymakers. Some years later, Van Peebles reflected on the film's initial release in Michael Singer's book *A Cut Above: 50 Film Directors Talk About Their Craft*:

> At first, only two theaters in the United States would show the picture: one in Detroit, and one in Atlanta. The first night in Detroit, it broke all the theater's records, and that was only on the strength of the title alone, since nobody had seen it yet. By the second day, people would take their lunch and sit through it three times. I knew that I was finally talking to my audience. *Sweet Sweetback's Badaasssss Song* made a zillion dollars before four white people had ever seen it.

After the success of *Sweet Sweetback's Baad Asssss Song*, the film industry opened its eyes and recognized an untapped demographic in black audiences. Coming up behind Van Peeble's film was *Shaft* (1971), another significant landmark in black cinema, written by Ernest Tidyman and directed by Gordon Parks. The story of a tough black gumshoe played by Richard Roundtree, *Shaft* was an extraordinary hit and, unlike Van Peeble's film, crossed over among white audiences and raked in more than $23 million at the box office. Like *Sweet Sweetback's Baad Asssss Song*, *Shaft* effectively laid the groundwork for the blaxploitation films to come through its depiction of a strong, flamboyant, antiestablishment black hero. By 1971, blacks were becoming increasingly tired of police brutality, of having to turn the other cheek to racial injustice, and of watching a constant barrage of submissive black characters on-screen. Director John Singleton, who would later direct a remake of *Shaft* starring Samuel L. Jackson, explained the original film's impact on black culture in Gerald Martinez's book *What It Is . . . What It Was*:

> You have a whole generation totally influenced by the image of a black man walking down the street in a leather coat, walking through Harlem; the close-ups on his face. When you think of *Shaft*, you think of that scene, don't you?

If *Sweet Sweetback's Baad Aasssss Song* unlocked the door for the blaxploitation films, *Shaft* kicked it open. Studios immediately began cranking out their own blaxploitation films in quick succession. In his excellent study of black cinema *From Sambo to Superspade*, Daniel J. Leab describes the stream of blaxploitation films produced in the wake of *Shaft*:

> Soon after . . . a veritable avalanche of black superheroes descended on the nation's screens. Thanks to the demise of the Code in the 1960s, its replacement by a weak industry-administered rating system, and a series of Supreme Court decisions relaxing the definition of obscenity, these films were filled with sadistic brutality, sleazy sex, venomous racial slurs, and the argot of the streets. Social commentary of any sort was kept to a minimum. Superspade was a violent man who lived a violent life in pursuit of black women, white sex, quick money, easy success, cheap "pot," and other pleasures. In these films white was synonymous with every conceivable kind of evil and villainy. Whites were moral lepers, most of

whom were psychotically antiblack and whose vocabulary was laced with the rhetoric of bigotry. Writing about the portrayal of whites in these movies, Pauline Kael charged that "except when we were at war, there has never been such racism in American films." She is right [up] to a point. These films are a mirror image of the way the black was for years treated on screen. It is only in our permissive society that the industry in its search for a black audience can carry the reversal much [further] than the original.

In 1972, the second blaxploitation film to become a huge crossover success was *Superfly*, the story of a cocaine dealer named Youngblood Priest. The film earned an astounding $11 million during its first two months in release and would end up earning more than $18 million. (The two biggest blaxploitation moneymakers were *Shaft* and *Superfly*, which were directed by Gordon Parks and Gordon Parks, Jr., respectively.) The film made a star of lead actor Ron O'Neal, and its platinum-selling soundtrack earned Curtis Mayfield consecutive hit singles with "Pusherman" and "Freddy's Dead." By the end of 1972, statistics showed that blacks represented nearly one half of the national moviegoing audience, which, according to James P. Murray's *The Subject Is Money*, amounted to approximately $110 million in ticket sales. At that time, this was the highest percentage of black moviegoers in the history of the cinema.

During the blaxploitation period—from 1970 to roughly 1975—more than two hundred of these films were made. As with all exploitation films, producers sought to cast recognizable names; the only problem was that there were very few established black actors in Hollywood. Because of this, producers began casting popular black athletes, such as Jim Brown, Fred Williamson, Rosie Grier, and baseballer Vida Blue. One such film, *The Black Six* (1974), featured six pro football players! So shameless were the producers in their exploitation of the athletes' status that each player's professional football team was listed in the opening credits alongside his name. The blaxploitation era also made actors of well-known comedians like Richard Pryor and popular soul singers like Isaac Hayes. Other notable stars to emerge from these films include the aforementioned Richard Roundtree, Jim Kelly, and Pam Grier (cousin of footballer Rosie Grier).

Soon, blaxploitation films in nearly every genre began to emerge, from Western to kung fu. Following the examples set by *Up Tight* and *Odd Man Out*, many were remakes, reworkings, or blatant ripoffs of preexisting films that had featured a predominantly white cast: *Hit Man* (1972) was a remake of the English crime drama *Get Carter* (1970); *Abby* (1974) was an unsubtle copy of *The Exorcist* (1973); with *Blacula* (1972) and *Blackenstein* (1973) American International Pictures simply retooled classic horror stories as blaxploitation films; and *Black Caesar* (1973) was little more than an obvious reworking of the Edward G. Robinson classic *Little Caesar* (1931). Most of the blaxploitation films that followed *Shaft* tended to depict blacks in a somewhat negative light; where the protagonist of *Shaft* had been a blue-collar joe who worked (mostly) within the lines of the law, many of these films featured black protagonists who worked as drug dealers, pimps, hookers, killers, and thieves. It is because of this that the blaxploitation cycle began to draw fire from groups such as the National Association for the Advancement of Colored People and the Coalition Against Blaxploitation. (Interestingly, it was Junius Griffin of the NAACP who first coined the term "blaxploitation.")

Filmmaker Larry Cohen, who directed the seminal blaxploitation films *Black Caesar* and *Hell Up in Harlem* (1973), believes the label blaxploitation ultimately damaged the public perception of the films. "*Every* movie is an exploitation movie," Cohen insists. "Every movie tries to get you to part with your eight dollars. Our job is to get you to spend your money and come into the theater, not unlike a barker at a carnival sideshow trying to entice you to come and see the fat lady or the dwarf. That's what the whole business is about. You do whatever you have to to sell tickets. Every picture is exploiting something and some audience. So what if you're making films for a black audience? Why shouldn't they have their cinema, anyway? There was a long period when there were no black pictures. So, as soon as they started making pictures for a black audience, somebody went around yelling, 'Blaxploitation!' It's rather foolish, obviously. I think it tainted the product, and people didn't look at the pictures more clearly until later on."

Defining the years in which the cycle rose and fell has always been a source of debate, but the number of blaxploitation films began to dwindle noticeably after 1975. Apart from a few stragglers, such as

*Car Wash* (1976), the cycle had wound down. Market research indicated that blacks had grown tired of ethnic films and preferred to spend their money on "white" movies like *Jaws* and *The Exorcist*. In the wake of Quentin Tarantino's *Jackie Brown* (1997) and Singleton's update of *Shaft*, there was a renewal of interest in blaxploitation films, and their legacy. But the question remains: Is that legacy a positive or negative one?

Rusty Cundieff, a black filmmaker whose *Tales from the Hood* (1995) is an homage to blaxploitation, sees the cycle in a positive light. "Overall the films were a positive thing," Cundieff says. "That was what was available at the time for black actors, writers, and a few directors. Ultimately, it is some type of window to black culture in the seventies. It may be a rather skewed version of it, but at least it's a version, which is more than you have when you try to look at films to give you an idea of what black culture in the fifties or sixties was about; there is nothing there. Also, in a broad sense, [these films] do give you a feeling of the black mindset at the time, which was very pro-active and militant and looking to overcome obstacles, which I think all those films had to some degree or another. They were gonna beat the system in this way, or they weren't going to be held down in that way. Even in some of the most inane of those films, that basic concept tends to present itself."

Roger Corman agrees. "I think [blaxploitation films] played a crucial role in allowing black actors, writers, producers, and directors to show their ability," Corman explains. "And they proved to Hollywood that a black-oriented film could be successful. I think they were very important on both of those levels."

In *Black Film/White Money*, scholar Jesse Algeron Rhines discounts the validity of arguments such as Corman's:

The blaxploitation period was not an example of African-American filmmaking. Much more often than not, whites were in control behind the camera reproducing their own point of view. In fact, of the hundred or so films featuring significant numbers of African-American characters and/or an African-American–derived storyline and produced during the blaxploitation period, roughly 1970 through 1974, fewer than one fifth were under African-American control. Even fewer came from black-owned production houses and fewer still were financed and/or distributed by African-Americans.

Although there is truth in Rhines's statements, they can be read as somewhat unfair if one considers just how few black-owned studios and distribution companies existed in the early 1970s. Rhines seems to imply that if blacks could not control the films in which they appear, it would have been better to have had absolutely no black cinema. However, culture wars must be fought and won battle by battle; they cannot be won overnight. David Walker, a black filmmaker who edits the blaxploitation magazine *Bad Azz Mofo*, disagrees with Rhines's assessment. "Despite the fact that whites did and continue to control the film industry, the blaxploitation era provided tremendous opportunities for African-Americans behind the camera," Walker says. "During this time directors, writers, and producers emerged that may not have had the chance to work in Hollywood otherwise—not to mention make-up artists, stuntmen, and editors. One could speculate that without films like *Shaft*, *Trouble Man* (1972), *Blacula*, or *Cooley High* (1975), the opportunity for many blacks in the film industry would have never opened up. Every generation that comes along benefits from the advances of the previous generation. The same is true for filmmakers like Spike Lee and John Singleton, who owe at least part of their careers to the advances and sacrifices made by the likes of Gordon Parks, Melvin Van Peebles, Oscar Williams, Fred Williamson, Michael Schultz, and Jamaa Fanaka. Ultimately, the blaxploitation era proved that there was an audience for black films, and that those films can make money. Hollywood chooses to

### Did You Know?

A number of stars from the blaxploitation cycle reunited in 1996 for *Original Gangstas*, among them Fred Williamson, Pam Grier, Jim Brown, Richard Roundtree, and Ron O'Neal. The film was directed by Larry Cohen, who had directed the blaxploitation films *Black Caesar* and *Hell Up in Harlem* (both 1973).

ignore that from time to time, but it's a truth that never goes away. The recent success of *Barbershop* (2002) proved it all over again."

There can be no doubt that blaxploitation films often presented their characters in a negative, immoral light. Nor can it be denied that, by and large, whites controlled most of these productions. But the value of these films—whether or not their makers intended for them to have value—cannot be dismissed. Nearly every black filmmaker working today has credited blaxploitation films as being an inspiration for their entry into the film industry: whether or not the blaxploitation films of the 1970s truly opened doors for blacks working in the industry today, it is clear that they encouraged a belief among these would-be filmmakers that careers in the film industry were possible. Either way, the blaxploitation cycle must be seen as a turning point.

# Chapter 25

# The Home Video Invasion

GERARD DAMIANO'S

DEEP THROAT

HOW FAR DOES A GIRL HAVE TO GO TO UNTANGLE HER TINGLE?

EASTMANCOLOR (X) ADULTS ONLY

PHOTOFEST

Adult films such as *Deep Throat* (1972) were largely responsible for the early popularity of the videocassette recorder.

IT MAY BE DIFFICULT for today's younger generations to imagine a time when films weren't available on videocassette and there weren't VCRs to record one's favorite television programs. As the history of home video isn't often recounted, these individuals may be inclined to think that this technology arrived on the market fully developed; this was not the case.

The notion of video technology goes back as far as 1899, when Vladimir Poulsen conceived the idea of magnetic information storage. By the mid-1940s, German scientists had developed a device called the Magnetophone, which was capable of recording and storing sound magnetically. This technology arrived in the United States after World War II, and led to the development of the audiotape recorder. Engineers at Ampex—the American company that had previously developed the audio recorder—then created the first videotape recorder in 1956, intended for use by television stations. Ampex offered the first videotape recorder for consumer's use in 1963, which was sold through the Neiman-Marcus department store catalog for the outrageous price of $30,000. The following year, two European companies, Philips and Loewe-Opta, introduced home video recorders, which retailed for approximately $2,500. That same year Paramount senior vice president Paul Raibourn predicted that the steadily improving video technology would give the "motion picture producer . . . another way of exhibiting his pictures to the public for direct payment."

Sony introduced its video tape recorder (VTR) in 1967. This problematic device was made available for home use within three years, but it failed commercially because of its unreasonable cost. (Early VTRs cost between $1,000 to $4,000.) In another innovative move, Ampex attempted to rent films on tape in 1968—the first company to do so. These tapes, designated as being "for educational purposes only," were rented as an entire series for fifteen days at a staggering cost of more than $1,500. Needless to say, the price tag was prohibitively expensive for most people. In 1969, Sony introduced a new device: the videocassette recorder (VCR), and in 1972, the U-Matic line of VCRs, which sold for approximately $1,500.

That same year, AVCO introduced the first prerecorded tapes in conjunction with Columbia Pictures. The AVCO video player—known as Cartrivision, or "cartridge television"—was offered in Sears and Roebuck stores for $1,600. Such titles as *High Noon* (1952), *Stagecoach* (1939), and *Bridge on the River Kwai* (1957) were available for rental at Sears stores for approximately five dollars each. These rental cassettes were engineered so that they could be watched only once, and had to be returned and checked out again for a second viewing. A number of factors—among them cost, the inability to screen a film more than once, the impending threat of competition, and overall shoddy quality of their product—caused Avco to cease manufacturing their Cartrivision line after only one year, incurring a loss of more than $1 million.

> ### *Did You Know?*
>
> Documentary filmmaker and *Time* critic Richard Corliss once said of video: "Today is a time of turbulence and stagnation, of threat and promise from a competitor: the magic omnivorous videocassette recorder. In other words, it's business as usual."

In 1975, Sony introduced the Betamax VCR, which, in addition to playback, possessed the capability to record for up to one hour. The following year, Sony introduced a line of Betamax VCRs that retailed for $1,300. In 1977, RCA introduced a VCR capable of recording up to four hours, but using a different, noncompatible format known as VHS. In 1976, Time-Life Multimedia announced that it would sell prerecorded Beta videocassettes by mail.

In October 1977, a Detroit entrepreneur named André Blay inked a deal with 20th Century-Fox for $500,000 a year (plus a royalty of $7.50 per tape), giving Blay the license to sell videocassettes of fifty 20th Century-Fox titles. Blay sold more than a quarter of a million tapes through a *TV Guide* advertisement in the first year alone. By 1979, approximately 800,000 Americans owned VCRs, and Blay was supplying more than three hundred distributors with tapes. Around 1983, the Los Angeles-based George Atkinson (who bought his tapes from Blay) established the first independently owned video rental business. Videocassettes at Atkinson's store were rented initially for $10 per day. Within three years the video rental business was booming across the nation.

In the mid-1980s, less-costly Korean-made VCRs flooded the market, dramatically reducing the average price. After a price and format battle between VHS and Betamax, Sony ceased the manufacture of Betamax. By 1987, the cost of the VCR had dropped to $250 and a blank videocassette could be purchased for five dollars. By this time, approximately one half of all U.S. homes owned a VCR. Interestingly, pornography played a major role in the early sales of the VCR. Thanks to this new device, viewers no longer had to embarrass themselves by traveling to seedy neighborhoods to attend screenings in darkened porn theaters. (In 1980, approximately sixty percent of all U.S. video sales were of pornographic movies.)

At first, the motion picture industry was apprehensive about the videocassette. In 1977, Universal sued Sony, claiming that the recording of television shows and films infringed upon copyrights of intellectual properties. (Sony won the case, but only after a seven-year-long court battle.) A statement made at that time by MPAA president Jack Valenti illustrates the film industry's early attitude toward this technology: "I say to you that the VCR is to the American film producer and the American public as the Boston Strangler is to the woman home alone."

Over time the motion picture industry would come to embrace the VCR (and later innovations such as the LaserDisc and the Digital Video Disc, or DVD). Each of the major studios established its own video distribution center, and served new domestic and international markets. The studios managed to reap huge profits from video rental businesses by charging exorbitant prices for tapes of new releases. (Video chains prepurchase videos for upwards of $75 each only to see them later sold to the public for somewhere around ten dollars.)

Video technology has also had a profound impact on network television, which has seen its viewership dwindle. This has meant bad news for advertisers; using the VCR's Fast Forward button, viewers can simply zip past bothersome commercials.

The videocassette has also proven to be important for the film industry. After the major studios began dominating the theatrical market in the 1970s, many independent film producers were unable to compete and were forced out of the business. However, the video market has changed that trend; video (and DVD)

### Cinematic Firsts

The first mainstream feature made expressly for release to video was *Tangier* (1982).

has provided an outlet for many lower-budget filmmakers who might not have been able to get their films seen otherwise. The major studios have also come to embrace the technology as most major films today earn the majority of their profits from video sales and rentals. Today, the video market accounts for more than $20 billion in sales annually.

# Chapter 26

# A Shark, a Jedi Knight, and the Modern Blockbuster

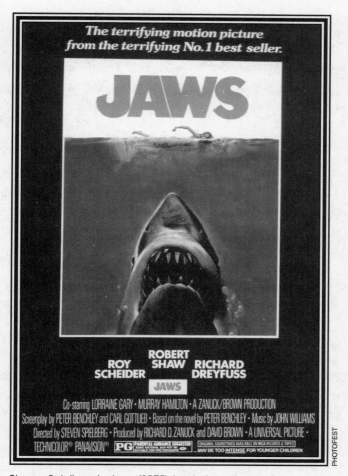

Steven Spielberg's *Jaws* (1975) kept viewers out of the water and influenced producers to stop making small, personal films.

HOLLYWOOD ENTERED the seventies facing a financial depression. The sixties had brought a breakdown of censorship restrictions and a multitude of big-budget flops. After seven decades, the film industry had learned only one thing: It knew nothing. Although studios always found it hard to predict what films would hit or miss, executives in the 1970s found this to be even more difficult than their predecessors. TV-movies had begun to cut into revenue earned from theatrical releases, and studio heads found themselves at a loss. They recognized only that the so-called "proven" ingredients for a potential hit film could now result in disaster (witness the remake of *Lost Horizon*, 1973, and *New York, New York*, 1977). As young blood was transfused into Hollywood's ruling class, the decisionmakers became more and more influenced by the counterculture of the time, and were more willing to take unprecedented risks. Thus, the seventies became a high-water mark for cinematic sex and bloodshed. Hardly any subject was considered too risqué or taboo to exploit during this experimental period. The era also ushered in a new generation of filmmakers collectively known as the "Movie Brats" (a list of whom appears in Chapter 23). Among these filmmakers were Steven Spielberg and George Lucas. Although no one knew it at the time, Spielberg and Lucas were about to revolutionize the film industry and create what would come to be known as the modern blockbuster.

The extraordinary success of *Jaws* (1975) began in 1971 when author Peter Benchley turned in a four-page outline of a proposed novel to an editor at Doubleday. A contract was then approved and Benchley was paid a $1,000 advance for the first four chapters. Eventually Doubleday published the book and Benchley was paid $10,000. After *Jaws* became an enormous bestseller, Bantam purchased the paperback rights for $575,000. Producers Richard D. Zanuck and David Brown optioned the film rights to the novel for the bargain-basement price of $175,000, which included a first-draft screenplay to be written by Benchley himself.

After viewing the dailies for Steven Spielberg's first theatrical film, *The Sugarland Express* (1974), Zanuck and Brown expressed an interest in working with him again. Spielberg was enthusiastic about the idea, but neither he nor the producers had a specific project in mind. It was then that Spielberg stumbled across *Jaws*. He would later recall (in *American Cinematographer*, February 1978):

[I] had a meeting with them on the first or second cut of *Sugarland* and I noticed in the outer office an unpublished book manuscript called *Jaws*. I don't know what seized me, but I thought the title was so fascinating—I thought it was about a dentist—that I picked up the book (actually swiped the damned thing), took it home, read it over the weekend, and knew that was what I wanted to do next. So I went to them on Monday and said, "We've been looking for a film to do together and I've found it in your office."

When its plot is boiled down to its barest elements, *Jaws* is thematically similar to Spielberg's 1971 telefilm *Duel*. Here, however, the menacing semi is replaced by an equally menacing great white shark. (Spielberg would later revisit these themes with *Jurassic Park*.)

The offer to reunite with Spielberg sounded great to the production team, but there was one problem: the project had come to them with another director attached. Spielberg was crushed. Fortunately, he was informed three weeks later that Dick Richards, the aforementioned director, had backed out of the project. Zanuck and Brown drew up the contracts and agreed to produce the film, which was to be shot in thirteen weeks, for $2.3 million. Universal promptly suggested Charlton Heston and Jan-Michael Vincent for the project, but Spielberg stuck to his guns and said no. "My goal was to find someone who had never been on the cover of *Rolling Stone*," he would later explain. "I wanted somewhat anonymous actors to be in it so you could believe this was happening to people like you and me. Stars bring a lot of memories with them, and those memories can sometimes, at least in the first ten minutes of the movie, corrupt the story." For his three leads Spielberg cast Roy Scheider, Richard Dreyfuss, and Robert Shaw.

Benchley quickly handed in a first draft of the script, which was extremely faithful to his novel. Spielberg rejected it. Instead of rehashing the pulpy, sex-drenched story from Benchley's book, Spielberg preferred to discard the first two thirds of the novel and then remain "very loyal to the third." In private, Spielberg said he hadn't liked any of the characters as they appeared in the novel, lamenting that he had rooted for the shark. Benchley went through three drafts of the script, all rejected, and upset that the impending film would bear little resemblance to his novel, spoke out against Spielberg in the *Los Ange-*

*les Times*, saying that the director had "no knowledge of reality but the movies. He is B-movie literate. . . . [H]e will one day be known as the greatest second unit director in America." The second writer to tackle *Jaws* was Pulitzer Prize-winning playwright Howard Sackler, who hammered out two more drafts. The script received further polish by Spielberg pal John Milius before being given to actor/screenwriter Carl Gottlieb, who wrote several more drafts. Although Gottlieb and Benchley received sole screenwriting credit, Spielberg and company rewrote the screenplay throughout the production. Spielberg would later explain (in *Sight and Sound*, Spring 1977):

> For some strange reason I got away with murder on *Jaws*. They just left me alone. I changed the script every day, but I never received a telephone call from any of the powerful executives on the West Coast. I don't think anybody was ever in love with any of the screenplays, and felt the story and script could only be improved.

The shoot was a particularly tough one for Spielberg and his crew, who filmed in the summer heat of Martha's Vineyard. Much of the film's cost could have been cut down had it been shot on a studio backlot, but Spielberg insisted that location shooting would give the film greater authenticity. The miniscule budget began to balloon, eventually reaching $8 million.

Special effects artist Bob Mattey realized that if the simulated creature was to appear real in the film, three separate mechanical sharks would be needed—each with its own specialized function. The sharks—nicknamed "Bruce"—would cost approximately $250,000 apiece. Each was operated by hydraulic pistons. The first time one of the sharks was used, it sank immediately to the bottom of the ocean. Then, as Mattey's technicians were retrieving it, its hydraulic system exploded. On other occasions the sharks crossed their eyes and refused to close their jaws.

Aside from problematic mechanical sharks, the film crew faced a number of other challenges. The weather was almost always disagreeable, the water would shift causing shots to change between takes, and sailboats and yachts routinely intruded into the background of the shots. Crew members began whispering about the film, referring to it as "Flaws." "I thought it would be a turkey," Spielberg later admitted. At several stages of production, he considered quitting. Still a young man at 26, Spielberg sometimes lost faith in his own vision; he had convinced himself that *Jaws* would be nothing more than an "exploitation movie, *Moby Dick* without Melville, without the eloquence." Despite such doubts, Spielberg stuck it out. Although no one will admit it today, it is well documented that Universal studio execs, as well as producers Zanuck and Brown, thought they had a flop on their hands, and considered pulling the plug on the project.

Filmmaker Alan Shapiro believes *Jaws* is a masterpiece, and credits Spielberg's persistence throughout the grueling film shoot. Shapiro, who directed *Flipper* (1997), has a firsthand knowledge of the horrors a director faces when shooting a film that takes place primarily on water. "You know how when you shoot on terra firma, the camera guys measure exact focal lengths, lay tape marks for actors, and get everything just perfect? Forget about that on water. Nothing stays put. As a director, coping with a live dolphin (and/or an animatronic one, with its attendant twelve-man crew), picture boats, crew boats, transport boats, actors getting seasick, the light, the power (remember, water and electricity don't mix), you want a half-decent performance, too? But, okay, everything comes together. You get the shot. Cut! It's perfect; a miracle. Only one problem: none of it was in focus! Or even in frame! Why? Because the goddamn water shifted. Now try to capture that lightning in a bottle for take two; and three, four, five, six, ad nauseum. And how many days is your schedule? How overbudget are you in the first week?"

When shooting on *Jaws* wrapped, the film was one hundred and four days behind schedule. Convinced that his career was over before it had properly begun, Spielberg experienced a severe anxiety attack. Spielberg recalls hearing "rumors from back in Hollywood that I would never work again because no one had ever taken a film a hundred days over schedule—let alone a director whose first film had failed at the box office!" Spielberg would then shoot for an additional three weeks at Universal.

Editing would not be any easier to bear. Because of the problematic shoot, Spielberg and editor Verna Fields found themselves often wondering how to cobble together pieces of unmatched footage.

Much of this was corrected by incorporating footage of real-life sharks and by reshooting some minor shots in Fields's swimming pool. Because so much of the footage of the mechanical sharks was flawed due to mechanical malfunction, Spielberg opted to avoid showing the entire shark in many scenes. This Hitchcockian effect—utilized initially for reasons of practicality—worked to the film's advantage; the shark seems more ominous and threatening because it is rarely shown.

Universal and producers Zanuck and Brown were more than happy with the resulting film. Universal then launched a promotional campaign the likes of which had never been seen before, including the unprecedented use of $700,000 worth of saturation television advertising. (With this campaign, Universal began the practice of assessing theater owners for a share of the film's advertising costs.) The film was then booked into 490 theaters—more than any film had ever been booked in simultaneously—for its opening weekend in June 1975. *Jaws* soon became the highest grossing film of all time and the first film ever to earn more than $100 million at the box office. It has since been dubbed the "first modern blockbuster" or the "first event picture."

In *Easy Riders, Raging Bulls* Peter Biskind explains the effect that the success of *Jaws* had on the film industry:

> *Jaws* changed the business forever, as the studios discovered the value of wide breaks—the number of theaters would rise to one thousand, two thousand, and more by the next decade—and massive TV advertising, both of which increased the costs of marketing and distribution, diminishing the importance of print reviews, making it virtually impossible for a film to build slowly, finding its audience by dint of mere quality. As costs mounted, the willingness to take risks diminished proportionately. Moreover, *Jaws* whet corporate appetites for big profits quickly, which is to say, studios wanted every film to be *Jaws*.

The second film to serve as a blueprint for the modern blockbuster was George Lucas's *Star Wars* (1977), which also began as a seemingly nondescript production. Having just scored a hit with *American Graffiti* (1973), Lucas set his sights on making a futuristic fairy tale, a project he saw as equal parts Errol Flynn, James Bond, and Buck Rogers.

(Interestingly, Lucas had previously attempted to purchase the rights to the 1939 *Buck Rogers* serial with a big-budget remake in mind, but was unsuccesful.) After fifteen months' work, Lucas had a mere thirteen-page treatment for *Star Wars* scribbled on notebook paper. The treatment was so bogged down with Lucas-invented sci-fi jargon that no one could understand a word of it. Because of the unfathomable nature of this treatment, Universal, for whom Lucas had just made *American Graffiti*, turned down the project—a decision that lost the studio several hundred million dollars in revenue.

A week later, Lucas and his representatives screened a bootleg print of the as-yet unreleased *American Graffiti* for 20th Century-Fox head Alan Ladd, Jr., who reportedly remarked that he wanted Lucas's next film to be a Fox release. Lucas then inked a deal with Fox that would pay him $175,000 to write and direct *Star Wars* (which ultimately grossed more than $250 million). In addition, Lucas's company, then known as the Star Wars Corporation, would receive 40 percent of the net. Lucas also insisted upon a deal which would grant him rights to the music, all monies earned from the soundtrack album, sequel rights, and merchandising rights.

According to Peter Biskind, Fox never batted an eye when granting Lucas's demands; Biskind writes:

> From Fox's point of view, Lucas's demands were a joke. Everyone knew that toys took eighteen months to design, manufacture, and distribute, and by that time the movie would be history. It was axiomatic that you couldn't make money on sequels, and the rights obviously didn't amount to much unless the movie was a huge hit, which nobody expected.

Lucas spent nearly three years crafting the screenplay for *Star Wars*. The basic plot was lifted from Akira Kurosawa's 1958 samurai film *Kakushi toride no san-akunin (The Hidden Fortress)*, and elements were borrowed from a number of other sources, such as Joseph Campbell's *The Hero with a Thousand Faces*, Carlos Castaneda's *Tales of Power*, and the works of Alex Raymond. After completing his third draft, Lucas convinced his *American Graffiti* cowriters Willard Huyck and Gloria Katz to polish the script. Although initially Lucas considered casting Amy Irving or Jodie Foster as Princess Leia, he was persuaded by production manager Don Roos to cast Carrie Fisher. Rounding out the principal cast was Harrison Ford, with whom Lucas worked on *American Graffiti*, and Mark Hamill, whom he'd spotted at a casting session for Brian De Palma's *Carrie* (1976). While the rest of the cast was made up of primarily unknown actors, Lucas wanted a distinguished player as his wise sage, Obi Wan Kenobi. Although Japanese actor Toshiro Mifune, the star of *The Hidden Fortress*, was among those considered, Lucas cast Alec Guinness in the role. To get him, however, Lucas had to give the hesitant actor a small piece of the film, which eventually earned him more than $6 million.

The atmosphere on the set was sometimes tense because Lucas—an introvert—sometimes found it difficult to express what he wanted from the actors. (It has frequently been remarked tha Lucas is a genius when working with technology; working with people gives him trouble.) To make matters worse, no one knew what the film or the dialogue was supposed to be about. Actor Harrison Ford later recalled, "We'd come into a scene and we're faced with dialogue straight out of Buck Rogers. I mean, I used to threaten George with tying him up and making him repeat his own dialogue!" Lucas's friend Steven Spielberg offered to help by shooting second unit, but Lucas refused. Spielberg insists this was out of jealousy and a sense of competition. According to Spielberg, Lucas kept saying, "I'm sure *Star Wars* is going to beat *Jaws* at some point."

After a rough cut of the film was assembled, Lucas invited Ladd, Spielberg, De Palma, Huyck, Katz, and Martin Scorsese to his home for a screening. The version shown still had very few special effects. When the screening ended, no one clapped. There was nothing but awkward silence. According to those who saw it, the film was "ridiculous" without the special effects. (Lucas had integrated dogfight sequences from old war films to give the viewers an idea of what would be inserted later; this footage meshed poorly with Lucas's film.) Fox now believed it had a disaster on its hands, and so did Lucas. However, Lucas's newly formed special effects company, Industrial Light & Magic, saved the day, providing many memorable, thrilling, and groundbreaking effects.

In his book *The Great Movies*, film critic and historian Roger Ebert lists *Star Wars* among the most important films ever produced:

Like *The Birth of a Nation* and *Citizen Kane*, *Star Wars* was a technical watershed that influenced many of the movies that came after. These films have little in common, except for the way they came along at a crucial moment in cinema history, when new methods were ripe for synthesis. *The Birth of a Nation* brought together the developing language of shots and editing. *Citizen Kane* married special effects, advanced sound, a new photographic style, and a freedom from linear story-telling. *Star Wars* combined a new generation of special effects with the high-energy action picture, and linked space opera and soap opera, fairy tales and legend, and packaged them as a wild visual ride.

When the film was completed, it had cost only $9.5 million to make. In less than three months *Star Wars* earned more than $100 million at the box office, becoming the second film to accomplish this feat. As with *Jaws*, many viewers returned to theaters to view *Star Wars* again and again. The Bantam Books novelization of the film (penned by an uncredited Alan Dean Foster) sold more than two million copies. John Williams's musical score became the best-selling soundtrack of all time, selling more than three million copies. Lucas made a fortune from merchandising when fans quickly snatched up seemingly any-thing and everything with the *Star Wars* logo on it, from lunch boxes to action figures. (A linen commer-cial proudly announced, "Now you can have scenes of Luke in action on your mattress!") The film made Dolby sound the success that it is today, introduced the special effects–laden film in which the human actors are secondary to the

### Cinematic Firsts

George Lucas insisted on recording the sound for *Star Wars* with Dolby technology. However, *Star Wars* was not the first film to use this technology— a distinction that belongs to Stanley Kubrick's *A Clockwork Orange* (1971).

effect, spawned two sequels and three prequels, was rereleased numer-ous times, and taught Hollywood just how lucrative movie tie-ins and merchandising can be. (Through 2003 it is estimated that merchandise from the first three *Star Wars* films alone will have generated nearly $3 billion, which is almost five times as much as the films themselves have earned.)

Naturally, Hollywood execs began working to devise a "foolproof" formula for manufacturing a blockbuster film, using *Jaws* and *Star Wars* as their models. (Composer John Williams, who scored both films, had little trouble finding work.) Today multimillion-dollar marketing campaigns are an everyday occurrence, films are booked into thousands of theaters and multiplexes for their opening weekend, and tie-in toys are manufactured and released into stores weeks before the films hit theaters. In their book *Steven Spielberg*, Donald R. Mott and Cheryl McAllister Saunders champion Spielberg and Lucas as saviors of the American film industry:

> *Jaws* really began a "renaissance" for the Hollywood film. Spielberg and Lucas were the guiding forces in "a rebirth and a revolution in the art of Hollywood" just as . . . Orson Welles (with *Citizen Kane*) had been for the postwar period.

Others disagree. "Spielberg and Lucas together have done more damage to the American cinema than any two other directors," says University of Nebraska film studies professor Wheeler Winston Dixon. "Spielberg is an excellent action director whose best movie is *Duel*. It's a small, modest, entirely action-oriented piece, and succeeds admirably. Lucas has never been a filmmaker; he is a technician who is a wizard at special effects, but has little grasp of human concerns. The public, however, embraced *Jaws*, *Star Wars*, and their successors with a frenzy, and films began a downward spiral toward comic book unreality, in which smaller films didn't have a chance of competing in the same marketplace. Once video came in, smaller films went straight

> ### *Did You Know?*
> After Steven Spielberg's *Jaws* and George Lucas's *Star Wars* became the first two films in the history of cinema to make more than $100 million, the two filmmakers joined forces for *Raiders of the Lost Ark*, which also broke the $100 million mark.

to video and DVD without ever getting a U.S. theatrical release. The public now expects blockbusters, and studios pour hundreds of millions into these 'summer event' movies, but the more thoughtful work gets lost in the shuffle."

While there is no doubting the artistry of *Jaws* and, to a much lesser extent, *Star Wars*, the "event films" that have succeeded them are largely inartistic, soulless productions. It's ironic that these two films, both expected to be failures early on, would end up serving as models for the sure-shot can't-miss films of many summers to come. Whereas the studios releasing *Jaws* and *Star Wars* (Universal and Fox respectively) had little faith in those projects, studios today make nothing but high demands on the blockbusters now produced.

In their book *Hit and Run*, Nancy Griffin and Kim Masters describe the continuing evolution of the "event picture" in the late 1980s and early 1990s:

> The blockbuster mentality had reached a fever pitch in Holly-wood. The studio hungered for hits that would not only top $100 million in box-office revenues but spawn sequels and a merchandising bonanza of toys, lunch boxes, and T-shirts. But, the game demanded big stars and breakthrough special effects as well as imaginative "event" marketing. A strong opening weekend was essential, and that required extensive saturation television advertising. Meanwhile, star salaries were rising and production costs were climbing faster than the rate of inflation. Steven Spielberg's *Jaws*—the picture that helped create the prevailing blockbuster fever—had a $10 million budget in 1975; it would have cost more than $40 million ten years later. And while Spielberg's film opened in just 409 theaters, major films now routinely opened on 1,000 screens or more.

Although the casts of *Jaws* and *Star Wars* were comprised largely of no-name players, the success of the blockbuster film set in motion a skyrocketing effect on the salaries of actors. (As of this writing, top fees are in the ballpark of $22 million.) However, the take-no-prisoners mentality of Hollywood heads of production now requires that a blockbuster be stocked with the most bankable marquee names; studio execs today will do anything they can to fill theater seats on opening weekend. The need to win and make money has become so fierce that the product—the films themselves—are now second in importance to the money they cost and earn. This has always been true to some extent; now it is the standard.

In 1989, Spielberg commented on Hollywood's obsession with the blockbuster film. "There's anxiety everywhere," he explained. "There's a palpable tension. Everything has to succeed—or else. I'm telling you, it's viral."

In the end, through no fault of their own, *Jaws* and *Star Wars* helped bring about an environment where art is sacrificed in the name of commerce. David Cook, author of *Lost Illusions: A History of American Cinema 1970–1979*, believes that the impact of these films, despite their negative ramifications, cannot be ignored. "I view movies like *Star Wars* as milestones in the history of cinema," Cook explains. "They changed the entire landscape of American film."

# Chapter 27

# Computer-Generated Imagery (CGI)

Even revolutionary computer-generated imagery couldn't save Disney's *Tron* (1982) from becoming a critical and commercial failure.

THE RESEARCH AND DEVELOPMENT that led to today's computer-generated imagery (CGI) systems began as early as the mid-1950s. Studies at the Massachusetts Institute of Technology (MIT) sought a method by which synthetic electronic imagery could be produced. The MIT team, led by Dr. Ivan Sutherland, developed a program known as CAD (computer-aided design). CAD, later renamed Sketchpad, was capable of producing 3-D images based on programmed coordinates. Richard Rickitt explains the earliest significant breakthroughs made with this technology in his book *Special Effects: The History and Technique*:

> In 1964 Sutherland used the Sketchpad tool to create a short film called *Sketchpad*. Though crude, the film was perhaps the first 3-D computer animation, and was the launchpad for the incredible CGI systems that are used today to create sophisticated 3-D graphics.

By 1965, further studies had significantly advanced this technology and software. Using a device known as the "graphic pen," graphic designers were able to draw images that appeared on the computer screen. This technology, deemed impractical due to its costliness, was bettered only a few years later when Boeing researcher William Fetter created a 30-second television commercial for Norelco that utilized 3-D modeling.

It wasn't until the seventies that computer-generated imagery (through high-resolution graphics) entered the field of motion pictures. John Whitney, Jr., and Gary Demos, working for partner companies Information International Incorporated ("Triple I") and Evans and Sutherland, were hired to work on the motion picture *Westworld* (1972). For this film they used full-screen raster graphics (images defined as a set of pixels or dots in a column and row format, also called bitmapped graphics) to produce scenes representing the perspective of a robot. With their work on *Westworld*, Whitney and Demos established themselves as the foremost computer graphics artists of the period, earning an Oscar nomination for their groundbreaking efforts. Whitney and Demos later coproduced a number of television commercials using computer graphics, and provided state-of-the-art computer imagery for such motion pictures such as *Futureworld* and *The Looker*.

In the late 1970s CGI was used effectively (although sparingly) in a number of films, including *Star Wars* (1977) and *The Black Hole* (1979). A London motion picture graphics firm called System Simulator Ltd. was hired to create a mountainous terrain for the film *Alien* (1979). During this period a number of animators—among them Loren Carpenter—experimented with computer-animated shorts. George Lucas, who'd recently scored a tremendous hit with his special-effects extravaganza *Star Wars*, consulted Triple I about working on its sequel, *The Empire Strikes Back* (1981). Although Triple I produced an elaborate scene depicting several X-Wing fighter pilots flying in formation, Lucas deleted the scene during postproduction. Still intrigued by the idea of utilizing this technology, Lucas established a graphics division of his own at Industrial Light and Magic (ILM), and hired New York Institute of Technology whiz kid Ed Catmull as head of this division, who brought with him a number of his brightest colleagues. In his book *Becoming a Computer Animator*, Mike Morrison explains:

> The advent of Lucasfilm's computer graphics division is viewed by many as a major milestone in the history of computer graphics. Here the researchers had access to funds, but at the same time they were working under a serious movie maker with real, definite goals.

During this period, breakthroughs in computer-generated imagery designed for arcade video games were made almost daily, and were applied subsequently to filmmaking. In the early 1980s, a handful of computer animation studios were established. John Whitney, Jr., and Gary Demos, the computer graphic designers who had first performed their magic on *Westworld*, were instrumental in realizing *Tron* (1982), the most significant CGI film yet produced. Whitney and Demos, however, left their posts to establish the Motion Picture Production Group before the film's production began.

**Did You Know?**

The title *Tron* (1982), comes from a BASIC command which means "trace on."

*Tron* isn't the first Hollywood film to utilize CGI technology, but it did feature more computer graphics than any previous film. So great was the task of producing these scenes that the work had to be divided between four graphic design houses: Digital Effects, Inc., Robert Abel & Associates, Mathematical Applications Group Inc. (MAGI), and Triple I. The $20 million Disney-produced film, which takes place "inside" a computer video game, was conceived by animator Steven Linsberger. Fifteen minutes of *Tron* is composed entirely of computer-generated imagery, and there are more than 200 additional scenes that utilize computer-generated backgrounds. Despite the successful application of CGI in *Tron*, the film's box-office failure damaged the industry's view of computer animation. In his book *Computer Graphics and Animation* Garth Gardner explains:

> As the first film to make extensive and widely-publicized use of digital graphics, much of the industry treated *Tron* as a test for the viability of computer-generated imagery. Although its computer animation was stunning, the film's failure at the box office was proof to many that the future for CGI was limited. The fact that computers had been used to recreate the world within a computer did nothing to alter people's opinion that computer graphics could only represent the artificial.

That same year, Lucasfilm created a one-minute sequence for *Star Trek II: The Wrath of Khan* (1982), that depicted the simulated birth of a planet. In 1983, Lucasfilm's CGI division created a computer system called Pixar, capable of creating detailed computer animation shorts. The following year Lucasfilm released the first Pixar short, *The Adventures of André and Wally B.* Although its success brought industry attention to computer animation, CGI experts were unhappy working for Lucasfilm. Many of them questioned Lucas's commitment to the utilization of this technology and openly discussed branching out on their own. Apple Computer chairman Steve Jobs made an offer to purchase the company, but Catmull and the other Lucasfilm designers rejected it. Jobs then agreed to provide the capital for the team to start their own company. Catmull and his colleagues broke ties with Lucasfilm and established a new computer graphics house, also named Pixar, and in 1985 the Pixar team created the first CGI character for a motion picture in the otherwise forgettable *Young Sherlock Holmes*. Their first short as an independent unit, *Luxo, Jr.* (1986), was about a father and son pair of table lamps. Although Pixar did not turn a profit for its first five years, the company played a key role in demonstrating the value of computer-generated imagery to the rest of the film industry.

By the end of the decade CGI had become firmly established within the industry, and had come to be accepted as a practical film-making tool. With each new commercial or feature film to utilize CGI, computer animators were able to hone their craft. More and more, computer-generated imagery and real-life images are combined seamlessly to create illusions that could never have been accomplished by older technology.

### Cinematic Firsts

The first computer-animated creature to appear in a motion picture was the unnamed sea beast in James Cameron's *The Abyss* (1989).

# Chapter 28

# "Toy Story" (1995)

Buzz Lightyear (voiced by Tim Allen) lifts Sheriff Woody (voiced by Tom Hanks) "to infinity and beyond" in *Toy Story* (1995).

THE STORY OF *TOY STORY* began with the establishment of the computer animation house Pixar in 1984. Also key were the creations of the computer programs Menv (Modeling Environment) and Render-Man ToolKit. Menv, a program that took nearly ten years to perfect, is an animation tool used to create 3-D models of characters with controls which articulate movement. (With these controls the artist is capable of isolating specific frames without having to alter the entire scene.) The equally important RenderMan ToolKit program pulls together all aspects of digital information for a 3-D animation scene, rendering it precisely into each frame with "chromatic opulence" to achieve a heightened appearance of reality. Using this technology, Pixar produced the short film *Tin Toy* in 1988. This short captured Hollywood's imagination and allowed the Pixar team to begin working in the field of television commercials.

Impressed with his work, Disney made a number of lucrative offers to Pixar animator John Lasseter to direct animated films for them. Much to their chagrin, however, Lasseter remained loyal to his colleagues at Pixar and turned Disney down. Finally, in 1990, Lasseter suggested that Pixar and Disney collaborate. This time Disney turned Lasseter down. "We do all our own animation at Disney," he was told. Then, to Lasseter's surprise, Disney reconsidered later that year. The studio contacted Pixar and informed them that they were interested in hearing any film ideas the computer graphics firm might have.

Drawing upon the strengths of *Tin Toy*, the Pixar team would suggest another storyline concerning living toys. The earliest ideas for this project involved a tin soldier who must find his way home after being left somewhere far away. The tin soldier soon became a ragdoll cowboy that was based partly on a pull-string Casper the Friendly Ghost doll Lasseter owned. It was then decided that this cowboy, Sheriff Woody, needed a buddy. After considering a number of ideas, it was decided that the buddy would be a space traveler named Lunar Larry. (The Pixar team later reconsidered this and renamed him Buzz Lightyear.) Lasseter and company then pitched the idea to Disney, who quickly bought the project. For the first time in Disney history their artwork would be done outside the studio. Disney did, however, insist upon the right to exert story control.

A number of accomplished screenwriters (Andrew Stanton, Joel Cohen, Alec Sokolow, and *Buffy the Vampire Slayer* creator Joss Whedon) were brought in to write a script based on the Pixar team's outline. Once they felt the film's storyline was solid, Pixar hired art director Ralph Eggleston to determine what the film should look like.

> ### *Did You Know?*
> The toolbox that Tim Allen's character Buzz Lightyear pushes from the milk crate is labeled "Binford Tools." This is the name of the fictitious company that sponsors "Tool Time" on Allen's television sitcom *Home Improvement.*

By coding articulation controls into each model the animators could synch the movements of the characters' mouths to the dialogue spoken. (The facial and bodily movements of the actors were filmed as they recorded their dialogue. The animators incorporated them into the characters.) Oscar-winning actor Tom Hanks was the unanimous choice for the role of Sheriff Woody, and comedian Tim Allen supplied the voice of Buzz Lightyear.

Just as Pixar had drawn on its ability to re-create toys when they had come up with the idea for *Toy Story*, the team also recognized its weaknesses. Because of CGI's inability to reproduce human characters that actually looked like human beings, it was decided that the human beings in the film should be depicted in a stylized manner. Lasseter explained this in *The Guardian* (November 19, 2001):

> At Pixar, we like to think we use our tools to make things look photo realistic, without trying to reproduce reality. We like to take those tools and make something that the audience knows does not exist. Every frame they know this is a cartoon. So you get the wonderful entertainment of, "I know this isn't real, but boy it sure looks real!" I think that's part of the fun of what we do. The closer you get to reproducing reality the much harder it is—especially human beings. The audience sees human beings everyday, so they know when it's not right. That's why we try to stay in the stylized world, which I think is successful. I don't see the point in reproducing a human

being because if you get a camera and a great actor—trust me, it's so much cheaper and easier, and it will be so much more successful.

Although *Toy Story* began life on storyboards as did all previous Disney films, the animation process would be somewhat different. The first step in the computer animation process is "modeling." This entails giving characters and objects shape and defining how they will occupy space. Approximately 90 percent of the characters in *Toy Story* began their existence as simple graphics primitives such as cylinders and spheres, which are elaborated on and transformed.

Another important element in the creation of a computer-animated film is "shading," by which filmmakers can manipulate the surface characteristics of created objects to give them a natural look. Rather than allowing a wooden bookshelf to look shiny and plastic as basic computer animation would, shading creates the grainy look associated with real wood. Shading is a long, tedious process, but it's needed to achieve a realistic look.

From the beginning, the Pixar team knew they needed a villain whose evil deeds would compel the two main characters—Sheriff Woody and Buzz Lightyear—to unite. *Toy Story*'s baddie would be Sid, an evil ten-year-old boy who resides next door to Woody and Buzz's owner, Andy. This child would have to be cruel and sadistic to make audiences dislike him, but what actions would make this child seem vicious in the eyes of the *toys*? Animator Andrew Stanton recounted his childhood pranks of tying M-80 firecrackers on to the backs of his toy soldiers. This idea appealed to Lasseter; when Sid first appears, he is shown tying a cherry bomb onto a Combat Carl action figure. Combat Carl then meets his demise as the helpless toys watch in horror. John Lasseter and Steve Daly describe Sid's evolution in their book *Toy Story: The Art and Making of the Animated Film*:

> As the staff unleashed a flood of childhood exploits to pour into Sid, the struggle to make the character work with the overall story proved difficult. At one point the story team tried beefing up Sid into a full-tilt bullying nemesis for his neighbor Andy. They began generating scenarios of jealousy and rivalry between Sid and Andy, but that approach threw the plot line

out of balance. Sid was taken "to just gruesome extremes," says Stanton. Various storyboards depicted him aiming staple guns, slingshots, and darts at the hapless dolls. "He got so sadistic, it was as if he understood that these toys would feel the pain, or that they would suffer."

In the end, it was decided that Sid should be depicted as an average ten-year-old kid who simply likes to pester his sister and destroy things. (Isn't this what all ten-year-old boys do?)

Editor Lee Unkrich was another invaluable member of the Pixar team. Unkrich, who would later serve as codirector on the Pixar films *Toy Story 2* (1999) and *Monsters, Inc.* (2001), had never before worked on an animated film. Unkrich later explained the differences between editing live action and computer animation in *The Motion Picture Editors Guild Newsletter* (January/February 1999):

> [I]n live action, the editing process is a game of taking a huge amount of material and wading through it, trying to find the best way to put it all together. If a director neglected to shoot a certain angle on the set, you have two options: try to work without the shot or, if you are working with a big budget, go out and shoot it. In my world I am not bound by that; the sky is really the limit. It is as simple as me getting together with the layout people and saying something like, "Hey, I need a shot of this length with these characters in it. And let's do a little camera move in it." They deliver it to me, and I work it into the scene. Keep in mind, this is all before any animation has actually happened; we're working with still figures or figures that have very rudimentary blocking. We're really building a solid template for the scene and the animation that is yet to come.

More than a hundred people worked on *Toy Story* for nearly four years and its creation was the result of more than 800,000 machine hours (at 300 megabytes per frame). The film contains 1,560 shots and 110,000 frames, all created on Silicon Graphics and Sun workstations. The shots were edited using Avid editing systems, and the film was rendered at a "farm" consisting of 87 dual-processor and 30 quad-processor 100-MHz SPARCstation 20s. "There is more computer power applied to this film than to any film in history," Pixar founder Ed Catmull would later explain.

So much meticulous attention to detail paid off for Pixar. When the film was released, *Toy Story* took in more than $350 million at the box office, was showered with critical praise, and received three Oscar nominations. Director Lasseter was presented with a Special Achievement Oscar "for the development and inspired application of techniques that have made possible the first feature-length computer-animated film." Ed Catmull sums up *Toy Story*'s achievement:

> The people behind *Toy Story* had been working for some twenty years to change the way films are made. When the chance finally came, there was a team of people including a remarkable group of creative storytellers with a passion for animation and many of the pioneers of computer animation. The whole was much greater than the sum of the parts. The creative group, led by John Lasseter, place story and character above all else. They didn't just talk the line, they walked it. The result was a film that exceeded everyone's expectations, except for John, who believed all along that this was going to be a film that people loved.

With the release of *Toy Story* the latest generation of the animated feature had arrived. Among the successful computer-animated films to have followed in its wake, those crafted by Pixar have consistently improved the craft and expanded the possibilities for such projects.

While the film utilizes CGI technology, it is clearly a turning point unto itself. *Toy Story* is as separate a landmark from the crea-

---

### Cinematic Firsts

The first CinemaScope animated film was Walt Disney's *Sleeping Beauty* (1959).

---

tion and implementation of CGI as the first close-up is from the creation of the first camera lens. It would be difficult to overestimate the impact *Toy Story* has had upon animation. In some ways, *Toy Story* might be seen as being far more revolutionary than *Snow White and the Seven Dwarfs* was in 1937. Where "Disney's Folly" primarily proved that a feature animated film—constructed largely the same way as previous animated shorts—could be successful, *Toy Story* changed the art form completely. By the beginning of the following decade, viewers had come to expect computer animation, making traditional animation nearly obsolete. In 2003, an additional nail was hammered into the coffin of traditional animation when Disney announced that it would no longer be producing traditionally animated films.

# Chapter 29

# Rules Are Made to Be Broken: Dogme 95

The communal residents of Lars von Trier's 1998 Dogme 95 film *Idioterne* (*The Idiots*) pretending to be mentally ill.

THE STORY OF THE DOGME 95 collective began in the middle of the night in 1993 aboard a moving train. Danish filmmaker Lars von Trier and producer Peter Aalbaek Jensen, who cofounded Zentropa Entertainment, were traveling together. "We were in the sleeping compartment of a train, and we had the kind of intimate moment that you get when two men are lying naked together in the dark," Jensen would later tell *Guardian* reporter Ryan Gilbey. "Then Lars piped up, 'I want to do something called Dogme.' I said, 'It's a stupid title, go back to sleep.'" (For the record, "Dogme" is a literary term meaning creative freedom through restraint.) According to Jensen, this was the last he heard of Dogme until 1995, when von Trier reportedly asked fellow filmmaker Thomas Vinterberg, "Do you want to start a movement?" This movement, as conceived and outlined by Trier and Vinterberg, would become known as Dogme 95, and be expressed by a collective made up of four Danish directors: Trier, Vinterberg, Kristian Leyring, and Soren Kragh-Jacobsen. Inspired by François Truffaut and the film-makers of the French New Wave, the collective set forth a set of rules for themselves (written by von Trier and Vinterberg) as a manifesto of sorts. These rules, which they referred to as their "Vow of Chastity," were as follows:

1.  Shooting must be done on location. Props and sets must not be brought in. (If a particular prop is necessary for the story, a location must be chosen where the prop is to be found.)

2.  The sound must never be produced apart from the images or vice versa. (Music must not be used unless it occurs where the scene is being shot.)

3.  The camera must be hand-held. Any movement or immobility attainable in the hand is permitted. (The film must not take place where the camera is standing; shooting must take place where the film takes place.)

4.  The film must be in color. Special lighting is not acceptable. (If there is too little light for exposure the scene must be cut or a single lamp attached to the camera.)

5.  Optical work and filters are forbidden.

6.  The film must not contain superficial action. (Murders, weapons, etc., must not occur.)

7.  Temporal and geographic alienation are forbidden. (That is to say, the film takes place here and now.)

8.  Genre movies are not acceptable.

9.  The film format must be Academy 35mm.

10. The director must not be credited.

Furthermore I swear as a director to refrain from personal taste! I am no longer an artist. I swear to refrain from creating a "work," as I regard the instant as more important than the whole. My supreme goal is to force the truth out of my characters and settings. I swear to do so by all the means available and at the cost of any good taste and aesthetic considerations. Thus I make my Vow of Chastity.

The idea of these "vows" was to find artistic liberation and breathe new life into the film medium in an era when big-budget blockbusters had become the norm. Dogme was conceived "to challenge the conventional film language—in order to make authentic films, in search of the truth." Referencing Truffaut's 1954 essay *Une certaine tendence du cinéma francais*, Dogme was touted as a "rescue bid" to counter "certain tendencies" found in cinema. According to the "Questions and Answers" section of the official Dogme 95 website, the rules of the manifesto were "intended to inspire and raise a debate about film in general and feature films in particular."

In the spring of 1995, von Trier agreed to participate in a symposium on the cinema in Paris. Von Trier, however, had a different agenda. He used the occasion to announce that he was appearing on behalf of the newly formed Dogme 95 collective. After announcing the formation of this group, von Trier read aloud the above ten rules and Vow of Chastity, and refused to answer any questions from the stunned crowd. Instead, he dropped hundreds of bright red leaflets on the audience, which explained the collective and their mission, and exited the building. When pressed for an explanation, von Trier gave reporters a juicy tale—that the other members of the collective had forbidden him to elaborate upon the rules. He later admitted, however, that he'd simply wanted to leave the conference quickly because it had been "very boring."

The response to von Trier's announcement was one of shock. No one had attempted to challenge the language of cinema so vocally since the French New Wave. In his book *Key Moments in Cinema: The History of Film and Filmmakers*, Geoffrey Macnab explains the reaction:

For some, the Vow was a wearisome retreading of a path already covered by the French New Wave forty years before.

Skeptics regarded it as a provocation . . . Others saw it as a practical guide to low-budget filmmaking. There was much talk of the "emperor's new clothes": older directors complained that they had been making Dogme-style films for years, but had not needed to draw up manifestos to justify themselves.

Comparisons to the French New Wave were inevitable (and invited), but although the philosophies of the two groups shared a few similarities, they were still very different. Like the New Wave filmmakers, the collective saw the camera as a means to record activities rather than make art. The "auteur theory"—a belief championed by New Wave filmmakers—was strongly opposed by the Dogme code, which stated that directors could not be credited for their work. Where the French New Wave upheld Truffaut's conclusion that a film should bear the signature of its director, the Dogme sought to make the director invisible. In his *Bright Lights Film Journal* essay "Dogme/Dogma," Eric Schlosser points out another key difference between the two schools of thought:

> ## Cinematic Firsts
>
> Paul Morrissey claims that his film *Trash* (1970) was, in actuality, the first film to apply all of the rules found in the Dogme 95 "Vow of Chastity."

Dogme is a New Wave. But this time, the wave is meant to be stronger than the men behind it. Copyright lawyers are out of luck. Anyone can obtain a Dogme certificate if he (or she) shoots a film in accordance with the ten rules . . .

Von Trier's collective soon dropped from the public's radar and debates regarding their rules and philosophies died down. The collective again reared its head at the 1998 Cannes film festival. There, Dogme 95 cofounders von Trier and Vinterberg introduced the first two Dogme films: Vinterberg's *Festen* (*The Celebration*) and von Trier's *Idioterne* (*The Idiots*). Interestingly, both films broke the rules as they were filmed on digital video. Despite Rule #9's strict prohibition of anything other than Academy 35mm, most of the Dogme films that followed would be shot digitally, as well. This, the collective decided, would be permitted as long as the footage was then transferred to Academy 35mm.

In fact, breaking one or two of the rules became a norm as long as the film adhered to the majority of the commandments, maintained the essence of Dogme, and was approved by the collective. American filmmaker Richard Martini, who later directed the fifteenth Dogme film, *Camera* (2000), believes that the Dogme Vow of Chastity, like all rules, was intended to be broken. "I think the underlying principle is to break the rules that bind you as a filmmaker," Martini explains. "It's hard to chastise someone for breaking the rules when the concept is based upon breaking the rules."

*The Celebration* tells the story of an unpleasant family dinner at which a man decides to expose his father as a child molester. The film was critically embraced and won the Jury Prize at Cannes. In his review, *Chicago Sun-Times* critic Roger Ebert observed of Dogme's rules: "It would be tiresome if enforced in the long run, but the style does work for this film." Von Trier's *The Idiots* was a much more difficult sell, and it was intended to be. The film follows a group of young people who establish a commune so that they may live in a nonmaterialistic utopia. The members of this commune then go out into the world and pretend to be mentally ill. As one might guess, *The Idiots* did not receive as warm a reception.

Nevertheless, Professor Peter Schepelern of the University of Copenhagen, who has written two volumes on von Trier's work, believes *The Idiots* to be the defining film of the movement. "*Festen*, of course, is a very powerful film and both the plot and the acting follow the spirit of Dogme—"to force the truth out of characters and settings," Schepelern observes. "But I would say that *Idioterne* is the most impressive Dogme film." In his essay "Film According to Dogme: Ground Rules, Obstacles, and Liberations," Schepelern expounds further:

> *Idioterne* stands out as the quintessential Dogme film because the technical and aesthetic rules are framed by a plot that also concerns an experiment with ground rules, about dealing with a challenging test: Does the teacher dare to "spasse" [act like an idiot] in front of the art class he teaches? Does the housewife dare to "spasse" when she returns home to her family?

Does Trier dare to "spasse" with the cinematic language? The group is searching for a primordial state, the inner idiot, just like Trier is looking for a primordial film art. Transgressing the bourgeois norms—including nakedness and sexual orgies—is matched by the transgression of the cinematic consensus of film art.

In hindsight, the Dogme filmmakers chose an interesting time to release the first two films. The simplicity of the Dogme films stood in direct opposition to the excesses of bloated Hollywood blockbusters like James Cameron's *Titanic* (1998)—upon its release, the most expensive film produced to date. The Dogme films also coincided with the release of an indie film from the United States, *The Blair Witch Project* (1998), also shot on digital video, which bore an uncanny resemblance aesthetically to the Dogme films. *The Blair Witch Project*, like those of the Dogme 95 collective, hinted at what might be achieved when filmmakers relied less on the conventions of storytelling and filmmaking.

> ### *Did You Know?*
>
> Paul Morrissey announced his intention to make a certified Dogme 95 film in the late nineties. It never materialized, as he was unable to find sufficient financing.

Hoping to spread the Dogme movement, its cofounders wrote letters inviting many of the world's foremost directors to fashion a Dogme film. Vinterberg even attempted to convince Steven Spielberg to make a Dogme film. (A number of Dogme films have been produced in the United States, but none were helmed by major Hollywood directors at the time of this writing.)

The third official Dogme film emerged the following year. *Mifune* (1999), the story of a young man forced to return home after the death of his father to tend the family farm and his retarded brother, was directed by cofounder Jacobsen. Humorously, *Mifune's* comical depiction of the mentally ill brought this comparison to *The Idiots* from *San Francisco Examiner* critic Wesley Strick:

These guys have a soft spot for the mentally ill that would make the Farrelly brothers roll their eyes. This brings us to the eleventh and unofficial Dogme commandment: Include one lovably unstable character or just ridicule them all. Sure, *The Idiots* mocks mental retardation in order to mock intellectuals, but nevertheless. . . .

In 2000, Kristian Levring became the fourth and final Dogme 95 founder to make a Dogme film. *The King Is Alive* was a quirky film about a group of bus passengers who stage a production of *King Lear* after their bus breaks down in the desert. It received mixed reactions, but everyone concurred that the acting was extraordinary. According to Peter Schepelern, this is one of several positive results when one works within the Dogme form:

> I think the Dogme method gives the actors more freedom, leading to more intensity in the acting. It can also manage to set a director free. [Vinterberg, after *Festen*, thanked Trier "for setting us free".] And Dogme has managed to give new attention and new inspiration to films that do not indulge in empty technique. I think it is an important point to demonstrate a type of filmmaking where the technical breaks down and the humane triumphs.

In 2002, the Dogme 95 collective issued a statement announcing that it would be withdrawing from the movement:

> In 1995 the Dogme brothers launched the groundbreaking manifesto "The Vow of Chastity," and made four films that were both critically and commercially acknowledged worldwide. They encouraged filmmakers all over the world to reconsider the conventions of moviemaking. The challenge was taken and by now thirty-one different Dogme films have been made in Korea, Argentina, Spain, USA, France, Switzerland, Norway, Italy, and, of course, Denmark. These films show the very diverse interpretations of ten Dogme rules, and perhaps the need of them.

Citing a fear that Dogme was becoming little more than a marketing tool, the pioneers planned to "move on with new experimental film projects." While this marked the "official" end of the movement, the collective encouraged filmmakers who wanted to make Dogme films to continue making them. "It was always meant to be a wave," Vinterberg said. "And they don't go on forever."

Dogme 95 has been pivotal in the introduction and acceptance of digital video as a legitimate piece of filmmaking equipment. Directors as diverse as Spike Lee, Gus Van Sant, and Mike Figgis have since made experimental films on digital video. Although the digital video revolution has not, as of yet, been quite as big as once predicted, it cannot be ignored. While Dogme was initially intended as a means of reacquainting established filmmakers with the cinema of reality, there can be no doubt that Dogme's biggest impact has been felt among lower-budget productions. The downside of digital video is that it has made filmmakers out of many who shouldn't be making films (thus polluting the market with even more unneeded garbage). On the other hand, Dogme has shown artists that films can be made with very little capital and/or technical knowledge. "Dogme shows that anyone can make a film," Martini explains. "As French filmmaker Jean Renoir said, 'When the cost of making a film is as much as a pencil and paper, then you'll find the true artists.'"

# Selected Bibliography

## Print Materials

Author unknown, "Oscars History," *Filmscape*, March 18, 2001.

Author unknown, "Oscar Wild: A Brief History," *The Guardian*, March 17, 2000.

Aberdeen, J.A., *Hollywood Renegades*, Cobblestone Enterprises, 2000.

Alexander, George, *Why We Make Movies: Black Filmmakers Talk About the Magic of Cinema*, Broadway Books, 2003.

Alleva, Richard, "And the Oscar Goes To . . . ," *Commonweal*, April 6, 2001.

Anderson, Jason, "Sweet Dogme," *Eye Weekly*, February 21, 2002.

Andrew, Dudley, *André Bazin*, Oxford University Press, 1978.

———, *Concepts in Film Theory*, Oxford University Press, 1984.

———, *The Major Film Theories: An Introduction*, Oxford University Press, 1976.

Anger, Kenneth, *Hollywood Babylon*, Straight Arrow Books, 1975.

Arkoff, Samuel, *Flying Through Hollywood by the Seat of My Pants*, Birch Lane Press, 1992.

Auster, Albert, and Leonard Quart, *American Film and Society Since 1945*, Praeger, 1991.

Austin, Bruce A., "The Influence of the MPAA's Film Rating System on Motion Picture Attendance: A Pilot Study," *The Journal of Psychology*, 1980.

Babitsky, Paul, and John Rimberg, *The Soviet Film Industry*, Praeger, 1955.

Baldwin, Neil, *Edison: Inventing the Century*, Hyperion Press, 1995.

Bardeche, Marcus, Iris Barry, and Robert Brasillach, *The History of Motion Pictures*, W.W. Norton, 1938.

Barol, Bill, "The Overstuffed World of AIP," *Slate*, October 29, 2001.

Barrier, Michael, *Hollywood Cartoons: American Animation in Its Golden Age*, Oxford University Press, 1999.

Barrios, Richard, *A Song in the Dark: The Birth of the Musical Film*, Oxford University Press, 1995.

Barry, Iris, *D. W. Griffith: American Film Master*, Museum of Modern Art, 1940.

———, *The History of Motion Pictures*, W. W. Norton, 1938.

Basinger, Jeanine, *American Cinema*, Rizzoli International Publications, 1994.

Baxter, John, *Steven Spielberg: The Unauthorized Biography*, HarperCollins, 1996.

Bazin, André, *What Is Cinema?*, University of California Press, 1967.

———, *What Is Cinema? Volume II*, University of California Press, 1971.

Beaver, Frank E., *Dictionary of Film Terms*, McGraw-Hill, 1983.

———, *On Film: A History of the Motion Picture*, McGraw-Hill, 1983.

Bendazzi, Giannalberto, *Cartoons: One Hundred Years of Cinema Animation*, John Libbey, 1994.

Biskind, Peter, *Easy Riders, Raging Bulls*, Simon & Schuster, 1998.

Black, Gregory D., *Hollywood Censored: Morality Codes, Catholics, and the Movies*, Cambridge University Press, 1994.

Blum, Daniel, *A Pictorial History of the Silent Screen*, Putnam, 1953.

Bogdanovich, Peter, *Who the Devil Made It?*, Alfred A. Knopf, 1997.

Bohn, Thomas N., and Richard L. Stromgren, *Light & Shadows*, Alfred Publishing Company, Inc., 1975.

Bondanella, Peter, *Italian Cinema: From Neorealism to the Present*, Continuum, 1983.

Bordwell, David, *The Cinema of Eisenstein*, Harvard University Press, 1993.

———, *On the History of Film Style*, Harvard University Press, 1997.

Braudy, Leo, and Morris Dickstein, *Great Film Directors: A Critical Anthology*, Oxford University Press, 1978.

Briggs, Joe Bob, *Profoundly Disturbing: Shocking Movies That Changed History*, Universe Publishing, 2003.

Brode, Douglas, *The Films of Steven Spielberg*, Citadel Press, 1995.

Brown, Karl, *Adventures with D.W. Griffith*, Farrar, Straus and Giroux, 1973.

Brown, Stacia, "Cook Outlines the Good, Bad of 1970s Hollywood," *Emory Report*, April 10, 2000.

Brownlow, Kevin, and John Kobal, *Hollywood: The Pioneers*, Alfred A. Knopf, 1979.

Buckland, Warren, *Film Studies*, Hodder & Stoughton, 1998.

Buhle, Paul, "The Hollywood Blacklist and the Jew," *Tikkun*, September-October 1995.

Burns, Arthur Robert, *The Decline of Competition: A Study of the Evolution of the American Industry*, McGraw-Hill, 1936.

Bywater, Tim, and Thomas Sobchack, *Introduction to Film Criticism*, Longman, 1989.

Callow, Simon, *Orson Welles: The Road to Xanadu*, Vintage, 1996.

Cardullo, Bert, "André Bazin on Film Technique: Two Seminal Essays," *Film Criticism*, 2000.

Carringer, Robert L., *The Making of Citizen Kane*, University of California Press, 1985.

Ceplair, Lary, and Steven Englund, *The Inquisition of Hollywood*, University of California Press, 1979.

Champlin, Charles, *George Lucas: The Creative Impulse*, Harry N. Abrams Inc., 1992.

Chester, Giraud, Garnet R. Garrison, and Edgar E. Willis, *Television and Radio*, Appleton-Century-Crofts, 1971.

Combs, Richard, "Primal Scream: An Interview with Steven Spielberg," *Sight and Sound*, Spring 1977.

Cook, David A., *A History of Narrative Film*, W. W. Norton, 1981.

————*Lost Illusions: A History of American Cinema 1970–1979*, Charles Scribner's Sons, 2000.

Copjec, Joan, *Shades of Noir: A Reader*, Verso, 1993.

Corman, Roger, *How I Made a Hundred Movies in Hollywood and Never Lost a Dime*, Da Capo Press, 1998.

Coursodon, Jean-Pierre, *American Directors Volume II*, McGraw-Hill, 1983.

Cowie, Peter, *A Concise History of the Cinema*, A. S. Barnes, 1971.

Culhane, Shamus, *Animation: From Script to Screen*, St. Martin's Press, 1988.

Deems, Taylor, and Marcelene Peterson, *A Pictorial History of the Movies*, Simon & Schuster, 1943.

Derry, T.K., and Trevor I. Williams, *A Short History of Technology from the Earliest Times to A.D. 1900*, Oxford University Press, 1961.

Deutelbaum, Marshall, *Image on the Art and Evolution of the Film*, Dover Publications, 1979.

Dewey, Donald, "East Meets West on the Silver Screen," *Russian Life*, December 1998.

Diawara, Manthia, *Black American Cinema*, Routledge, 1993.

Dick, Bernard F., *Anatomy of Film*, St. Martin's Press, 1978.

Dobrow, Julia R., *Social and Cultural Aspects of VCR Use*, L. Erlbaum Associates, 1990.

Doherty, Thomas, *Pre-Code Hollywood*, Columbia University Press, 1999.

Douglas, Kirk, *The Ragman's Son*, Simon & Schuster, 1988.

Dyer, Frank Lewis, and Thomas Commerford Martin, *Edison: His Life and Inventions Vol. 2*, Harper & Brothers, 1910.

Ebert, Roger, *The Great Movies*, Broadway Books, 2002.

————, "Snow White and the Seven Dwarfs," *Chicago Sun-Times*, October 14, 2001.

Edwards, Ted, *The Unauthorized Star Wars Compendium*, Time Warner Books, 1998.

Eisenstein, Sergei, *Film Form*, Harcourt, Brace, 1949.

————, *Notes of a Film Director*, Dover Publications, 1970.

Eisner, Lotte H., *The Haunted Screen: Expressionism in the German Cinema and the Influence of Max Reinhardt*, University of California Press, 1973.

Eliot, Marc, *Walt Disney: Hollywood's Dark Prince*, Birch Lane Press, 1983.

Fell, John L., *Film and the Narrative Tradition*, University of Oklahoma Press, 1974.

Flaherty, Robert, "How I Filmed *Nanook of the North*", *World's Work*, October 1922.

Flynn, John, "The Origins of *Star Wars*: Evolution of a Space Saga," *Not of This Earth*, Summer, 1994.

Flynn, Peter, "The Silent Western As Mythmaker," *Images*, April 17, 2000.

Foss, Kim, "Journal: Copenhagen," *Film Comment*, July 8, 2003.

Frazer, John, *Artificially Arranged Scenes: The Films of Georges Méliès*, G. K. Hall, 1980.

Friedman, Lester D., and Brent Notbohm, *Steven Spielberg Interviews*, University Press of Mississippi, 2000.

Fulton, A. R., *Motion Pictures: The Development of an Art from Silent Films to the Age of Television*, University of Oklahoma Press, 1960.

Gehring, Wes D., *Handbook of American Film Genres*, Greenwood Press, 1988.

Giannetti, Louis, *Understanding Movies*, Prentice-Hall, 1993.

Gilbey, Ryan, "Dogme Is Dead. Long Live Dogme," *Guardian Unlimited*, April 19, 2002.

Gish, Lillian, *The Movies, Mr. Griffith and Me*, Prentice-Hall, 1969.

Goldwyn, Samuel, "Hollywood in the Television Age," *Hollywood Quarterly*, Winter, 1949/1950.

Gomery, Douglas, *The Hollywood Studio System*, St. Martin's Pres, 1986.

———, *Movie History: A Survey*, Wadsworth, 1991.

Gottlieb, Carl, *The Jaws Log*, Newmarket Press, 1975.

Grace, Helen, "Battleship Potemkin," *Senses of Cinema*, February 11, 2004.

Graham, Cooper C., Steven Higgins, Elaine Mancini, and Joao Luiz Viera, *D. W. Griffith and the Biograph Company*, Scarecrow Press, 1985.

Greer, Darroch, "Anthony Dod Mantle," *Hollywood Industry*, April, 2000.

Gregg, Martha Case, and Paul Davis, "Mathematics Meets Film Animation in Kansas City Community Lecture," *SIAM News*, September, 1996.

Griffin, Nancy, and Kim Masters, *Hit and Run*, Simon & Schuster, 1996.

Griffith, Richard, and Arthur Mayer, *The Movies*, Simon & Schuster, 1957.

Gronemeyer, Andréa, *Film*, Barron's Educational Series, 1998.

Hamlin, Andrew, "It Came from Roger Corman," *MovieMaker*, Issue #42.

Hampton, Benjamin B., *History of the American Film Industry*, Dover Publications, 1970.

Hays, Will H., *See and Hear*, Motion Picture Producers and Distributors of America, 1929.

Henderson, Robert M., *D. W. Griffith: His Life and Work*, Oxford University Press, 1972.

Hickenlooper, George, *Reel Conversations*, Citadel Press, 1991.

Hirsch, Foster, *Film Noir: The Dark Side of the Screen*, Da Capo Press, 1981.

Jacob, Gilles, and Claude De Givray, *François Truffaut: Correspondence 1945–1984*, Cooper Square Press, 1988.

Jacobs, Lewis, *The Emergence of Film Art*, Hopkinson and Blake, 1969.

———, *The Rise of the American Film: A Critical History*, Harcourt, Brace, 1939.

James, Darius, *That's Blaxploitation!*, St. Martin's Press, 1995.

Kaplan, E. Ann, *Women in Film Noir*, British Film Institute, 1978.

Karney, Robyn, *Cinema Year by Year 1894–2002*, Dorling Kindersley, 2002.

Kauffmann, Stanley, *Living Images*, Harper & Row, 1973.

Kazan, Elia, and Michel Ciment, *Kazan on Kazan*, Secker and Warburg, 1974.

Kehr, Dave, "*Cahiers* Back in the Day," *Film Comment*, September/October 2001.

Kenny, Glenn, *A Galaxy Not So Far Away*, Henry Holt, 2002.

Keylin, Arleen, and Christine Bent, *The New York Times at the Movies*, Arno Press, 1979.

Kindem, Gorham Anders, *The International Movie Industry*, Southern Illinois University Press, 2000.

Kinney, Jack, *Walt Disney and Other Assorted Characters*, Harmony Books, 1988.

Kirschner, Allen, and Linda Kirschner, *Film*, Odyssey Press, 1971.

Knight, Arthur, *The Liveliest Art*, Macmillan, 1957.

Koszarski, Richard, *An Evening's Entertainment: The Age of the Silent Picture 1915–1928*, Charles Scribner's Sons, 1990.

Koven, Michael J., *Blaxploitation Films*, Pocket Essentials, 2001.

Kracauer, Siegfried, *Theory of Film: The Redemption of Physical Reality*, Oxford University Press, 1974.

Kramer, Stanley, and Thomas W. Coffey, *It's a Mad, Mad, Mad, Mad World*, Harcourt Brace, 1997.

Krenz, Carol, *100 Years of Hollywood*, MetroBooks, 1999.

Krutnik, Frank, *In a Lonely Street: Film Noir, Genre, Masculinity*, Routledge, 1991.

Lasseter, John, and Steve Daly, *Toy Story: The Art and Making of the Animated Film*, Hyperion, 1995.

Leab, Daniel J., *From Sambo to Superspade*, Houghton Mifflin, 1975.

Lebo, Harlan, *Citizen Kane*, Doubleday, 1990.

Leff, Leonard J., and Jerold L. Simmons, *The Dame in the Kimono*, Anchor Books, 1991.

Leish, Kenneth W., *Cinema*, Newsweek Books, 1974.

Leopold, Todd, "When Independents Took Over," CNN.com, February 23, 2004.

Lewis, Jon, *Whom God Wishes to Destroy: Francis Coppola and the New Hollywood*, Duke University Press, 1995.

Lindgren, Ernest, *The Art of Film*, Macmillan, 1963.

Lucas, George, *The Adventures of the Starkiller* (second draft, January 1975), unpublished.

———, *The Star Wars* (treatment, May 1973), unpublished.

———, *The Star Wars* (first draft, May 1974), unpublished.

Lyons, Mike, "Toon Story: John Lasseter's Animated Life," *Animation World*, November 1, 1998.

MacCann, Richard Dyer, *Film: A Montage of Theories*, E. P. Dutton & Co., Inc., 1966.

Macnab, Geoffrey, *Key Moments in Cinema*, Hamlyn, 2002.

Magill, Frank N., *Magill's Survey of Cinema*, Salem Pres, 1980.

Major, Wade, "To 'B' or Not to Be," *Boxoffice*, date unknown.

Malcolm, Derek, "Auteur, Auteur," *The Guardian*, May 7, 1999.

———, "Robert Flaherty: *Nanook of the North*," *The Guardian*, April 13, 2000.

Maltin, Leonard, *The Disney Films*, Crown, 1973.

———, *Of Mice and Magic*, Von Hoffman Press, 1980.

Manvell, Roger, *Experiment in the Film*, Grey Walls Press, 1949.

Marlow, Eugene, and Eugene Secunda, *Shifting Time and Space: The Story of Videotape*, Praeger, 1991.

Martinez, Gerald, Diana Martinez, and Andrés Chavez, *What It Is . . . What It Was*, Hyperion, 1998.

Mast, Gerald, Marshall Cohen, and Leo Braudy, *Film Theory and Criticism*, Oxford University Press, 1992.

———, *A Short History of the Movies*, Bobbs-Merrill, 1976.

McBride, Joseph, *Steven Spielberg: A Biography*, Simon & Schuster, 1997.

McCann, Richard Dyer, *The First Filmmakers*, Scarecrow Press, 1989.

McCracken, Harry, "Luxo Sr.: An Interview with John Lasseter," *Animator*, Winter 1990.

McGee, Mark Thomas, *Fast and Furious: The Story of American International Pictures*, McFarland & Company, 1984.

Means, Loren, "Some Notes on Noir and Hard-Boiled," original publication and year unknown.

Mellencamp, Patricia, and Phillip Rosen, *Cinema Histories, Cinema Practices*, American Film Institute, 1984.

Michael, Paul, *The Academy Awards: A Pictorial History*, Crown, 1964.

Miller, Mark Crispin, *Seeing Through Movies*, Pantheon, 1990.

Mitchell, Elvis, "No Greenlight on Road from 'Hood to Hollywood," *The New York Times*, May 30, 2004.

Morrison, George, "The French Avant-Garde," *Sequence*, Fall 1948.

Mott, Donald R., and Cheryl McAllister Saunders, *Steven Spielberg*, Twayne, 1986.

Muller, Eddie, *Dark City: The Lost World of Film Noir*, St. Martin's Press, 1998.

Mulvey, Laura, *Citizen Kane*, British Film Institute, 1992.

Munshower, Suzanne, *Warren Beatty: His Life, His Loves, His Work*, St. Martin's Press, 1983.

Murphy, Richard J., "Carnival Desire and the Sideshow of Fantasy: Dream, Duplicity, and Representational Instability in *The Cabinet of Dr. Caligari*," *Germanic Review*, 1991.

Murray, Bruce A., and Christopher J. Wickham, *Framing the Past: The Historiography of German Cinema and Television*, Southern Illinois University Press, 1992.

Naha, Ed, *The Films of Roger Corman*, Arco, 1982.

Nowell-Smith, Geoffrey, *The Oxford History of World Cinema*, Oxford University Press, 1996.

Oliver, John W., *History of American Technology*, Ronald Press, 1956.

O'Reilly, Kenneth, *Hoover and the Un-Americans: The FBI, HUAC, and the Red Menace*, Temple University Press, 1983.

Osborne, Robert, *Academy Awards Illustrated*, ESE California, 1969.

Palmer, R. Barton, *Hollywood's Dark Cinema: The American Film Noir*, Twayne, 1994.

Parker, John, *Warren Beatty: The Last Great Lover of Hollywood*, Carroll & Graf, 1993.

Parkinson, David, *History of Film*, Thames and Hudson, 1995.

Patterson, Lindsay, *Black Films and Filmmakers*, Cornwall Press, 1975.

Peary, Gerald, "Elia Kazan," *Boston Phoenix*, March 14, 1999.

Phillips, Julia, *You'll Never Eat Lunch in this Town Again*, Random House, 1991.

Phipps, Keith, "Roger Corman," *The Onion A.V. Club*, April 1, 1999.

Picard, Laura, "Frank Capra: Public Enemy No. 1," *Morphizm*, February 20, 2004.

Pickford, Mary, "The Big Bad Wolf Has Been Muzzled," *Hollywood Reporter*, December 1934.

Poster, Steve, "The Man Behind *Close Encounters of the Third Kind*," *American Cinematographer*, February 1978.

Powdermaker, Hortense, *Hollywood, the Dream Factory: An Anthropologist Looks at the Movie-Makers*, Little, Brown, 1950.

Preminger, Otto, *Preminger: An Autobiography*, Doubleday, 1977.

Quigley, Martin, Jr., *Magic Shadows: The Story of the Origin of Motion Pictures*, Georgetown University Press, 1948.

Ramsaye, Terry, *A Million and One Nights*, Simon & Schuster, 1926.

Randall, Richard S., *Censorship of the Movies*, University of Wisconsin Press, 1970.

Ramos, Steve, "Understanding Dogme," *City Beat*, April 20, 2000.

Rawlence, Christopher, *The Missing Reel*, Atheneum, 1990.

Rhimes, Jesse Algeron, *Black Film/White Money*, Rutgers University Press, 1996.

Rhode, Eric, *A History of the Cinema*, Farrar, Straus and Giroux, 1976.

Richardson, Paul E., "The First Master of Russian Film," *Russian Life*, February 1998.

Robertson, Patrick, *Film Facts*, Billboard Books, 2001.

Robinson, David, *From Peep Show to Palace: The Birth of American Film*, Columbia University Press, 1997.

———, *History of World Cinema*, Stein and Day, 1973.

Rodriguez, Elena, *Dennis Hopper: A Madness to His Method*, St. Martin's Press, 1988.

Romney, Jonathan, "Citizen Kane," *New Statesman*, June 7, 1999.

Ross, Jonathan, "John Lasseter," *Guardian Unlimited*, November 19, 2001.

Rotha, Paul, *The Film Till Now*, Funk and Wagnalls, 1949.

———, *Robert J. Flaherty: A Biography*, University of Pennsylvania Press, 1983.

Ruby, Jay, "A Re-examination of the Early Career of Robert J. Flaherty," *Quarterly Review of Film Studies*, Fall 1980.

Russell, Jamie, "Dogme for Beginners," *BBC Film*, April 25, 2002.

Sackett, Susan, *The Hollywood Reporter Book of Box Office Hits*, Billboard Books, 1990.

Sarris, Andrew, *You Ain't Heard Nothin' Yet: The American Talking Film: History & Memory, 1927–1949*, Oxford University Press, 1998.

Schatz, Thomas, *Boom and Bust: The American Cinema in the 1940s*, Charles Scribner's Sons, 1997.

———, *The Genius of the System*, Pantheon, 1988.

Schepelern, Peter, "Film According to Dogme: Ground Rules, Obstacles, and Liberations," unpublished, 2003.

Schickel, Richard, *The Disney Version*, Simon & Schuster, 1968.

———, *D. W. Griffith: An American Life*, Simon & Schuster, 1984.

Schlosser, Eric, "Dogme/Dogma," *Bright Lights Film Journal*, date unknown.

Schumach, Murray, *The Face on the Cutting Room Floor*, Morrow, 1964.

Schwarz, Ronald, *Noir, Now and Then*, Greenwood Press, 2001.

Selby, Spencer, *Dark City: The Film Noir*, McFarland, 1984.

Seton, Marie, *Sergei M. Eisenstein: A Life*, A. A. Wyn, 1952.

Sherman, Eric, and Martin Rubin, *The Director's Event*, Atheneum, 1970.

Shiach, Don, *The Movie Book*, Anness Publishing, 1992.

Silver, Alain, "Nanook of the North," *One World*, 1996.

———, and James Ursini, *Film Noir Reader*, Limelight Editions, 1996.

———, and Elizabeth Ward, *Film Noir: An Encyclopedic Reference to the American Style*, Overlook Press, 1993.

Singer, Michael, *A Cut Above*, Lone Eagle, 1998.

Sitney, P. Adams, *The Essential Cinema*, New York University Press, 1976.

———, *Vital Crises in Italian Cinema*, University of Texas Press, 1995.

Skinner, Kiron K., Annelise Anderson, Martin Anderson, and George P. Schultz, *Reagan: A Life in Letters*, Free Press, 2003.

Slide, Anthony, *Aspects of American Film History Prior to 1920*, Scarecrow Press, 1978.

———, *The Griffith Actresses*, A. S. Barnes, 1973.

———, *The International Film Industry: A Historical Dictionary*, Greenwood Press, 1989.

Snider, Burr, "The *Toy Story* Story," *Wired*, December 1995.

Solmon, Gregory, "Fancy Math," *Film Comment*, July/August, 2002.

Spark, Nick T., "Working Out the Bugs," *The Motion Picture Editors Guild Newsletter*, January/February, 1999.

Spehr, Paul C., *The Movies Begin*, Newark Museum, 1977.

Stankowski, Rebecca House, "Night of the Soul: American Film Noir," *Studies in Popular Culture*, 1986.

Stephenson, Mark, "Interview with Kristian Levring," *Netribution*, 2001.

Spicer, Andrew, *Film Noir*, Longman, 2002.

Stern, Seymour, "Griffith: The Birth of a Nation," *Film Culture*, 1965.

Street, Sarah, "Citizen Kane", *History Today*, March, 1996.

Talbot, Daniel, *Film: An Anthology*, Simon & Schuster, 1959.

Taylor, John Russell, *Cinema Eye, Cinema Ear: Some Key Filmmakers of the Sixties*, Hill & Wang, 1964.

Thomas, Bob, *Walt Disney: An American Original*, Simon & Schuster, 1976.

Thomas, Dana, "Directing in the Dark," *Newsweek*, June 16, 2003.

Thomas, Frank, and Ollie Johnston, *Disney Animation: The Illusion of Life*, Abbeville, 1981.

Thompson, Kristin, and David Bordwell, *Film History: An Introduction*, McGraw-Hill, 1994.

Thomson, David, *Rosebud: The Story of Orson Welles*, Alfred A. Knopf, 1996.

Thurman, Judith, and Jonathan David, *The Magic Lantern: How Movies Got to Move*, Atheneum, 1978.

Tudor, Andrew, *Theories of Film*, Viking Press, 1974.

Tuska, Jon, *Dark Cinema: American Film Noir in Cultural Perspective*, Greenwood Press, 1984.

Ubois, Jeff, "Sun Goes Hollywood," *Sun World*, November 1995.

Van Gelder, Peter, *That's Hollywood*, HarperCollins, 1990.

Vizzard, Jack, *See No Evil: Life Inside a Hollywood Censor*, Simon & Schuster, 1970.

Wagenknecht, Edward, and Anthony Slide, *The Films of D. W. Griffith*, Crown, 1975.

Waxman, Sharon, "Hollywood's Casting Problem: Who Will Run the M.P.A.A.?" *New York Times*, May 30, 2004.

Welles, Orson, and Peter Bogdanovich, *This Is Orson Welles*, De Capo Press, 1992.

Williams, Martin, *D. W. Griffith: First Artist of the Movies*, Oxford University Press, 1980.

Williams, Trevor I., *A Short History of Twentieth Century Technology c. 1900–c. 1950*, Clarendon Press, 1982.

Winokur, Mark, and Bruce Holsinger, *The Complete Idiot's Guide to Movies, Flicks and Film*, Alpha Books, 2001.

Wyatt, Ed, "Was *The Great Train Robbery* Really the First Western?," *Classic Images*, May 1999.

Young, Jeff, *Kazan: The Master Director Discusses His Films*, Newmarket Press, 1999.

Zavattini, Cesare, "Some Ideas on the Cinema," *Sight and Sound*, October 1953.

Zwick, Steve, "Lights, Camera, Family," *Time*, January 16, 2001.

## Websites

Academy of Motion Picture Arts and Sciences
www.oscars.org

American International Pictures
www.houseofhorrors.com/aip.htm

The Art and Culture Network
www.artandculture.com

Becker Films
www.beckerfilms.com

Behind the Scenes
www.ex.ac.uk/bill.douglas/Schools/behind.htm

Biography
www.biography.com

Blaxploitation
blaxploitation.com

British Film Institute
www.bfi.org.uk

Cinema Web
www.cinemaweb.com

Dogme 95 Official Website
www.Dogme95.dk

Film Fodder
www.filmfodder.com

Film Site
www.filmsite.org

The German-Hollywood Connection
www.germanhollywood.com/index.html

Historical Events
www.philately.com/philately/19th_century.htm

History of *Star Wars*
www.supershadow.com/starwars/history.html

Hollywood Renegades Archive
www.cobbles.com/simpp_archive

Horror-Wood Webzine
www.horror-wood.com/arkoff.htm

Internet Movie Database
www.imdb.com

Inventing Entertainment: The Motion Pictures and Sound Recordings
    of the Edison Companies
memory.loc.gov/ammem/edhtml/edhome.html

Let's Go to the Movies: The Mechanics of Moving Images
www.moah.org/exhibits/archives/movies/introduction.html

Los Angeles Almanac
www.losangelesalmanac.com

Lumière Brothers
www.terrace.qld.edu.au/academic/lote/french/yr5lumi.htm

Motion Picture Association of America
www.museum.tv/archives/etv/M/htmlM/motionpictur/
    motionpictur.htm

Motion Picture Association of America (official site)
www.mpaa.org

Movie Maker: Lone Scherfig Interview
www.moviemaker.com/hop/09/directing.html

Oscar info
www.oscarinfo.com

Pixar: Official Website
www.pixar.com

The Political Economy of the New Hollywood and the Rise of the
    Science Fiction Film
www.hannapok.com

Questia
www.questia.com

Silent Movie Monsters
silentmoviemonsters.tripod.com/germanexpressionism.html

Teenage Horror Factory: The Unofficial Website for AIP and the Teenage
    Monster Movies of the 1950s
www.horrorseek.com/horror/tonyrivers/homepage.html

A Tribute to Sam Arkoff and AIP
www.badmovieplanet.com/3btheater/stuff/arkoff.html

The University of Aldera
www.aldera.net/scripts

Wikipedia
www.wikipedia.org

## Documentaries

Demme, Ted, and Richard LaGravenese, *A Decade Under the Influence*, IFC Films, 2003.

Epstein, Michael, and Thomas Lennon, *The Battle Over Citizen Kane*, Lennon Documentary Group, 1995.

Rice, Craig, *Half Past Autumn: A Look at the Life and Works of Gordon Parks*, HBO Films, 2000.

Story, David, *The Blockbuster Imperative*, Trio Network, 2003.

Toubiana, Serge, and Michel Pascal, *François Truffaut: Stolen Portraits*, Myrict Pictures, 1993.

## Original Interviews Conducted by Author

J. A. Aberdeen, 2003

Dudley Andrew, 2003

Damien Bona, 2003

Peter Bondanella, 2003

Joe Bob Briggs, 2003

Peter Buhle, 2003

Jeff Burr, 2000

John Canemaker, 2003

Ed Catmull, 2003

Larry Cohen, 2000

Roger Corman, 1999

Rusty Cundieff, 1999

Wheeler Winston Dixon, 2003

Elizabeth Ezra, 2003

Harry M. Geduld, 2003

Marjorie Heins, 2003

Millicent Marcus, 2003

Richard Martini, 2003

Charles Musser, 2003

Richard Neupert, 2003

Jay Ruby, 2003

Peter Schepelern, 2003

Alan Shapiro, 2003

Alain Silver, 2003

Bill Unger, 2000

David Walker, 2003

Robert Wise, 2001

# Acknowledgments

The author would like to thank the following individuals for their assistance, encouragement, and patience: God, Kerri, Dan and Sherry Rausch, Norman and Marion Leistikow, Mary, John White, Steve Spignesi, Michael Dequina, Mike White, Fred Rosenberg, John Perkins, Chris Watson, Ronald Riley, Ryan Hixon, Keith Gordon, Henry Nash, Peter Modesitt, Cyndee and Sam Timmerman, and Aron Taylor. I would also like to thank my three beautiful daughters, Jordan, Jaiden, and Jalyn, for bringing so much sunshine into my life; without you, I'm nothing.

Despite the silly disputes we've all had, I cannot forget the crew: Josh, Ryan K., Stephanie, Ryan R., Laura, Sean, Amy, Mark, Shelly, and Cherie. I love you guys, and I always will.

I would like to give extra special thanks to my editor Richard Ember for not dispatching the squad of hit men to my door when this manuscript was late. Instead, he offered assistance, suggestions, and friendship. Thanks, Richard.

R.I.P.: Tim Yeager, Randy Bradfield, Laron Denmon, and Damon Gross. I miss you all.

# Index

# About the Author

**Andrew J. Rausch** is a freelance writer and film critic whose articles, essays, reviews, and celebrity interviews have appeared in numerous publications, including *Film Threat, Ain't It Cool News, Bright Lights Film Journal, Shock Cinema, Micro-Film, The Joe Bob Briggs Report, Creative Screenwriting,* and *Images: A Journal of Film and Popular Culture.* Rausch is also the author of *The 100 Greatest American Films, Hollywood's All-Time Greatest Stars,* and *The Greatest War Films of All Time.* In addition, Rausch has worked on a number of B movies in various capacities, including executive producer, screenwriter, and actor. He resides in Parsons, Kansas, with his three daughters, Jordan, Jaiden, and Jalyn, and a dog named Kesey (after novelist Ken Kesey). His ten favorite films (in no particular order) are: *The Godfather Part II* (1974), *Goodfellas* (1990), *Sunset Boulevard* (1950), *Pulp Fiction* (1994), *Penny Serenade* (1941), *Solaris* (2002), *Casablanca* (1942), *The Thin Red Line* (1998), *All the President's Men* (1976), and *Yojimbo* (1961).